WAR IN THE LAND OF THE MORNING CALM

JIM CAMPBELL

BOOKLOGIX®

Alpharetta, Georgia

Copyright ©2012 by Jim Campbell.

All rights reserved. No part of this book may be reproduced or transmitted in any form or by any means, electronic or mechanical, including photocopying, recording, or any information storage and retrieval system, without permission in writing from Jim Campbell.

ISBN: 978-1-61005-175-0

Printed in the United States of America

∞This paper meets the requirements of ANSI/NISO Z39.48-1992 (Permanence of Paper)

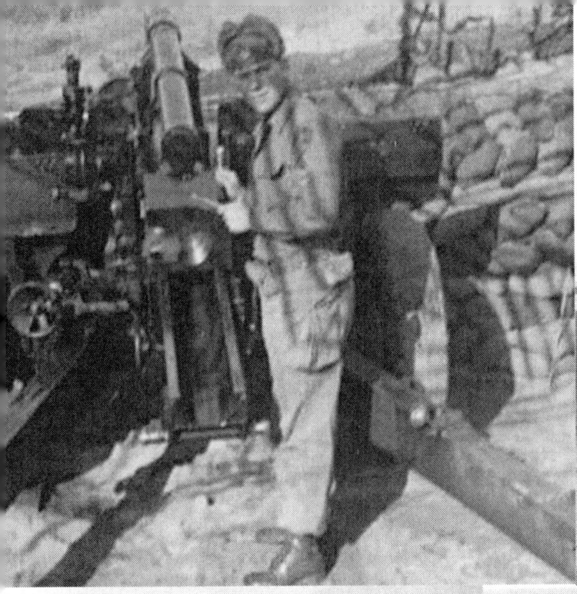
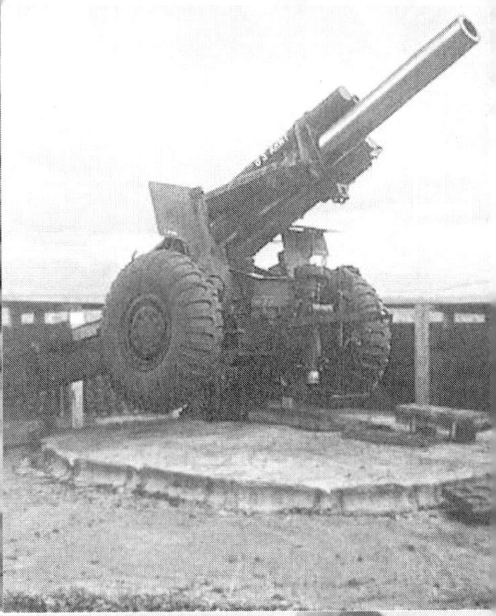
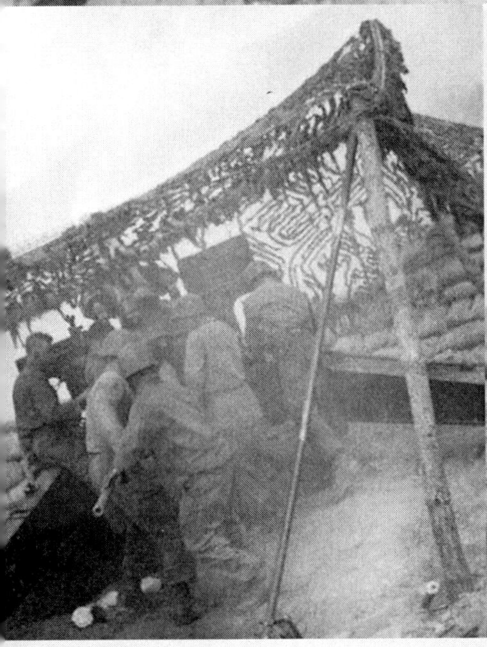
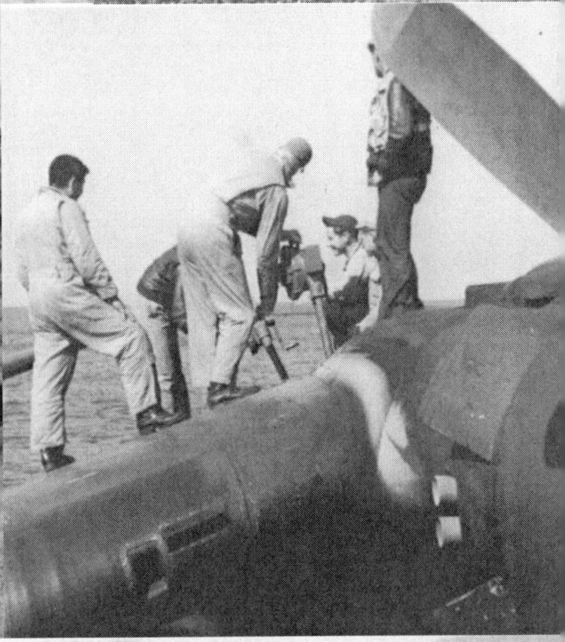
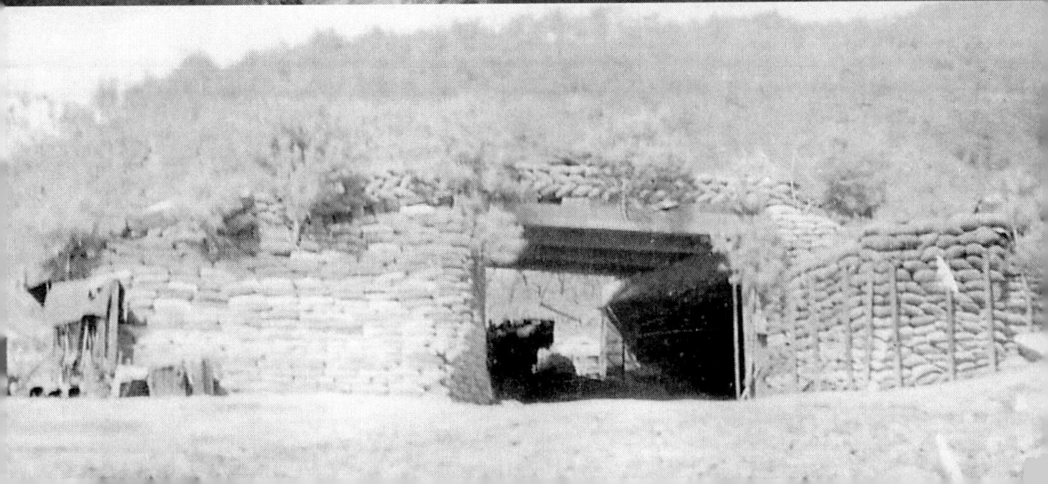

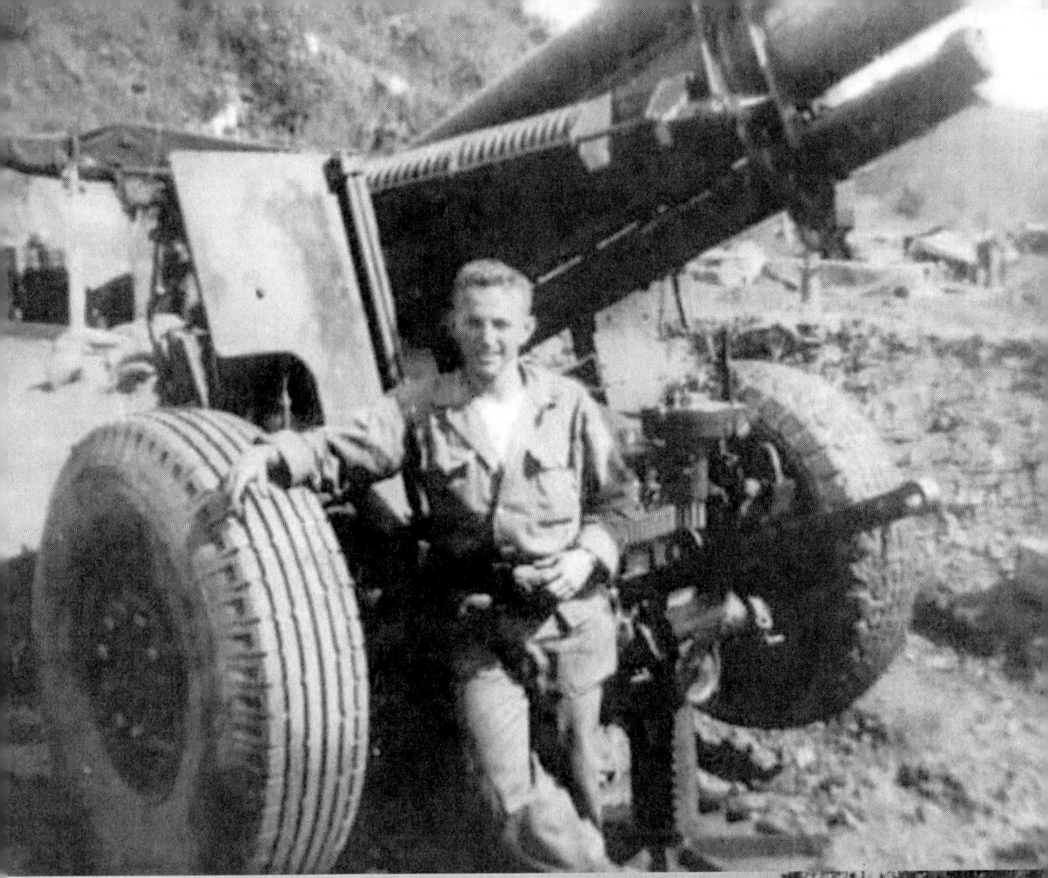

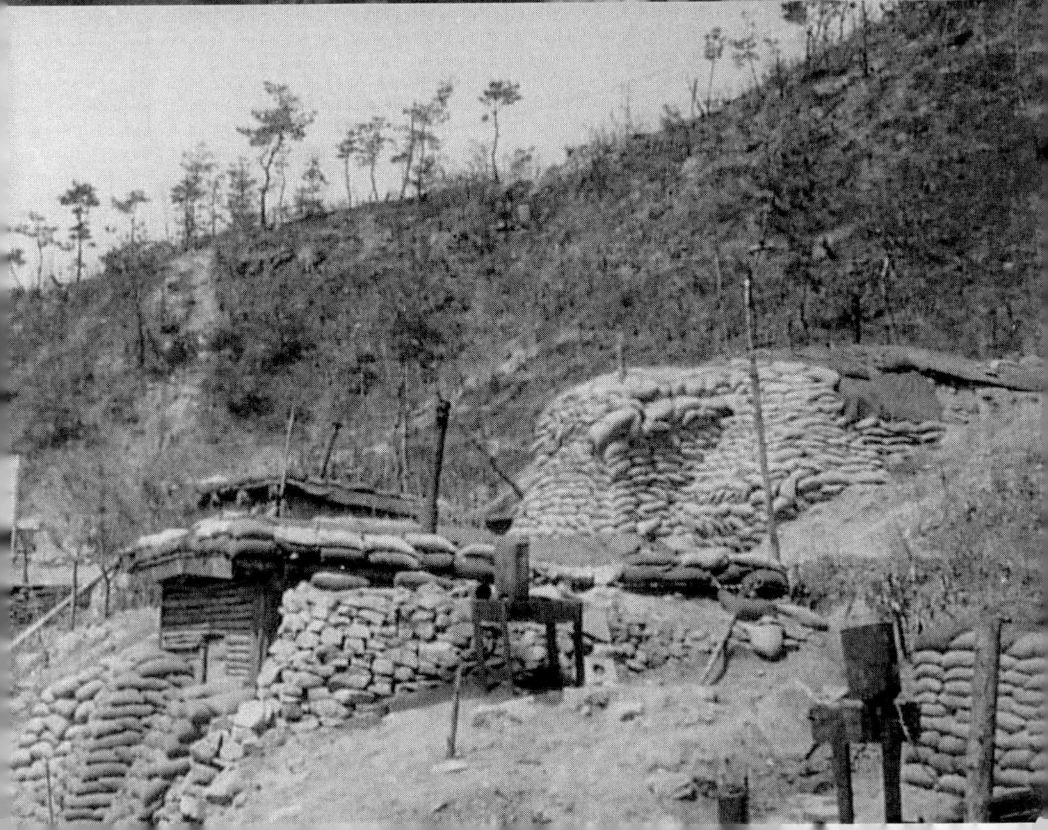

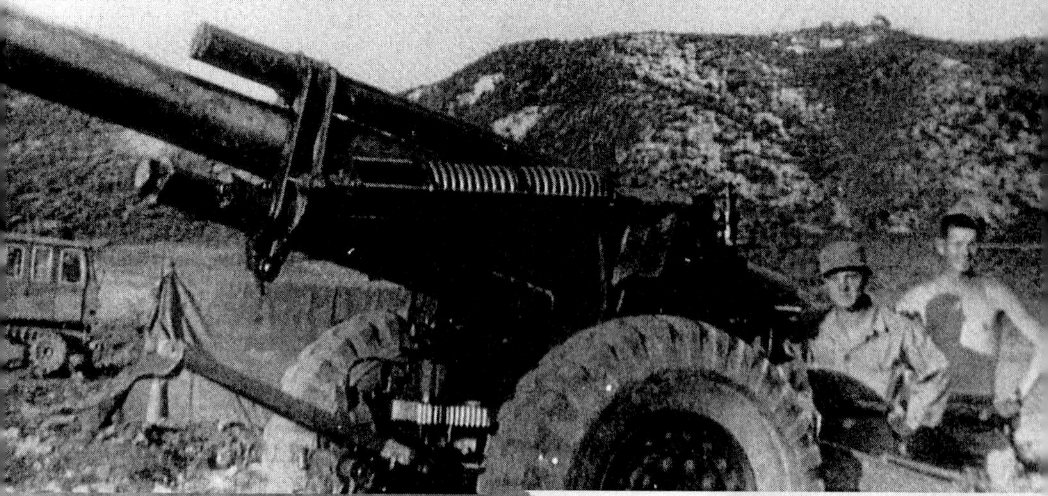

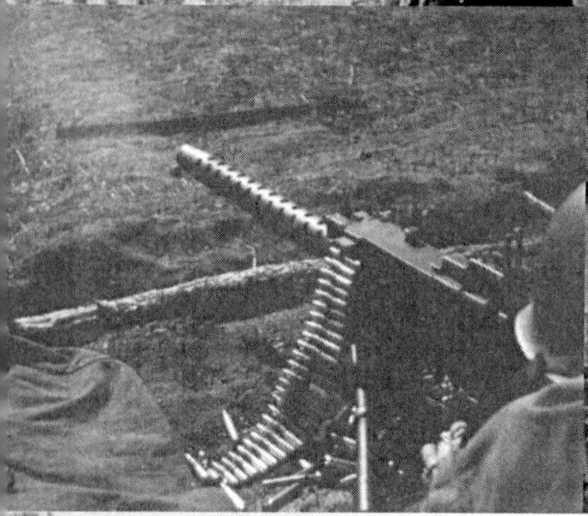

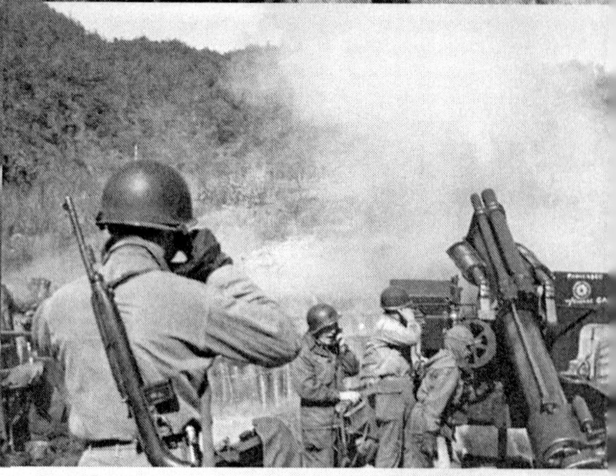

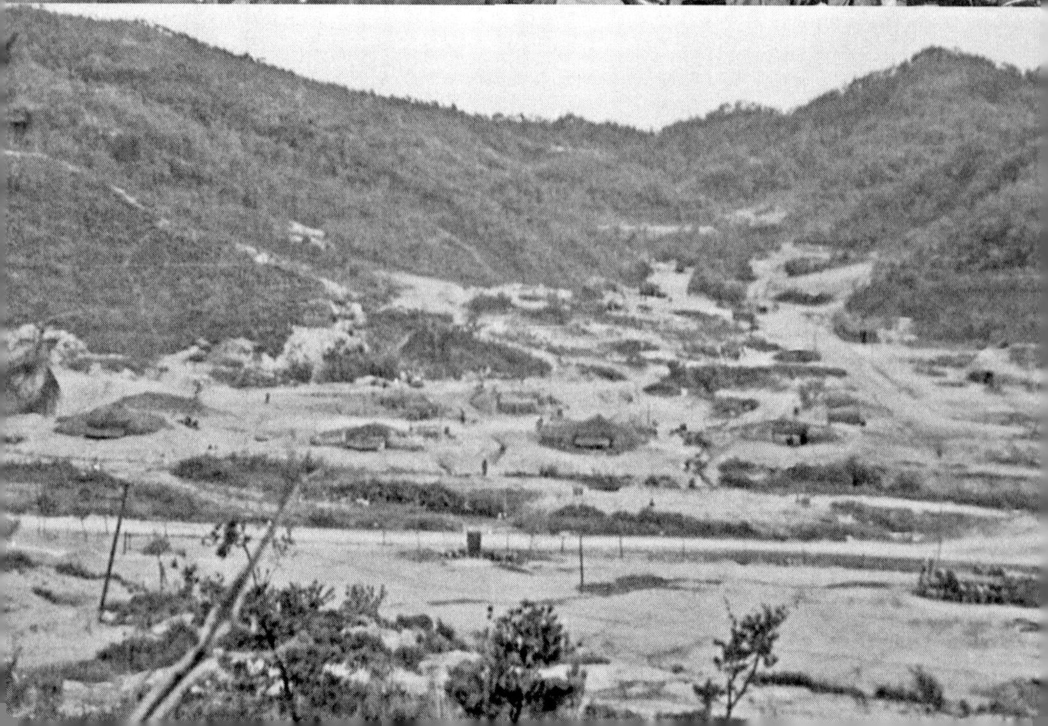

TABLE OF CONTENTS

Acknowledgements...xi
In Memoriam...xiii
Glossary...xv
Statistics..xxi
Introduction...xxiii

EPISODES

1 **LIFE ON THE LINE**
   Jim Campbell 1

2 **SHIPPING OUT**
   George Brittany 9

3 **THE QUARTERMASTER MAJOR**
   Bob Lombard 13

4 **THE HOENSONG MASSACRE**
   Robert W. Gross 15

5 **PTSD**
   Robert W. Gross 19

6 **THE 5TH RCT**
   Jack Enkeman 25

7 **THE BURKE BOYS**
   Henry And John Burke 29

8 HILL ONE ONE SEVEN
  DANIEL WOLFE 35

9 SILVER STAR LOST
  BEN FARNAN 39

10 BATTLE OF CHANGTO
  MARTIN LEE BROUSSARD 45

11 RADIO OPERATOR, TAC
  ANONYMOUS 51

12 THE MP
  WALTER WALLACE LEE 59

13 THE VOLUNTEER
  AL TAYLOR 67

14 THANKSGIVING IN KOREA
  EUGENIO QUEVEDO 77

15 THE BORINQUENEERS
  EUGENIO QUEVEDO 79

16 SERGEANT RECKLESS
  ROBIN L. HUTTON 83

17 SQUAD LEADER - WEAPONS PLATOON
  CHARLES MORGAN 93

18 GRAVES REGISTRATION
  JOHN E. MOORE 97

19 A HARD DAYS' NIGHT
  BILL INGBRETSEN 99

20	THE B-26 MARAUDER PILOT	
	Al Van Aman	105
21	THE BIRD COLONEL	
	Bob Moore	109
22	THE BLADE MAN	
	William J. Carter	113
23	THE 145TH FIELD ARTILLERY BATTALION	
	Robert Warilow	119
24	190 PROOF	
	Walter Adams	125
25	NO PURPLE HEART TODAY	
	Joe Jones	127
26	FORT RUCKER STORY	
	Bill Williamson	129
27	DEAR JOHN	
	Bill Williamson	131
28	DETECTIVE STORY	
	Jim Campbell	135
29	MEDAL OF HONOR	
	John Meyers	139
30	DEATH ON THE IMJIN	
	Dale Geise	149
31	THE ENGINEERS	
	George Collett	151

32 WATER, WATER, EVERYWHERE
DALE GEISE 161

33 LABOR SAVING DEVICE
DALE GEISE 163

34 BEWARE THE CAN IN THE BUSH
DALE GEISE 165

35 CBR WARFARE
WALTER ADAMS 167

36 CBR, SEARS, AND THE ENGINEERS
WALTER ADAMS 179

37 THE MOSQUITO PILOT
JOE HOLDEN 183

38 TWO HUNDRED CHINESE
JIM CAMPBELL 195

39 BROTHERS
PERRY RUBART 197

40 AMBUSH PATROL
BILL MITCHELL 199

41 RAID ON HILL 412
JACK GREENE 201

42 ROCKET ATTACK
ROGER WARD 205

43 SILVER STAR TARNISHED
ANONYMOUS 207

44 KUMHWA VALLEY PATROL
    BILL JORGENSEN 209

45 SNOOPER SCOPE
    ROGER BEATTY 211

46 THE 38TH FIELD ARTILLERY BATTALION
    BOB MEHLER 215

47 THE STRAWBERRY GRENADE
    JOHN GIRARD 217

48 LIFE OF AN ARTILLERYMAN
    PAUL BONHAM 219

49 CHINESE BREAKTHROUGH
    ROGER BLAKENEY 233

50 THE FOG OF WAR ON HILL 620
    ROBERT D. HESLEP 237

51 THE MiG AND ME
    RON HILL 241

52 R AND R
    BILL JAMISON 245

53 THE MEDIC CAPTAIN
    ROGER JENKINS 247

54 THE SEAPLANE PILOT
    ANONYMOUS 249

55 STEVEDORES
    BILL MASON 259

56 TRAGEDY
   BRAD WILLIAMS 261

57 AIDE DE CAMP
   ROBERT MILNE 265

58 THE SWAGGER STICK
   JIM CAMPBELL 269

59 THE OFFICERS CLUB
   ROBERT LUDLAM 273

60 KIM Q. BONG
   AL TAYLOR 277

61 THE PROVOST MARSHALL
   AL TAYLOR 279

62 HOMEWARD BOUND
   JIM CAMPBELL 281

63 MY GUARDIAN ANGEL
   JIM CAMPBELL 285

64 EPILOGUE
   JIM CAMPBELL 289

ACKNOWLEDGEMENTS

WAR IN THE LAND OF THE MORNING CALM
JAMES P. CAMPBELL

FIRST HAND ACCOUNTS OF THOSE WHO WERE THERE...

Many thanks to all of my fellow veterans who participated in the writing of this book. We hope that readers will find our accounts interesting and informative. Those of you who served will find many explanations of events, equipment, etc., somewhat basic. I hope, however, that most of the readers will be persons who have never been in the military and for that reason elaborated on some points that might otherwise be confusing to the average civilian. For the same reason, the glossary of terms is somewhat overdone.

There are hundreds of other stories left untold which is unfortunate since they are a part of the history of our nation and our military. I met men who could not speak of their experiences. Some were prisoners of the North Koreans or Chinese; others participated in battles of unimaginable slaughter and horror. They can never forget, nor should we... Let our prayers be with them...

DEDICATED TO THOSE WHO FOUGHT FOR FREEDOM

And many thanks to my daughter Winde Sullivan, who tirelessly proofread, made many good suggestions, and kept our grammar reasonably correct.

IN MEMORIAM

Every nation honors its warriors with plaques and memorials of one kind or another. These, I find particularly touching:

A Plaque at the Korean War Memorial in Washington, District of Columbia, United States of America:

"OUR NATION HONORS HER SONS AND DAUGHTERS WHO ANSWERED THE CALL TO DEFEND A COUNTRY THEY NEVER KNEW AND A PEOPLE THEY NEVER MET."

A monument on the John Cabot Trail, at the northern tip of Nova Scotia, over-looking the Gulf of St. Lawrence reads:

"THEY WILL NEVER KNOW THE BEAUTY OF THIS PLACE, SEE THE SEASONS CHANGE, ENJOY NATURE'S CHORUS. ALL WE ENJOY WE OWE TO THEM, MEN AND WOMEN WHO LIE BURIED IN THE EARTH OF FOREIGN LANDS AND IN THE SEVEN SEAS. DEDICATED TO THE MEMORY OF THE CANADIANS WHO DIED OVERSEAS IN THE SERVICE OF THEIR COUNTRY AND SO PRESERVE THEIR HERITAGE."

Sir William Stephenson, Head of British Intelligence during WWII, wrote this short poem. It is said that Lady Churchill carried a copy in her purse throughout the war years. It should be inscribed on a monument somewhere:

"DEAR LORD, LEST I CONTINUE MY COMPLACENT WAY, HELP ME TO REMEMBER THAT SOMEWHERE OUT THERE A MAN DIED FOR ME TODAY. AS LONG AS THERE MUST BE WAR, I THEN MUST ASK AND ANSWER - AM I WORTH DYING FOR?"

GLOSSARY OF TERMS

NOTE: Purposely the explanations and definitions that follow are sometimes lengthy and detailed so the reader who may never have served in the military will better understand the arcane, strange, and confusing words and phrases used. These date back to WWII and Korea so many have changed or have been dropped over the years as other wars (with different weapons, technology, tactics, etc.) have created their own peculiar language.

A/N PRC 10	Army/Navy Portable Radio Communications. Backpack radio used during WWII and Korea. Weighed about 35 pounds. Dependable with a range of about five miles with no weather interference.
BAR	Browning Automatic Rifle .30 calibers. WWI vintage but was a basic infantry weapon during WWII and Korea. Fed from 20 round clips. Range 5-600 yards plus. Very accurate. Weighed about 22 pounds.
Bronze Star with V for Valor	The fourth highest award for an act of bravery in combat; a Meritorious Bronze Star was also awarded.
Bunker	In simplest terms, a cavity dug into the side of a hill or mountain reinforced with logs and sandbags. Depending on location, etc., freestanding bunkers were sometimes constructed above ground again using logs for sides and roof and reinforced with sandbags.
Burp Gun	Chinese fully automatic sub-machine gun. Rate of fire approximately 900 rounds per minute. 50 round drum fed. Copy of Russian weapon of WWII. Short range, not very accurate but at that rate of fire accuracy is not too important.

CO	Commanding Officer
DSC	The Distinguished Service Cross is the second highest award for bravery in combat.
Direct and Indirect fire	Direct fire as the name implies consists of firing a weapon at a target (usually visible) on a flat trajectory; in other words, the round travels pretty much parallel to the ground. Indirect fire, on the other hand, normally comes from high-angle of fire weapons such as mortars and artillery, with the round making a high arcing flight before impacting the target. These weapons have a range a thousand yards or so for mortars and up to 14 miles or more for the heavy artillery pieces.
Deuce and a half	Army truck capable of carrying two and a half tons of cargo. Depending on conditions, could carry much more. As a troop carrier it could handle a couple of squads of men and their equipment - uncomfortably. . .
EE8	Field telephone, battery operated, connected by communication wire, which was easily cut by artillery fire, shrapnel, etc. Had a hand crank, which rang the connected phone. Short range. Also known as the Double E8.
FO	Forward Observer. Generally from an artillery outfit whose job is to direct and correct artillery fire. Our artillery is referred to as the infantryman's best friend.
GI	Government Issue. Includes everything from under shorts to the man wearing them.
Gun	In the military, a rifle is never referred to as a gun. It is a rifle, a weapon, an M-1 but never a gun.

Glossary of Terms

Interdiction fire	Generally speaking, this is artillery fired at random targets at random intervals. Roads for example, are easy marks and incoming rounds can cause damage and interruptions. Also known as harassing fire.
KATUSA	Korean Augmentation Troops to United States Army. Some young Korean troops were placed in our units partially as a training program for them.
KIA	Killed in Action.
Line Crosser	A South Korean national who goes undercover into enemy territory to gather information and intelligence.
LP	Listening Post. Usually one or two men in a position to the front of the main defensive line. Early warning system in case of attack. Used EE8 phones or radio to communicate with CO.
LD	Line of Departure. A point at which a patrol or other unit would cross at a given time on their way to perform a mission. Used as a method of control to prevent confusion with other units.
M-1	Basic infantry rifle of WWII and Korea. Semi-automatic. Clip held 8 rounds. .30 caliber. Range 500 yards plus. Very accurate. Weighed about 9 lbs. loaded. Known as the Garand after its inventor, John Garand.
M-2 or M-deuce	.30 caliber carbine (short-barreled rifle) that also saw duty in WWII. Lightweight, about 7 pounds. Fired either semi-automatic or full automatic mode. Rate of fire about 600 rounds per minute. Fed by ten round clip, 20 round magazine, or 30 round magazine. Accurate to one hundred yards plus.
MIA	Missing in Action

MLR	Main Line of Resistance. In civilian language would be referred to as the front line.
MSR	Main Supply Route.
MOH	Medal of Honor. Nation's highest award for bravery in combat.
Navy Cross	Second highest award for valor given by the Navy.
OP	Out post. Generally thought of as defensive positions on the perimeter of a units area of responsibility. The men on outpost duty would allow the rest of the company to get some sleep, depending on circumstances. Also used in the context of an area of tactical importance as in the case if a large hill mass needed for observation or to block an important approach toward the MLR, etc. Often manned by a larger unit such as a rifle company with supporting fire as needed.
Phonetic Alphabet	Words representing letters for sake of clarity particularly useful in radio communications. Able, Baker, Dog, Easy, Fox, etc.
Purple Heart	Established by George Washington, August 7, 1782. Awarded to men and women in uniform for wounds or death sustained in action against an enemy of the United States.
PTSD	Post-traumatic stress disorder or syndrome. A severe anxiety disorder due to psychological trauma causing flashbacks, nightmares, anger, sleeplessness, inability to concentrate, etc. Can be extremely debilitating.
Quad 50	Four .50 caliber machine guns mounted in a turret generally on the the back of a half-track armored vehicle. Originally designed as an anti-aircraft

Glossary of Terms

	weapon, it quickly found use in WWII and Korea as an Infantry support weapon. Rate of fire is well over 500 rounds per minute. Range up to four miles, effective range 1500 yards plus.
ROTC	Reserve Officer Training Program. Junior ROTC programs are available in some high schools. College ROTC provides a person the opportunity to become a commissioned officer and follow a career in the military. The Distinguished Military Graduate program (restricted to the top 5 or 10 percent of military graduates) provides the student an opportunity to become a Regular Army Officer as opposed to a reservist. Regular Army meaning a 30-year career with the military. About the only other way to receive a Regular Army commission is through West Point.
Round	One of those oddities that's hard to explain to someone who has never been in the military. A civilian would probably say "bullet." In the service it is called a round - as in a rifle round, an artillery round, a mortar round, etc. One rifle round, one shot. Probably a holdover from the days of the round cannon ball?
Recoilless Rifle	Might be called a cannon without the kick. The projectile and Rifle propellant were as one when loaded into the breach. When fired a large portion of the blast escaped to the rear of the weapon offsetting the forward momentum (and the resulting kick) of the projectile.
R and R	Rest and Recreation (and maybe recuperation). Usually meant a seven-day pass to a nice place - like Tokyo.
RCT	Regimental Combat Team. An Infantry Regiment

xix

	with additional support units attached such as armor, artillery, etc.
ROK	Republic of Korea.
Range	As in rifle range, pistol range, machine gun range, etc. Infantry training during the era (WWII and Korea) was done mostly on known distance ranges meaning the firing lines would be from 100 yards, 200 yards, 500 yards etc., depending on the weapon being used.
Sharpshooter	An Infantryman had to qualify with his basic weapon meaning he had to fire a certain score on the rifle range. The basic weapon for a rifleman was the M-1 Garand. Firing (using different positions) was done from 100 yards, 200 yards, and 500 yards. The lowest qualification award was Marksman, the next Sharpshooter, and the highest was Expert. I don't remember the numerical scoring but to fire Expert was very difficult. At 500 yards, the rifleman would fire at a 12-inch bulls eye and had to hit it quite consistently to attain the Expert's medal. And this was without telescopic sights or any method of bracing the rifle except for using the sling.
Silver Star	Third highest award for bravery in combat.
TOT	Time on Target. An artillery barrage or concentration whereby rounds from varying caliber weapons are timed to hit the target at the same moment regardless of their distance and location from that target. Very devastating.
WIA	Wounded in action.

STATISTICS

The problem with statistics and warfare is that it is sometimes difficult to remember that each of those numbers represents a tragedy. The Chinese or North Korean mother who lost a son in combat was probably no less grief-stricken than an American mother in the same circumstances. Such thoughts would not be on the mind of the combatants. No quarter asked, none given.

The loss of lives resulting from war is so great that the brain can hardly comprehend the magnitude of such horrors. For example, 85 million human beings died in WWII. With all the advances made in nuclear weaponry since then, and similar improvements in other means of killing one another, the next world war will probably be the last one.

HERE ARE SOME OF THE STATISTICS OF THE FORGOTTEN WAR:

- 33,629 Americans died in Korea. 105,785 were wounded.
- 415,000 of the South Korean Army died. 429,000 were wounded.
- 1,263 of the British Commonwealth died - Britain, Canada, Australia, and New Zealand. 4,817 were wounded.
- 1.5 million (approximately) Chinese and North Koreans died though the total is not known.
- 450,000 South Korean civilians died. (estimated.)
- Total MIA US forces 8,176. Included 2,045 POWs; 1,794 KIA bodies never recovered; 4,245, MIA and 92 missing non-battle casualties.
- By comparison, the total MIA in Viet Nam was 1,799. 58,270 Americans died in Vietnam. 153,300 were wounded. The Korean War lasted three Years, Viet Nam ten years.
- Of the UN Forces, the United States provided 90% of all army personnel, 93% of all Air power, and 86% of all naval forces.

Our nation has been involved in 14 wars with Iraq and Afghanistan still on going as of this writing. Approximately 1,125,500 members of our military died in all those conflicts. Sadly, more than half of that total (564,000) were killed in our own Civil War.

War is a necessary evil. As long as there are those who would seek to destroy the freedoms we enjoy and the freedoms of our friends and neighbors, conflicts of one magnitude or another will go on until mankind someday realizes the futility of killing one another. That seems an unlikely scenario…

INTRODUCTION

Jim still wears the uniform as he serves with a local veterans organization that provides the Honor Guard for a fallen comrade.

The name of Korea was once Hankook. When it was conquered and occupied by Japan, the ancient name of Chosun was revived meaning, "Land of the Morning Calm." It was also known as the Hermit Kingdom and later, of course, "Frozen Chosun." I'm sure during the war period there were many other names given by our GIs to that destitute country, but not printable in a polite society. The calm of the Land of the Morning Calm came to an end in 1950 when North Korea invaded the Republic of South Korea.

Our United Nation allies and we responded not only because of treaty obligations but to prevent an ally and a fledgling democracy from being enslaved by a vicious Communist dictatorship. 33,650 American military personnel died in the conflict - not to make South Korea the 51st state or to occupy it or to subjugate it - but to give a downtrodden people a chance at freedom and a democratic form of government. To the people of South Korea, it is not the Forgotten War - nor should it ever be considered so in our country.

One can understand why it was called the Forgotten War. It began only five years after the end of WWII, a fight for the survival of Western Civilization, as we know it. Our population was tired of war, grateful it was over, and we wanted only to put our lives back together. Peace and prosperity reigned. And it was not a "popular" war, not to mention that probably half our population never heard of

xxiii

Korea. Little did we realize that it was also the beginning of the Cold War - in fact, it was the first significant ground conflict of that long drawn out confrontation.

It seems odd now but there was a period of time in which home bomb shelters were a thriving business. Children practice drilled at school on how to get under their desks for protection in event of an attack. Our daughters and other children wore identification bracelets if the unthinkable occurred. Public and government buildings in every city were designated as fallout shelters and were stocked with food and water in case of a nuclear strike. There was the Cuban missile crisis. This was all part of the Cold War.

I had long been out of the service but received a notification that I, along with many others, was being called back to active duty (for the coming invasion of Cuba). As it turned out, the Army had the wrong man and I remained a civilian.

Thousands of books and articles have been written about wars. Probably more than any other topic except perhaps romance and love. And the two seem irrevocably entwined.

I wonder, for example, what the rate of marriages might have been in our nation during the WWII era as opposed to the four-year period prior to the war. An odd thought but I suspect it jumped by 50%. I did read that marriages were at an all-time high in the 40's. So many GI's marrying their sweethearts before going into harm's way. Or those who waited until they were safely home. And it was the same during the Korean War. In 1950, the year "our" war began, 3,548,000 babies were born in this country. That was the largest birth rate in a single year ever known in history. The Baby Boomers had arrived thanks to WWII and the peace that followed.

Eighty-five million human beings perished during the Second World War. To put that in perspective, the population of the United States in 1941 was 133,400,000. Maybe those three million plus babies that were born was God's way of balancing the scales.

So why publish another book about war - any war? They are all the same - someone wins, someone loses, someone dies. Simply put, I hope to give the civilian reader an insight of what combat is about from a personal standpoint. We are fortunate to live in a reasonably prosperous country so many of our younger people know little of discomfort. I want them to read of the hardships that are endured and the fear, loneliness, sorrow, despair, camaraderie, bravery, and terror and occasional bits of humor that occur under such conditions. Not to mention rarely having a bath, or a change of clothes, or passing sleepless nights huddled in a hole in the ground, or eating only food from a can and other such minor discomforts! And did we pray? Yes, never a day passed that I did not ask for the safety of my young men and that they would return to their loved ones unharmed and unscarred.

These stories are first person accounts of men and women who were there. There is no plot. There are no explanations of grand strategies or political policies or any of the other bewildering activities behind the scenes of a nation at war. I simply hope that these vignettes, and brief accounts will convey the feelings and experiences of those of us who served.

Not all narratives will be of combat. Some will be of everyday life under conditions that are foreign to the average civilian. But combat is a strange world - a horrific battle can be in progress while only a mile away, all is quiet. Or one man can live through the most vicious of combat time after time while all around him friends fall and die. We read of those who have won the Medal of Honor or other awards for bravery and can only wonder at their gallantry and selflessness.

Wars are fought to be won. We did not totally achieve that in the Korean conflict though the North Korean army was crushed. Our Air Force decimated the North Korean Air Command, which consisted not only of North Korean pilots, but hundreds of Russians as well. Russia also supplied North Korea with the latest of their aircraft and equipment. Perhaps they too, found that we Americans could be tough adversaries when aroused. And finally, we fought the million-man Chinese Army to a draw resulting in the accomplishment of our initial objective - freedom for the people of South Korea.

My contribution to that effort was, to say the least, minimal. However, to this day, I am proud of the fact that I served, and in some small way helped to give the citizens of South Korea a better life. Look at their nation today - a dynamic economic success, a democracy, a capitalist society where the average person can prosper and finally, a strong ally. I feel certain my comrades-in-arms feel that same sense of pride and accomplishment.

For those of you who served, you may find discrepancies or inaccuracies. If so, I believe they will be errors of the memory with no intention to mislead or exaggerate. After all, we are going back some 60 plus years. There will be mistakes perhaps, in my transcribing of the events through personal interviews. I tried as best I could to accurately relate these stories that my fellow veterans contributed. I am deeply indebted to them for sharing their experiences. And my heart goes out to those whom I contacted but could not speak of their lives under fire as they still suffer from post-traumatic stress syndrome. In my own case, some things come readily to mind as though they happened yesterday - others are just long forgotten. "More often than not, we put our memories in a duffel bag rather than in a filing cabinet." I do not know where I read that but it seems appropriate.

James (Jim) P. Campbell
Former Rifle Platoon Leader
1st Platoon, L (Love) Company
3rd Battalion, 65th Infantry Regiment
Third Infantry Division

LIFE ON THE LINE
Jim Campbell

I will try to describe what daily life was like under somewhat normal but adverse conditions. In other words, not in a bloody combat situation at that time. Many hours were downright dull. We filled them by trying to improve our trenches or observing our opponents across the valley. There were no facilities for bathing or cooking so those details took little of our time. We did try to catch some sleep during the day as Chinese artillery or the possibility of an attack kept us awake and alert at night. As said in the Introduction, we might be bored while less than a mile away our counterparts could be involved in a life or death struggle.

The first position we held on the MLR was a ridgeline high atop a very large mountain - which was one gigantic rock. It was near impossible to dig trenches or bunkers so our protection from incoming fire was minimal. My command post consisted of a rectangular hole dug into the reverse side of the ridge. It was about 6 feet square with a table, our EE8 telephone, a Coleman lantern, and a bunk made of a frame laced with communication wire to support one person. I don't ever remember sleeping on it, at night we never slept. We'd catnap during the day. It wasn't much of a bunker but did provide some protection from flying shrapnel.

Unfortunately, my men were pretty much exposed, as our trenches (if you could call them that) were very shallow because we were sitting on solid granite. My first night on the line, a Chinese artillery shell landed close to one of my boys and the explosion took one of his legs. He was at the far end of my area and fortunately near the company command post where the company commanders' Jeep was located. By the time I reached his position (a matter of two or three minutes in the darkness), he had been loaded in the Jeep and was on his way to the rear. He survived, thankfully, and ultimately arrived home - safe but severely damaged.

For some reason, I had an experienced Engineer attached to my platoon. I suppose the Engineer Battalion didn't have much going on so some of their guys were farmed out to help improve our positions. It was kind of funny - we didn't have any material for such improvements. However, one sunny afternoon I was looking down on the dirt road that wound its way to the top of our rock, probably a distance of a half-mile or more from the valley behind us. Two Korean workers had a 10-foot log suspended between them and were making their way to our position. It was obviously for a future bunker in our company area. How they made it up that twisting road with that very heavy chunk of wood was amazing. I guess it took them three or four hours. We would have needed about 50 more that size to do us much good.

Our engineer decided that he would start blasting just in case more bunker building equipment was on the way. However, breaking into our rock was not that simple. He used a shaped charge (an explosive charge shaped so the force of the blast was centered on one point - imagine a funnel) which he detonated into the side of our mountain. The blast drilled a hole a couple of inches in diameter and a few inches into the rock. He shoved in a stick of dynamite and detonated it. The resulting blast dug a bigger hole - about a foot deep and a foot wide! Impressive.

We considered his efforts great entertainment but also surmised that it would take about ten years and a couple of tons of dynamite to improve our positions. And I never did see another log being hand-delivered to our unit. I still marvel at the two Koreans who carried that one up a very steep, long and torturous road. I hope they were well paid.

Our engineer did help me with one of my crazy ideas. We put two or three sticks of dynamite in an old ammo crate and filled it with rocks, empty rifle cartridges, scrap metal of any kind, etc. We placed it a few yards in front of my platoon position leaning against a large rock facing down one of the avenues of approach. We wired it and concealed it with brush and put the detonator in one of our foxholes to be exploded if we were attacked. The back-up rock would, hopefully direct all the shrapnel toward the attacking enemy. Fortunately, we never had to use it but I often wonder how effective it would have been. Improvisation is the name of the game.

My engineer was soon transferred to another unit and I was sorry to see him go - along with his bag of tricks. Unfortunately, I learned later that he was killed in a premature explosion of his own making while working on another hoped for bunker. It saddened me greatly when told of his death. I'm sure he left a young grief stricken wife.

On another occasion two young soldiers came into my platoon area carrying some kind of equipment and proceeded to set up a canvas shelter of sorts. I had no idea who they were or what they were doing. As they didn't have the courtesy to introduce themselves I being the polite individual that I am, said, "Who the hell are you guys and what are you doing in MY platoon area?"

They were a couple of nice kids from our Field Artillery Battalion and explained that they and two other teams from the FA were setting up a triangulation pattern to locate Chinese artillery positions. The three teams were spread several hundred yards apart on the MLR. Each team had listening devices with earphones and direction finders of some sort. When the Chinese artillery fired, each team would use their equipment to triangulate on the sound and thus pinpoint the Chinese position. Using their maps, they would then radio the coordinates of those gun emplacements to their FDC (Fire Direction Center). The FDC would give the firing information to our howitzer batteries and they would blaze away hoping to hit the enemy. I guess that was high-tech for those days. Compared to our current technology, that quaint system was primitive and laughable - but better than nothing. And who knows - it might have been very effective.

One of the odd things that one of our superiors back in the rear came up with was called the "Mad Minute." Every afternoon at 1500 hours (3 P.M.) all weapons on the line were to be fired for 60

War in the Land of the Morning Calm

Live fire mission.

seconds. Each rifleman, machine gunner, BAR man, and all the weapons of a rifle company were to blast away in the direction of the enemy, none of whom were visible. I'm sure our Chinese opponents must have thought we were a bit crazy not to mention the fact that it was a terrible waste of ammunition. The only reason I could think of that made sense was that by firing we were pretty much reminded or forced to clean our weapons daily. Who knows?

Friends have asked me about personal hygiene, showers, latrines, food, etc., under the circumstances in which we found ourselves. In a nutshell, living conditions were primitive. We had no showers or any way to bathe except to pour water into our helmets and sponge off as best we could. The strange thing is that I have no recollection of where we got the water, drinking or otherwise. I vaguely remember a large canvas bag hanging from a tripod close to my platoon area. Who kept if full of water or where it came from I have no idea.

Episode One - Life on the Line

Obviously, someone from the rear took care of it for us. Sanitary facilities such as latrines were non-existent. As for a change of clothes, uniform or underwear, when any of that occurred it was a real treat.

On one occasion, I was ordered to take a squad from my platoon back to Battalion Headquarters to rehearse for a patrol that was scheduled for that night. There we had the opportunity to bathe, have a hot meal, and receive a change of clothes. Wonder of wonders. We returned to our company and I took the ambush patrol out as ordered. The next morning we returned filthy dirty. It all seemed backward to me - I could have rehearsed the patrol in our company area, gone out that night, and then headed back to Battalion for a shower, etc. That way the shower and clean clothes would have lasted a couple of days!

Speaking of incoming (as we referred to Chinese artillery fire), our company Executive Officer shared a pretty substantial bunker (the only one in our area) with the Company Commander. The Execs form of entertainment was to count the number of incoming rounds we received during the night. Each morning, he would call the platoon leaders and announce, "Lt., we received one thousand rounds last night - not much damage, etc., etc." I think he was prone to exaggerate - I never counted but if we had received that much artillery fire directly on our positions we'd have all been dead or wounded in a couple of nights. If that entertained our Exec far be it for me to complain.

On one notable occasion, we had moved from one area to another a considerable distance from our previous location. We were grungy. Upon arrival, our company commander ordered every man to shave - all 180 (more or less) of us. He figured that would be a morale booster. Only one problem - no one had razors or blades. But he was insistent and finally found two or three. So we started, fortunately, most of the guys were just youngsters so there were no heavy beards to speak of. I guess we got it done but I'm sure there were many nicked jaws and a lot of tender skin when it was all over.

Food was a problem. Some units had field kitchens that were able to prepare and serve hot meals. We were not that fortunate and lived on C-rations pretty much the same as were the mainstay of front-line troops in WWII. I don't remember much about them except that they were packaged as a one-meal deal. The main entrees for dinner, for example, would be cans of beans and franks, or pork and beans, spaghetti and meatballs, and other forgettable items. There were some little things thrown in such as crackers, maybe a sweet of some sort, etc. Breakfast was powdered milk with a strange cereal mix, powdered coffee, an ounce or so tin of jelly, Spam and maybe some kind of fake egg mess. I think I existed on powdered milk and cereal. There was also an ignitable heat tab that could be placed under a canteen cup full of coffee or stew. Worked pretty good.

However, my platoon sergeant was from Puerto Rico and every few days he received some condiments from home - chili peppers, hot sauce, rice, whatever his sweet wife could think to send. We then took two or three different cans of the C-rations and dumped them in a pot with whatever goodies his wife had provided and proceeded to heat the mixture. Not exactly haute cuisine but better than nothing. He rotated home shortly after I arrived so our tasty dishes came to an end.

One other note about food - my young platoon medic was a great kid and for some reason was always at my side. He was very conscientious and would do anything I asked. But he was addicted to the horrible C-ration powdered coffee. In my book, it was akin to drinking mud but I believe he consumed 20 canteen cups a day. Mike mixed it with stale water, heated it, and consumed it promptly. One day I said to him, "Mike, if one of our guys gets hit while you're fixin' your coffee, which comes first - your wounded buddy or your coffee?" He looked at me stone-faced and with his Alabama drawl replied, "LOO-tin-unt, gonna depend on how bad he's ahurtin." A sense of humor is a requirement.

Episode One - Life on the Line

As I said above, my platoon sergeant was a Puerto Rican. Our Regiment; the 65th Infantry, was originally a National Guard unit from the island. They entered the war in the very early stages, and saw a lot of bloody combat and acquitted themselves very well. However, due to attrition and very few replacements, by the time I joined the regiment it was like any other stateside unit. I had a couple of KATUSA's, two black kids, two young Puerto Ricans and the rest were white youngsters from all over the states. They were all my boys! I was the "old man" of 24.

I had been with the company only a short time. One night as I was checking our positions, I heard guitar music close by. I went to investigate and of course, there were my two Puerto Rican lads, Miguel and Rafael, singing and plucking away. "Look guys," I said, "Don't you think it's a little dangerous making a bit of noise so close to our Chinese friends." Miguel looked at me and replied, "Si, Teniente but the Chinks know we are here, we know they are dere - it make no difference. Es verdad?" "True," I said, "but what if they get off a lucky shot and hit one of you guys. Then your duet becomes a solo. Or even worse, what if they put a slug right through that beautiful guitar?" That did it - guitar went back in the case and silence reigned once again. I snapped them a salute and said in my limited Spanish, "Buenos noches, bravo soldatas," and went on down the line. But I knew I was gonna miss that music.

Another (of many) incidents that I recall concerned a couple of Koreans approaching my platoon position late one evening. The war was winding down and we expected peace within a matter of days. The two were coming in from enemy territory but were unarmed and pretty bedraggled looking. We were in another area of the MLR at that time and in a fairly heavily wooded position at a low elevation. They seemed pretty worn out and struggling to reach us. I figured on letting them come on in but decided that I'd better call my company commander and inform him of the situation. His order was quick and simple: "Kill 'em."

7

I gave our company clerk the mission, as he was also my 57mm gunner. A 57mm recoilless rifle might be described as a fairly small portable cannon that packed a sizeable wallop. I also knew that the clerk could not hit the proverbial barn door if he were inside the barn. I stood beside him to make certain that his poor aim was as poor as what I expected. He fired and missed the two Koreans by about 30 yards. They promptly took off at a run and we never saw them again. I could not disobey my CO but I really didn't want to kill those two. So I thought my solution was a good one. No hits, no runs, no errors. And I truly believe they were a couple of South Korean line-crossers coming back from an intelligence-gathering mission. I hope they appreciated my concern for their safety! I don't recall what my CO said when I told him we missed. Probably something unprintable.

The war did end just a day or so after that incident. Trucks came in to carry us off the line and back to a reserve area. Our outfit loaded up and we slowly began moving down a dusty, dirt road. Much to my surprise, a company of Chinese fell in behind us strolling along as though we were one big, happy family. I was seated at the tailgate of the truck and they were so close I could have reached out and given them a high-five.

I took my 35mm camera and snapped a couple of pictures. One of their officers seemed to take offense and covered his face reaching for my camera as well. We were eye-ball to eye-ball. Had he snatched it the war might have started again right then and there. One of my friends had lost a lot of money in a poker game so he sold me that camera at a good price but still a lot of money. It was a Japanese 35mm Canon - very good for its day and I was not about to let our former adversary have it. Our convoy picked up speed and we left them in the dust. The war was over.

- JIM CAMPBELL

SHIPPING OUT
George Brittany

My first assignment as an officer was at Fort McClellan, Alabama, then an Infantry training facility. I was there several months as we turned out one group of trainees after another. It wasn't bad duty though sometimes tiresome. One night, out of boredom, I went to the Officers Club and played bingo. I won a table radio. The next day, my orders for Korea came through. I think that radio was the only prize I had ever won in my life so I could never separate the two events!

We shipped out from Camp Stoneman, California, on what probably was a troop ship used during WWII. I think the capacity was probably around three to four thousand troops. Being an officer, the accommodations weren't too bad. Much better than I had experienced seven years prior when I made the same trip as a young private. I shared a "stateroom" - a cubicle about 7 x 7 with two bunks, one over the other, a toilet and washbasin - with a good friend.

We had known each other for quite a while and the days passed fairly pleasantly. Enjoyed the weather, spent a lot of time on deck, placed cards, etc., and the food was pretty good. I think the length of the voyage was close to two weeks. Finally, we made port at Inchon, Korea.

Our first stop was the Replacement Depot where we received orders to report to the Seventh Infantry Division. I don't know where the Division Headquarters were located at that time but it was a fairly long jeep drive. We checked in and the two of us were assigned to one of the division's infantry regiments. As I remember, we boarded a train - it was small with wooden coaches, wood seats, broken windows, sooty and uncomfortable. As we moved north, we could see the flashes of distant artillery lighting the night sky and hear the

War in the Land of the Morning Calm

thunder of their explosions. It was like a scene out of a WWI movie, but this was real.

We arrived at Regimental Headquarters after quite a journey - but it was not over. The two of us were sent to the Third Battalion of the regiment. There we met the Battalion Commanding Officer who (at daylight) took us on a tour (on foot) of our battalion positions. We were holding a line in a very mountainous area, facing our Chinese opponents who held equally high, if not higher, terrain.

We returned to battalion headquarters where the Colonel assigned me to I (Item) Company and Ben to K (King) Company. There we parted to report to our respective units as rifle platoon leaders. Oddly, that was the very job I wanted. I immediately liked my company commander. He had been in Korea for several months and impressed me as being a good leader. He showed me around and gave me free reign to get oriented. Combat wise there wasn't much going on except incoming artillery fire.

My friend, Ben, however met a different situation. His very first night on the MLR, he was ordered to take a reconnaissance patrol into enemy territory to check out some reported Chinese activity. His patrol was ambushed and he suffered severe wounds to his abdomen from a Chinese burp gun but somehow his men got him back to their company where he was evacuated. When I heard of his bad luck I wondered why he would have been sent on such a mission his very first night. His company must have been very shorthanded. I ran into him several months later. His wounds were serious to the point that he had been airlifted to Japan for recovery. He told me that the flak jacket (which we all wore) saved his life. He rotated home and unfortunately we lost touch.

That's one of those situations where one cannot but help but wonder what would have happened had our assignments been reversed? After all, we had gone together to division, to regiment, to battalion and finally to our respective companies. He was immediately placed in harm's way while I got a free pass. But there is no point in dwelling on that sort of situation - that's a case whereby a person can play the "what if" game forever and to no avail, but I think of him from time to time and hope that he returned home to a full and happy life.

- GEORGE BRITTANY

THE QUARTERMASTER MAJOR
Bob Lombard

I was on my way to Fort Benning, Georgia, to attend 16 weeks of Basic Infantry Officers Training. I had received my commission after having completed only two years of college ROTC. Normally, that would have been a four-year requirement but I had joined the Army at age 17, serving 18 months on a short term enlistment, came home and got my college degree courtesy of the GI Bill. I never understood the generosity of the government, as I had not participated in WWII due to my age - 16 when it ended. But now it was payback time so off to Fort Benning I went as ordered.

We were all out of the same mold - young college grads that were about to serve our commitment of two or three years depending on whether we were reserve our regular officers. I was Regular Army and planned on making it a career.

The one exception to our group of neophytes was our company commander who was a Major from the Quartermaster Corp. For some reason, at his request, he transferred to the Infantry. In our book, he was an old guy - probably around 43 years of age! But he was exceedingly nice, very patient and did all the same training that we endured. In my somewhat juvenile mind, he just didn't add up to be a combat soldier. Way too soft.

Months later, I was in Korea serving on the MLR as a platoon leader. At the time we were in the Chorwon Valley area not far from OP Harry. I learned through a friend that our Major had just joined the regiment as S-3 (Operations) officer. That is a very responsible job so apparently our "old" ex-company commander had proved himself to be a very competent officer. I wish I could remember his name but that was too long ago.

13

Days later, I learned that he was KIA. He and a couple of other officers were inspecting the line. They stopped off at an artillery forward observation post in one of our adjacent companies. The bunker was on the forward slope of our ridge and the Chinese put a direct fire artillery round right through the aperture killing the FO and all others inside. The Chinese would cut a tunnel through a mountain, roll up one of their artillery pieces, get off a few shots and disappear behind the camouflage. They were deadly with their mortars and artillery. We were pounded every night and that was probably our greatest danger.

The major's death saddened me and I still think about him. Here was a man who could have finished his army career in relative safety, probably behind a desk somewhere stateside. For whatever reason, he wanted to become a combat Infantryman - and did.

I'm sure he left behind a wife and perhaps children. I wish I knew who they were so that I could personally tell them that their father and husband was a very brave man. We underestimated him.

- BOB LOMBARD

THE HOENSONG MASSACRE
ROBERT W. GROSS

On my second "unplanned" tour of combat in Korea I was assigned to Weapons Company, 3rd Battalion, 7th Regiment, 1st Marine Division. I had been in Japan recovering from wounds received at the battle of the Pusan perimeter and later at Inchon. The enemy drive on Pusan stopped and we were soon aboard ship heading to Inchon to participate in the famous end run to cut off the North Korean Army. Wounded again, I soon found myself in that hospital in Japan.

Not long after my arrival there, non-coms and officers came through the wards looking for any of us who were in any way, shape or form able to carry a rifle and fight. The million-man Chinese "Volunteer" Army had invaded across the Yalu River and our Army and Marine units were involved in vicious fighting. Many were surrounded and near annihilation. Although I had been slated to return to a stateside hospital I had healed enough to be deemed combat ready. So all of us walking wounded headed back to join the fight.

Combat operations were launched on January 4th, 1951 from Pohang, Korea, in what was called "Operation Killer." The enemy had finally been stopped and this was part of the United Nations counter offensive against the North Korean Peoples' Army and the soldiers of the Chinese Army.

The job of the Marine Infantry was to stop the enemy's momentum, push them back north killing as many of them as we could in the process and taking as few prisoners as possible. Our trigger pullers moved fast once the enemy was engaged. As the invaders retreated, it was then that we got our greatest kill ratio - up to twenty of them for each brave Marine lost.

On one gray, dismal, and drizzly afternoon we stopped for the day as it was quickly becoming too dark for any forward visibility.

We had also reached our objective that was a long, high ridge. We were the new owners of the high ground, at least on our side of that mountain.

The next morning at the break of day, we were testing to see if there were any enemy troops dug in and waiting for us to come down as we continued our advance northward. The terrain was favorable for them to attempt a surprise attack as we came clamoring down from that ridge - and we sure as hell did not want to give them the opportunity to cut us to pieces.

Fortunately, there were no enemy forces downhill, across the valley or even on the next ridge. What they did leave for us to see as they retreated was a horrible sight I can never forget. There was roughly a one-mile stretch of a gravel road running through the valley. All along that road lay over 300 dead American soldiers. They had been shot, bayoneted, dismembered, and tortured.

They were stone cold naked as the North Koreans and Chinese troops had stripped them of every stitch of their clothing, boots, weapons, and ammunition. It was bitter cold so no doubt our enemy would put their loot to good use. All of the dead were frozen in various positions - some sitting, some laying frozen to the ground while others hung haphazardly from personnel carriers, trucks and jeeps.

Most of the bodies were of very young soldiers but some were much older, indicating senior non-commissioned officers and officers who died with their men. After the bodies were identified, I learned that the most senior officer was a major, and there were a few captains and lieutenants scattered amongst the bodies. We were warned not to touch anything, as it was probable that the bodies might be booby-trapped. As it turned out, the entire convoy was loaded with such explosives.

Apparently, the Chinese had taken road signs placed by our MPs and used them to misdirect that convoy into a box canyon where it was trapped and every man annihilated. That scene and other horrible combat memories are etched forever in my brain with indelible ink... would that I could forever erase them.

After walking the entire length of this massacre, we went after the enemy with fierce determination in hopes of returning in kind... we wanted to revenge our fallen comrades. Unfortunate for us, the enemy troops had high tailed it back north and we never had the opportunity for payback time. Probably a good thing as we were bloodthirsty.

There was no mention of this episode back in the States until after the war. This was not the only incident of this type. There were several others such as those at the Sunchon Tunnel, Taegu. Kaesong, not to mention the deplorable way our POW's were treated. Many died in captivity of starvation, dysentery, torture, and disease. Our Senate later held hearings on these atrocities interviewing many of the men who had the good fortune to survive. I do not know the purpose or the results of such hearings, other than to expose to our fellow countrymen and to the world, the viciousness of our enemies.

I am grateful that I returned home, but memories such as these and many others equally as horrible have forever affected my life. With the aid of counseling and help from the Veterans Administration, I (and others like me) have found some solace and peace. But Korea is never far from our minds.

- ROBERT W. GROSS

PTSD
Robert W. Gross

Note: Bob wrote the following as a requirement from the Veterans Administration during his hearing on disability benefits. It was written, and presented to the VA in March of 2002. Here is his letter that he was kind enough to share. It is not for the faint of heart.

My introduction to post traumatic stress disorder occurred on the morning of 17th of August 1950, near the base of a mountain called No Name Ridge and listed as the most critical battle of the whole Korean War: "Never afterwards were conditions as critical, never again did the North Koreans come as close to victory."[1]

I was a Marine rifleman in a front line combat infantry company, part of the "Fire Brigade," Marines rushed from the United States to South Korea to stop the onslaught of the North Korean Peoples' Army that had overrun the Korean peninsula down to the Naktong River. It was here that Army and Marine generals had withdrawn all U.S. troops into a "last stand enclave called the Pusan Perimeter to be held at all cost."[1]

The fifteen previous days of fierce fighting, long marches under extreme conditions of water, food, and sleep deprivation quoted as, "It had taken nine grueling hours with great suffering from lack of water, heat exhaustion and over exertion in the stifling weather, the men almost went mad for water."[1] This left me ill prepared for what was about to befall me at the battle of No Name Ridge, also called Obang-ni Ridge, and on military maps as simply Hill 117.

During the frontal attack on Hill 117 a single incident changed my life forever. One of my fellow riflemen was so close to an exploding 82mm mortar round that his body was totally disintegrated. Just seconds later another 82mm mortar round landed

---

[1] Quotes from U.S. Marine Operations in Korea, Washington, D.C. Historical Branch G-3 Div. HQMC, 1954 The Pusan Perimeter.

19

right in back of a crouching Marine in front of me. That blast lifted me off the ground and when I regained my senses I noticed only a pair of legs attached at the pelvis and about 10 feet of intestines stretched forward up the hill. The rest of his body was gone.

The moment I could stagger up to him and saw what remained, I fell to my knees and could not move. My mind went crazy with fear and anger as how this could happen to a human being and it could have well been me. After a few moments, my platoon leader, 2nd Lieutenant Francis W. Muetzel, came upon the scene and literally pulled me away and back into the ongoing battle. Before the next morning was over, the battle proved to be far worse and bloodier than what we both had just encountered.

It happened at 0230. (2:30 AM) A green signal flare soared into the sky and the enemy hit - hit hard directly in front of A Company, my company, and soon we were over-run with enemy soldiers spraying the battlefield with submachine gun fire and hundreds of hand grenades in a massive close quarter combat zone of 20 feet or less.

It is here in the dark of night that my body was imprinted with the ultimate horror of lying in a shallow fox hole, both of my hand grenades long gone, and now I've used up all my ammo - I was 17 years of age and forced to make a personal decision. Do I attack the enemy bare handed and be dead in seconds or maybe if I lay motionless and appear dead perhaps I can survive this night. If I move, I'll be killed by the enemy or mistaken for the enemy and killed by my own marines.

As the battle played out, I was forced to listen to the chaos of combat and it is so terrible that the English language provides me with no words to speak the unspeakable. The sights, sounds, smells of it all haunts me to this very day as it has every day of my life for fifty years.

The sounds are unshakable of dying men's last sounds, the wounded crying out for help, even help from their mothers and wives. But no help comes as anything that moves is killed either by the enemy or in the dark of night, shot by friendly fire. As I lay there and listened to those sounds 'till daybreak, knowing there was nothing I could do to help my buddies, my mind and body was so consumed with guilt that even now I am frequently and totally incapacitated by those feelings. In a more sanitized version of what happened I leave to Marine historians who simply said that the Marines of Companies A and B stood, fought and died but held their ground.

One of the most somber moments of my life came during the morning report (a log of the previous day's events) pertaining to the night of August 17th and 18th. The sun was just breaking over the horizon and beginning to illuminate the battlefield. The sight was horrifying as there was not a tree standing. Only the blown off stubs of trunks remained and every ten feet or so were huge holes in the ground from artillery, mortars and grenades. The stench of smoke, burning flesh and other matter filled the air.

Most horrible of all was the body count as listed in that report. Graves Registration teams moved in to pick up the dead and dismembered body parts. There were only 90 of us remaining alive from the 185 at the start of the night. I cannot to this day forget those memories and frequently those memories have caused me major personal problems such as the shakes and lack of focus on anything.

The constant ringing in my ears is an ever present reminder of what caused it - a 500 pound bomb exploding a mere 100 feet from where I lay. The blast and concussion perforated my right eardrum. So intense was the blast that it literally lifted our bodies off the ground and into a semi-conscious state after which my sense of hearing, as I knew it, was gone forever. My ears continued to bleed for several weeks.

I continued to fight the enemy as a rifleman until I was pulled from the front lines on the 15th of September because of my age (17) and injuries. A few days later, I was on my way to Japan for medical care and processing back to the U.S. Instead, I was ordered back to Korea on the 4th of January 1951, to a front line unit, Weapons Company, 3rd Battalion, 7th Marine Regiment. This was the beginning of the first United Nations counter-offensive against the Chinese. It began in the mountains near the 38th Parallel. The weather that day was 12° below zero. Cold weather gear did not arrive in Korea until the spring of 1951. Most of my company, including me, suffered frostbite to some degree.

After 70 days of cold weather mountain combat my luck played out as we attacked Hill 356. I was badly wounded by an enemy mortar shell that knocked me unconscious and left pieces of shrapnel in my chest. I was airlifted to the naval hospital ship U.S.S. Repose standing off the coast of Korea where the largest shards of metal were removed from and my eardrums inserted with tubes to relieve the pressure.

From the Repose, I went to hospitals in Japan and then on to the U.S. Naval Hospital at Portsmouth, Virginia. There I was finally transferred to Fleet Marine Force disability retired list as a result of my combat wounds. I suffered from hearing loss, tinnitus, anxiety reaction, bad nerves and some shrapnel still imbedded in my chest. I was then twenty years of age. Five year later, I was found unfit for duty and was turned over to the Veterans Administration.

For the last 50 years, I have suffered physically, emotionally and financially as a direct result of my combat experiences. As a young man, the tinnitus was of such severe nature as to almost drive me crazy. Now as an old man it has kept me from concentrating, staying focused, or studying for better opportunities under the GI Bill. This has caused me to move all over the U.S. from job to job always trying.

Episode Five - PTSD

The PTSD has caused me to have no normal routine as I could not to this day develop a pattern of regular sleep. I was nervous and jumpy and I tried to self-medicate with alcohol and a myriad of over the counter drugs such as barbiturates, etc., which only compounded my problems. I never knew from day to day what I wanted to be or where I wanted to stay. I had no pleasure being in the company of others as they made my problems worse. I isolated myself from my family, especially my children, who were left to my wife to be raised without a father. This has always caused me much remorse. PTSD follows a former combatant into old age like a steel ball chained to his leg, always there, always heavy, always bad...

Then one day in 1994, the stress of trying to carry on a job as a commissioned sales man became too overwhelming, and I simply walked out of the building. And I continued walking for several miles until totally exhausted and then called for my wife to come and get me.

To this day, the problems of trying for one good-nights rest, the nightmares, the sweats, flashbacks, the washed out feeling, hangovers from medications, being unnerved around people, not being able to suppress the terrible ringing in both ears, and finally having to live with a low grade continuous ache in my right ear was more than I was able to handle alone.

So, for most of this past year I have been attending PTSD group therapy sessions at the VA Clinic in Orlando, Florida. I also attend bi-weekly individual therapy sessions at the VA Center with Bill Sautner. Only time will tell.

- ROBERT W. GROSS

FOOTNOTE FROM BOB GROSS:

A few days before the first Provisional Marine Brigade was to dock at Pusan, Korea, August 2nd, 1950, all Marines on all the ships were lined up on deck and were told the following:

A. You are to sign your Last Will and Testament naming a beneficiary in the event of your death.

B. You are to divest yourselves of all billfolds, photos, paper money or coins and either send them home in a mailing pouch or throw the contents of your billfold into a G. I. can provided for that purpose.

C. We were then give a laminated card with necklace stating that if taken a Prisoner of War we were by the Geneva Articles of War required only to give our name, rank, serial number and nothing else.

D. We were then issued an M-1 rifle, ammo, and two hand grenades.

This episode brought home the grim reality of mortal combat that was soon to befall each and every one of us.

THE 5TH REGIMENTAL COMBAT TEAM
JACK ENKEMAN

My name is Jack Enkemann. I was one of the many who were drafted for service during the Korean War. The conflict in Korea started in late June 1950, and I was conscripted in late summer of that year and reported for duty in early December 1950, for a two-year period.

Along with several other friends we were assigned to the 114th Combat Engineers at Camp (now Fort) McCoy, Wisconsin. Engineers build roads, airstrips, etc., and part of the battalion was a Medical Detachment. I became part of that unit and our responsibility was to learn to be medics and care for the men who did the construction work. It seemed like a very good deal and I quickly grew to like my assignment. I even had the opportunity to go to Fort Sam Houston, San Antonio, Texas, and qualify as an Operating Room Technician.

The two years seemed to pass rather quickly and as I neared the end of spring in 1952, I envisioned December and the end of my obligation to the Army. However, while on leave in late May, I was "rescued" by the Michigan State Police and ordered to report back to Camp McCoy for assignment to FECOM (Far East Command).

By Special Orders I went from McCoy by train to Fort Lewis, Washington; by troop ship to Yokohama, Japan; by train to Sasebo, Japan; and by boat to Pusan, Korea. And finally, by truck to the combat zone in the north. I was assigned to the 5th Regimental Combat Team, a beefed up Infantry Regiment that had seen a great deal of action in the earlier days of the North Korean invasion.

Oddly enough, when I joined the regiment I was informed that there was not a need for combat medics at that time. By then I was a sergeant, but suddenly found myself to be a rifleman. In short order however, I was assigned to a weapons platoon and became a squad leader of a 57mm recoilless rifle section. I also had a couple of heavy

.30 caliber water-cooled machine guns under my command. They were of WWII vintage and were very cumbersome. The downside of all this was that I had had absolutely no training in any of this sort of thing. I knew nothing about my new job. Needless to say I was a bit nervous.

The 5th RCT had been in reserve for a short time but we received orders to relieve a unit of the 24th Infantry Division, which was leaving the MLR. We started receiving heavy artillery fire immediately upon our arrival and my guys were scared witless - most of us were new to combat. As the squad leader, I had to appear fearless but it was difficult.

In June of 1952, we became part of the 25th Infantry Division since what was left of the original 5th RCT was pretty well beaten down and there were a lot of short timers and many new men in the unit. We were back on line in new defensive positions consisting of shallow trenches. Incoming mortar and artillery fire seemed endless. My guys were nervous and would shoot at anything. I tried to calm them but part of the problem was, of all things, rats!

We were living on C rations so we would throw the empty cans, uneaten food, etc., out in front of our positions. At night, the rats came out in force and their foraging and rattling of tin containers brought on unwarranted machine gun and rifle fire. If killing rats had been our objective, my guys were doing a great job. Eventually, we became accustomed to our situation and settled in. But we never got over the fear of constant incoming Chinese mortar and artillery concentrations. Only those who have suffered through these things can understand the sheer terror of simply trying and hoping to survive.

On a lighter side, once a week I was allowed to go back to the supply point and buy beer for those who wanted it. Those who didn't drink would allow one of his buddies to buy his share. I thought it sold at six cans for a dollar but as it turned out, it was six cans for seventy-five cents. I collected the money but pocketed the extra quarter. Seemed only fair, as I had to make the long trip! And I didn't get rich.

Early October of 1952, I was transferred back to being a Combat Medic. I suppose I am probably one of the few men who can wear both the Combat Infantryman Badge and the Combat Medic Badge. I'm proud of that fact and I'm also proud of the fact that I served. We gave the people of South Korea a chance at a better life and they certainly made the best of it. I know they are grateful.

- JACK ENKEMAN

THE BURKE BOYS
Henry H. Burke

My name is Henry Burke. I enlisted in the Army from my hometown of Burlington, N.C. I knew I was going to be drafted and I didn't have a job so I went ahead and enlisted to get it over with. I went to Raleigh where we were inducted and met a guy there whose name was John Burke. He had volunteered also. We were not related but discovered that we lived only 45 miles from one another. We've been friends ever since as you will learn.

We went to Fort Jackson, S.C. where we got our shots, uniforms, and equipment and then boarded a bus for Fort Benning, Georgia. We arrived there a day or so later and drove past these big, brick four story buildings that looked like an old fort or something like that. We drove around this area and I said, "My Gawd, this ain't the Army, this is a college!" Those old buildings must have dated back to the '30s.

John and I started our basic training with the 30th Infantry Regiment. We stayed there about three weeks and then moved down to the airfield at Ft. Benning, Lawson Field. Then we were moved to the Harmony Church area and those of you who took your training know where that is. It's about as far as you can get from those nice brick buildings of "the college" into the back woods of Georgia. The middle of nowhere.

We were in that area to take our advanced Infantry training. Soon after, orders for Korea came down. There was an airline strike so we were bussed to San Francisco and then to Camp Stoneman. We were given a short leave, which we spent in Frisco. There I rode my first trolley and went down on the wharf and swam in the bay! Made a real day of it.

Then we were on our way to Japan where we were issued equipment, weapons, etc. From there we headed for Korea making port at Inchon and on to the Replacement Depot. I was assigned to the Third Infantry Division, along with John. If fact we were both assigned to G (George) Company, 2nd Battalion, of the 15th Infantry Regiment. We were sent up to the line almost immediately. A rifle company consists of about 200 men. The company when we arrived was down to nineteen! They had just come back from combat on Hills 477 and 487, September 1951.

We started training again and familiarized ourselves with some of the weapons used by the enemy. A few days later we were sent to a rear area where we received more combat training including working with the tanks of our armor battalion. Then we moved back on line on Thanksgiving Day, 1951. We moved into a blocking position and my first job was to go on LP (Listening Post) duty with another guy.

We went out at midnight and we were supposed to be relieved in two hours. It was 6° below zero, snow on the ground, and no one came to take over the position. We sat in that hole for five hours before relief came. When we finally got out, my feet felt like I was walking on razor blades or something. We 'bout froze to death. I went back to my other hole inside the company perimeter, pulled my parka close around me, and fell asleep. When I awoke this time, my feet and legs were numb.

Knew I had to walk to get some circulation going so I headed down the road to where the Brits had built a nice fire. I tramped around that fire for two hours thawing my feet out. Then lo and behold, the rear echelon guys brought Thanksgiving dinner up to us right there beside that road. Artillery fire started coming in and nobody was going to eat under those circumstances.

I said, "Well, there were twelve in my family so no one was bashful at our table." It was first come first served and I wasn't going to miss out on this meal. I went ahead and started helping myself to that turkey, dressing, gravy, mashed potatoes, and all that good stuff. An artillery round hit a little close and a piece of shrapnel smacked me in the butt. It didn't break the skin so I just kept on eatin'! It was a great Thanksgiving meal.

That evening we got orders to take a crucial hill. We were under strength, our company consisting of only 150 men. There should have been 200 of us. We moved out and attacked the highest point on the central front know as Little Gibraltar, Hill 355. It was about dusk and we had been fighting there for about five hours.

The Chinese hit us with a reinforced regiment - over 1,500 men. Bugles blowing, whistles shrilling. We had eight killed, 64 wounded, running out of ammunition, one officer left - pick up the wounded and withdraw. We went back down the hill and thanked God they didn't follow us.

The next morning the 7th Regiment moved through us and retook the objective without a shot being fired. By three o'clock that afternoon, they counted 1,500 dead Chinese. What happened was this - after we pulled off the hill, artillery was called in and with air bursts and high explosives decimated the Chinese forces. Those airbursts would mop out anything. An airburst was fused to explode a few feet above the ground instead of on impact. That way, shrapnel flew in all directions cutting down anyone in its path.

We went back into reserve. Some of our wounded came back from the hospital and we had some new replacements come in. From there we moved over to OP 200 and occupied that position for about two months, to the left of the Imjin River. On Christmas night, about five of us put on white snow gear, as there was about two feet of snow on the ground. And again, about five degrees below zero.

We headed for the river on a normal patrol mission. When we got there, the Chinese had hung Christmas cards saying, "Your friends back home are partying," "They don't care about you." "Come on over to our side, etc. etc." We collected those cards and I still have some at home.

We went back into reserves for a while and then went to relieve the Marines at Kimpo air base, near Seoul. We were there about three weeks and then moved back up on line to find ourselves once again in combat at OP Kelly. I don't remember where Kelly was located. We had come in off of another hill, which we had just lost, but with no casualties. My buddy, John Burke, had been my squad leader and I was his assistant. He later became a platoon sergeant and was occupying the hill that we had lost three times. The Chinese hit his position with a reinforced battalion and in the fight, John took shrapnel from a grenade to his back. He was evacuated by helicopter. Almost 50 years to the day, that piece of shrapnel surfaced. It was about an inch and a quarter long and a quarter inch wide. It was removed surgically and he carries it in his wallet as a memento.

He retired a major, a fine soldier. We've stayed in touch all these years and see one another from time to time. I retired after 24 years of service. I am proud to have served and consider myself fortunate. I had men fall on my right and my left but I never received a scratch. On three occasions, I was blown away from my weapon. So I thank God that I was able to do my job and return home safely.

- HENRY H. BURKE

ADDENDUM FROM JOHN
John Burke

Sometime during 1952 Henry and I were transported back to the rear were we got a much needed shower and a change of clothes. We were then "escorted" to a tent, given some paper and a pencil, and asked to write anything that came to mind about our experiences to date. It seems that a book concerning the History of the Third Infantry Division in Korea was in progress. This is what I wrote and, in fact, two or three years later found the book and there was my write-up:

"That old saying, 'a feller needs a friend" is more true here than any place I can think about. I'm lucky, because I don't need one. I already have a good friend.

My buddy and I bumped into each other the first day I came in the army and we've been together ever since. We're not related but have the same last name 'Burke,' only my first name is John and his is Henry. We took our basic training together, came to Korea together, and were sent to the same company and even the same squad. I'm squad leader and Henry is assistant squad leader. It's always seemed sort of natural for us to just stay together a good part of the time. Work gets done much easier when we can both do it. We take care of each other. And usually, when someone yells, "Burke," we both answer.

One time or battalion was sent in to support another regiment. Everyone was in a dither. No one exactly knew what was about to come off. All of a sudden, the CO came storming up with the order to attack Hill 355. We knew it was going to be bad.

We made the attack and never were far apart. I kept calling Henry's name to make sure he was still all right and every now and then he would call me. Knowing he was there made me feel more secure and more confident.

That fight was fierce. The Chinks threw in a big counterattack and we were ordered to pull back down the hill. We called back and forth occasionally all the way down to make sure we both were making it.

Since then, we've been on numerous patrols together. We take frequent looks to check on each other. I always feel better when Henry grins or waves back.

Friends are valuable anywhere, but I thank God especially that I have one here. When the chips are down, a buddy is just like money in the bank - you can count on him.

Obviously, there is a bond forged between men together in combat that transcends most any experience one might have in civilian life. John and I have enjoyed our friendship these many, many years.

- JOHN BURKE

HILL ONE-ONE-SEVEN
Daniel Wolfe

NOTE: I ran across Dan's poem in another publication. I contacted him and asked his permission to use it here and he was kind enough to do so. I also discovered that he authored a book of his experiences while in Korea entitled COLD GROUND'S BEEN MY BED. It is available on Amazon.com and well-worth reading. By the way, Dan was awarded the Bronze Star for Valor for his actions depicted in his poem. Here it is:

Korea, August 8th, 1952 - On this date I was a draftee with Love Company (L), 15th Infantry Regiment, Third Infantry Division. Charley Kauneckis was point man, I was the runner, Lt. W. A. Sidney was our intrepid Company Commander, and Sgt. Robert Massengale was out Assistant Platoon Sergeant.

Hill One-One-Seven was only a wart of a hill
Artillery would level it before we go in for the kill
We'll cross the Imjin; it'll be a walk in the park
My vest and helmet won't be seen in the dark.

Two bandoliers, two grenades are enough for this mission
Let's be off to the Chaplain before we head for perdition
The Lord is my Shepherd…was his solemn prayer
Will those words shield me while I'm a target out there?

What will Ma do if she gets the sad news?
Your son was a hero, but we have some bad news
Dusk over the Imjin helps our jon boats get through
We assembled at the Bubble for another review.

With Charley at the point and Sid leading the raid
I unlatched my safety and secured each grenade
A trail matted with wire led us along a steep cliff
It was here Charley whispered, "Come close, have a whiff."

It's kim chi, it's garlic; it stinks up the air
Run and tell Sid the Gooks are out there
Into the ditch shouted Sid, the artillery will blast 'em
A round plunged into the Imjin, another flew past them.

So much for the shells; let's move up the Hill
I hurled the grenades; whose blood did I spill?
Bullets from burp guns buzzed overhead
Some buddies lay wounded; how many were dead?

Down the cliff yelled Sid, our ammo is low
The men skidded and slid to the Imjin below
When I began to descend, Poodles ran up and said
"Massengale's out there, I think he's dead."

Follow me, Poodles, and keep your head down
I crawled under fire but Poodles was gone.
Massengale's collar in hand, I dragged him away
My heart beat like thunder, will I see another day?

I buckled his ankles with my web GI belt
We tumbled to the Imjin, what a hand I was dealt
His helmet was gone; his vest was in shreds
My O.D. fatigues were a pallet of reds.

Bullets pockmarked the Imjin; will we ever reach a boat
I edged closer to the cliff with Massengale afloat
They didn't see us; they missed us amid all the slaughter
He was a hero on the cliff but cold dead in the water.

Episode Eight - Hill 117

Ah, there's a jon boat; I towed him across
Graves Registration was waiting to record Love Company's loss
Swaddled in a body bag, its zipper tolled the knell
Massengale was at rest after his visit to Hell.

Wet in my bunker I zipped up my sack
The zip of the zipper zipped I was back
I survived through the night; I'll never know why
Maybe the old adage was true, I was too mean to die.

Dear Ma, Dear Pa, nothing's going on here
I'm far south of Seoul, way back in the rear
I'll send a few photos, show the guys my great tan
Tell them I'm a hero, your rear-echelon Dan.

- DANIEL WOLFE

SILVER STAR LOST
BERNARD J. FARNAN

My name is Bernard (Ben) J. Farnan. I am a first generation American, my parents having emigrated from Ireland. I know the Emerald Isles must be beautiful but for me to have been born in the United States of America was a privilege for which I shall forever be grateful.

I had a good childhood, growing up in Glen Cove, N.Y. where I was born. I went to public schools there and participated in sports, particularly baseball, basketball and football. After graduating, I worked alongside my mason father as a bricklayer and cement finisher and continued my interest in football. In fact, I had just finished the playoffs of my semi-pro football season when I was drafted in November of 1951.

Several us were sent to Fort Knox, Kentucky, for basic training. Fort Knox was the main base for the Army's armored forces. Our training there emphasized reconnaissance missions along with standard infantry operations.

We shipped out in June of 1952 and upon arrival in Korea, our unit was assigned to the 3rd Reconnaissance Company (Scout Section) of the Third Infantry Division. Sometime in September of that year we were attached to the 65th Infantry Regiment, a Puerto Rican National Guard outfit, now part of the division. The 65th was having some problems and seemed to be in need of assistance.

On September 18th, 1952, our Scout Section was to set up an ambush at the base of Outpost Kelly located in the Yonchon area of North Korea. A buddy of mine, an American Indian, was selected

War in the Land of the Morning Calm

from my platoon to go on this assignment. He was somewhat concerned as he was scheduled to rotate home in two weeks. I volunteered to replace him as he was truly a "short-timer." I know he was very grateful.

We moved out at dusk through a safe-lane in the MLR that had been marked as a pathway out to the valley. We were all decked out for battle - blacked out faces, taped dog tags, camouflage on our helmets, extra ammo, etc. We waited for the chaplain who made it a practice to say a few words on our behalf before we headed out. On this particular evening, we were greeted instead by a rabbi. This was a first for us but he graciously bestowed an ecumenical blessing on our group for which we were very thankful.

We crossed the LD and headed for our objective. The silence was broken a little later when one of my buddies (who came from the deep, deep south) turned to me and whispered, "Ben, what the hell is a rabbi?" Knowing his background, I told him that since I was a New Yorker I knew all about rabbis so, "trust me, we were in good hands." That pacified him and we continued on our way.

As darkness settled we set up in a skirmish line at the base of Hill Kelly. Between 2000 and 2100 hours we would occasionally get showered with rocks and dirt rolling down from above. Suddenly, the bugles and horns began to blare as Kelly was surrounded and under attack by the Chinese. Flares lit up the sky and the blasts of burp guns and small arms fire filled the air. Our artillery began dropping pre-planned concentrations with the shells screaming in over our heads and slamming into the Chinese troops.

While this was taking place, our squad was hit from our left flank. Our NCO in charge became disoriented and unceremoniously left us. Two ROK soldiers in our squad left as well. Not a good situation. Now I was in charge.

I led what was left of the squad into a deep ravine that had a fair amount of water caused by run off from the mountains and high terrain on our right flank. I placed the remainder of the squad on both sides of the gully hoping that we were pretty well concealed. Unfortunately, I was wrong - a grenade came bouncing into our midst. I was blown back against the bank but the waist deep water absorbed most of the explosion and shrapnel. One of the guys got a sliver in his upper lip and a large piece ripped the burlap cover on my helmet and dented it as well.

I realized that we had to move again to escape the Chinese patrol. We scrambled to another area that provided more concealment with bushes and reeds in the area. To our good fortune, the Chinese left and I asked another close buddy, Jim Wheeles, to assist me in finding our way back to the MLR the following morning.

Jim took point and I took rear guard position and we made our way back safely with no further incidents. We learned that we were the only patrol in the valley that night and we had been given up for dead. We were happy to report that such was not the case but the men defending OP Kelly did not fare as well. There were few survivors of that engagement.

I did tell Arnold, my Georgia pal, that I was right - the rabbi had done a good job for us and saw our squad to safety. I do believe Arnold was truly grateful. We all were!

Jim Wheeles and I were written up for the Bronze Star, the Army's fourth highest award for valor. (When our son was born, we named him Kelly in honor of those brave men who fought and died on OP Kelly.)

A month later, we were moved to the Chorwon Valley area, I believe near Kumhwa. The date sticks in my mind - 28th of October 1952. Our mission was to help retake Iron Horse Mountain, also known as Jackson Heights. It seems that a battalion of the 65th Infantry Regiment refused to assault the Chinese positions and 97 Puerto Ricans were placed under arrest and court martialed for disobeying a direct order. Much later I learned that there was considerable dispute about the fairness of the charges.

We moved into our positions at nightfall. Severe fighting was in full progress on the mountain. Somehow, I heard moans coming from directly in front of my position - apparently in the middle of a minefield. There was a very thick fog throughout the night and visibility was much impeded. As the fog began to thin, I shimmied up a thin sapling to get a better view. I was able to see a figure sprawled on the ground obviously in pain.

I notified my platoon leader. Jim Wheeles and a buddy, Henry Davis, joined me as we made our way toward the wounded man. He was one of the 65th Infantry guys and was laying in a slight depression made by the detonated mine. It appeared that one leg was partially blown off and he was surely in shock. Time, for him, was running out.

The fog began to lift and the sun was rising. I noticed that the very thin trip wires in the minefield (just at grass level) stood out distinctly because of the shimmering dewdrops dripping from them. Like tiny birds on a telephone wire. I told our Captain that I would go in and make pronounced footprints so that Henry could follow me hopefully without any danger. Of course, if I were to step on a buried mine that game would be over.

The rabbi must have still been with us for I reached the wounded man safely and Henry followed with a stretcher. We followed our foot steps back out and a MASH chopper evacuated him. I don't know to this day if he survived - I pray that he did. For that episode, I was recommended for the Silver Star and Henry, for the Bronze. But my records were later destroyed in a fire at the St. Louis, Missouri, records center so I never received the awards.

Some fifty years later I began searching and located Jim in Alaska and another buddy in South Carolina. The Military Historian in my city became interested in my story and wrote of it in local papers, which created some helpful interest for my cause. My buddies produced eyewitness affidavits and Congressman Peter Kind has taken up my quest. Whether or not I receive the Silver and Bronze Star is of no great importance to me - but I would like for my

Episode Nine - Silver Star Lost

children and grandchildren to see them and hold them. I would like them to know that men and women of our military are brave and selfless and many have sacrificed their lives so that others could live in peace. And I am certain that the people of South Korea will never forget what our allies and we did for their fledgling nation.

- BERNARD J. FARNAN

Ben Farnan's family and 50th Anniversary in 2006.

BATTLE OF CHANGTO
MARTIN LEE BROUSSARD

Martin Lee on the left.

My name is Martin Lee Broussard of St. Martinville, Louisiana. I was a member of GHQ First Raider Company. The company was formed shortly after the outbreak of the Korean War in June of 1950. It was said that ours was the only unit reported in combat from the day it arrived in Korea until the day it left in April 1951. Our first mission was related to Inchon.

The Inchon landing had been planned and General McArthur had been warned that the port was heavily defended by the North Korean Army. Furthermore, the huge rise and fall of the tide, some 12 to 24 feet, would make it very difficult for assault barges to land troops ashore. So it was decided by our high command to make a diversionary raid on the Korean coast in the area of Kunsan, some 100 miles south of Inchon. It was hoped that the raid would draw the North Korean forces away from the actual landing site.

My outfit was given the task of taking a look at that proposed fake site. We went by sea aboard a Navy ship and some distance offshore, put our rubber rafts in the water. There were three teams, 12 of us per raft. Each boat had a swimmer. That was my initial task. The three of us dropped off our respective rafts about 300 yards from shore and swam in. Our exposed skin was blackened and we carried penlights on our headgear and a bayonet on our belt. Our task was to scout the area and if there seemed to be no problems, signal the assault rafts to come in. With approximately 36 of us ashore, we were able to make a more extensive recon of the area. Shortly, however, we came under heavy enemy fire and our reconnaissance ended as we retreated back to sea.

War in the Land of the Morning Calm

For whatever reason, the Inchon landing proceeded as originally planned. Our company took part and as it turned out, the port was not heavily defended as had been anticipated. The objective of the unit to which we were attached was Kimpo Airfield, several miles south of Seoul.

On our way, we came upon a South Korean Army unit that was surrounded and being attacked by a larger North Korean force. We went to their aid with the intention of breaking the South Koreans from their trap. When we finally joined forces, the ROK (Republic of South Korea) Commanding Officer said, "What the Hell are you doing here?!" Our CO replied, "We just thought you might need some help." The ROK's reply was something to the effect that the officer leading the North Korean attack was his brother and it was his, the ROK CO's desire to kick his brother's ass! Didn't need our help - so we departed.

Sometime after that little dustup we found ourselves on the move and heading into North Korea. I don't know exactly where we were other than heading north. We came into an area where we looked down on a rather small valley. It was full of harvested sheaves of rice all stacked and wrapped looking like teepees. As the company struggled along, one of the guys yelled, "Hey, those damned bunches of rice are moving." We stopped and sure enough, one would move a few feet and then another - heading toward the high ground.

Our CO immediately called for an air strike and fortunately, a flight of P-51 fighter-bombers was on station. In a matter of minutes, they were making strafing runs with their four .50 caliber machine guns blazing away. We joined the fight pouring rifle and machine gun fire into the rice stacks. Oddly enough, the sheaves of rice quit moving! In fact, rice and bodies were scattered all over that valley. We moved on.

Sometime during the last days of March 1951, our raider company made a recon patrol about seven miles behind enemy lines.

Episode Ten - Battle of Changto

The purpose of the raid was to determine the strength of the Chinese and North Korean units facing our forces in that area. My good friends, Jamie Lee, Jack Harper and Cecil Kimrey (I had not been invited!) had stopped to take a rest.

It was a bright moonlit night and the three of them were on a hillside observing some enemy troops mining a road. Suddenly, a North Korean patrol stumbled into the area and their Lieutenant was calling out for their password. Jamie was resting on the slope holding his rifle with his left hand, butt of the weapon on the ground, muzzle pointed straight up. The Korean officer reached for his Burp gun slung over his shoulder but didn't move quite fast enough. Jamie had no time to aim, just slid has hand down to the trigger, canted the M-1 toward the Korean officer and snapped off a shot. It took him square in the chest. The other two North Koreans were dispatched quickly.

Our unit (with the Burp gun and the shoulder patch of the Korean officer to identify his division) headed back toward friendly lines. A snapshot of the patrol upon their return appeared years later on the cover of a book written by George Forty. In that picture Jamie has that Burp gun slung across his chest with a bullet hole in the leather sling clearly showing the entry point, which killed the NK officer.

Eventually, we fought our way across Korea all the way north to the Yalu River. Arguably we were the first unit to reach it in November 1950. Also, we may have been the first unit to make contact with the Chinese that same month. One thing for certain, all Hell broke loose with the invasion of that million-man Chinese Army. The cold was unbelievable. Water froze in our canteens but that was a minor thing. On one occasion, as we were advancing one of my buddies said tracers were going between my legs! I heard later that there was a meteorological specialist with the Marines. During the 17-day battle and retreat from the Chosin Reservoir he recorded temperatures of 20 to 40 degrees below zero. On one night, it hit 60 below with sixty MPH wind gusts. The aid stations were filled with so many wounded that little if anything could be done for those with

War in the Land of the Morning Calm

frozen feet, legs and hands. Many of those who survived suffered their entire lives as a result of frostbite and frozen limbs.

We made it back to the port of Hamnung where the evacuation of our troops and civilians was underway. There were some 90,000 Korean refugees trying to flee to the South. Mixed in with them were North Korean infiltrators so a thorough screening was taking place. Eventually, the withdrawal was completed and the port destroyed. My unit, along with others, was airlifted out on C-54 Air Force transport planes.

All too soon, we were back in the fight. This time at a place called Changto, a small hamlet, in North Korea. Changto had been a rice growing and storage area and was apparently still productive. After the expulsion of our forces from the north, the North Koreans wanted it and sent two regiments (around four to five thousand men) to pillage and secure it. The defense force consisted of a couple of hundred South Korean Marines. Our Raider unit of roughly 200 arrived to reinforce and aid in the defense.

We got there tired and hungry and took up temporary quarters in a small house in the schoolyard that was surrounded by a three-foot high stone wall. The South Koreans occupied an old-time earthen fort north of a dry streambed separating the schoolyard from the fort. Our rest ended abruptly with enemy bullets whizzing through the frail walls of the schoolhouse. The Battle of Changto was on. The North Koreans controlled the high ground to our east, south and west.

The fight started the morning of the 13th of January 1951. The weather was brutally cold and snowy. As the morning turned to evening, firing increased from sporadic to intense and more so as nighttime approached. What was fairly long-range mortar and 61-caliber machine gun fire during the first day turned into the first of fourteen mostly nighttime Banzai attacks. Screaming and shrieking hordes of North Koreans came streaming down the hillsides wielding

Episode Ten - Battle of Changto

burp guns, rifles, bayonets, and grenades. They attacked primarily from the northeast, east, and southeast quadrants.

Both sides realized quickly that this was a battle to the death, no quarter asked or given. By the end of the second day, it was obvious that ammo would soon be in short supply. We called for airdrops to replenish it. The effort was undertaken with limited success as the wind and falling snow made target identification difficult. And the wind caused significant amounts to drift toward our enemies and away from our forces.

During the afternoon of the second day, a small helicopter landed by our rock wall south of the perimeter to bring in ammo and take out some of our wounded. I learned later that this was the first time a chopper had ever been used to evacuate wounded from an active battle zone. Unfortunately, on this first attempt the chopper would not start, it had a dead battery. The pilots were forced to spend the night as infantrymen armed with no more than .45 caliber pistols. On the third day, another copter came in with a spare battery and both left carrying out the wounded.

As midnight of the second night approached there was no let-up in the intensity of the fight. With ammo running even lower, orders came down from Hqs. for our unit to make our way across the dry streambed just north of our position and join the South Koreans in the old mud fort. We attempted to do so, starting on the south side of the schoolyard perimeter.

Unfortunately, the North Koreans had infiltrated the streambed making our crossing impossible. Again, lack of ammo was a problem so we redistributed it from the "haves" to the "have-not's" to compensate as best we could for a serious problem. Night turned to day with no slow-down in the intensity of repeated attacks until the following morning.

Fortunately, clearing weather allowed us to call in a flight of Marine Corsair ground attack planes. They made strafing and napalm runs; that combined with a relief column coming to our aid from the south, convinced the North Koreans that they had had enough. They began retreating to the northeast leaving by South Korean count, more than 1,200 plus bodies in the snow, 870 wounded and many POWs taken. Despite the fact that the enemy had the advantage of the high ground and great superiority in numbers, we suffered fewer than twenty dead and wounded. Of course, that was twenty too many.

In April of 1951, I was rotated back to Japan and a few months later shipped out for the states. A slow train across country and finally I was back in Cajun country, New Iberia and home, Loreauville, Louisiana. Population about 500. It was 4:00 A.M. when we pulled into the station in New Iberia. I called my brother and he was there in a matter of minutes. We drove over to Aunt T's restaurant and there was my Dad's Chrysler out front. We walked in and heard the voices of my Mother and Aunt T in the kitchen. Hugs, crying, screams and pans hitting the floor, gumbo flying. It was good to be home and as we say in Cajun Country, "Laissez les bons temps rouler!"

- MARTIN LEE BROUSSARD

RADIO OPERATOR
Tactical Air Control Party

EDITORS' NOTE: The contributor of the following story chose to remain anonymous and his wish will be granted. However, I would like to mention that he was the recipient of the Silver Star, the Navy Cross, several Purple Hearts (he admitted to three), nine Battle Stars, two Unit Citations, a Korean Presidential Unit Citation, and probably several other decorations that he was too modest to mention. The following is his story:

The draft was in full swing, but with me it was never a consideration. I liked the Marine Corps reputation for their esprit de corps and promptly joined at age 17. First stop, of course, was Parris Island where I received my boot training and then on to radio school at Fort Del Mar, California.

We shipped out in August of 1950 arriving in Pusan, Korea, where we went into a staging area for a couple of days. We could hear artillery fire off in the distance and to say we were nervous would be a serious understatement. We strung tin cans around our perimeter to alert us to any infiltrators. Truthfully, we were all scared to death; that first night we were engaged in a firefight with anything that moved. I think we killed two goats and a cow. We shot at shadows and anything else that looked or sounded threatening. That was our initiation to war.

Shortly after, we moved north and relieved an Army unit that had taken a ridge and then been driven off by the North Koreans. We retook the position; the Army unit moved back in and lost it a second time. We went back in and I think that before it was all over that ridge changed hands three times. Casualties were heavy on both sides.

The North Koreans called us the Yellow Leg Devils as we wore the old style lace-up leggings instead of combat boots. We called ourselves the Fire Brigade, as it seems we were assigned to plug holes, or whatever was needed. I was with the 1st Battalion of the 5th Marine Regiment and as my training suggests, I was a Tactical Air Controller. My primary job as such was to call in air or naval strikes on targets of opportunity.

The sweetest hit was near the Naktong River. I believe the 25th Infantry Division was holding a line in that area and had withdrawn to the south side of the river. We had been in the area about 30 days, 18 of which had been in heavy combat. Our unit, a portion of the 1st Battalion, was on a ridge facing the Naktong, which was very shallow at that point. The North Koreans had come across but retreated during the night.

Sunrise the next morning they tried to cross the river again in force. We were ready and waiting and I was able to call in a flight of Marine Corsair fighter planes standing by on station. They caught the North Koreans in mid-river as they attempted that crossing. The Corsairs made one strafing run after another until the river truly ran red with blood. It was all over in a matter of minutes and I would guess that probably a thousand North Koreans died that morning.

Our Regiment also made the landing at Inchon. Our unit went in at sunset and I was in one of the command boats of the second wave. There was very little resistance. We stepped off the boat on to the seawall and headed for our assembly area in a railroad yard a couple of hundred yards ahead of us. I was loaded with a radio on my chest and my backpack, weapon, ammo belt, etc., making it difficult to move quickly. Suddenly, there was a stream of tracer rounds bracketing me; a couple of North Korean machine guns were laying down suppressing fire and it seemed to me those rounds were missing me by inches. I knew if I stumbled and fell in the wrong direction, I'd be dead - so I did the logical thing and hit the dirt - face down and scared out of my wits.

With all the noise and confusion, I didn't realize that their gunners had ceased firing. They were apparently overrun by some of our guys. So I was still flat on my face when I got a swift boot in the

Episode Eleven - Radio Operator

butt and my Captain said, "Get up, Marine, we can't win this damned war with you laying there on your ass." I guess I should have been embarrassed but I was too happy to be in one piece.

That night we holed up in what had been a brewery. There was beer in some of the tanks and we were tempted to imbibe a bit. Our Captain said we had better hold off until he looked around. Then he announced, "I don't think we'll be sampling any tonight, there's a North Korean body in that tank over there." That kind of killed our thirst.

It rained all night, making our lives even more miserable. I had dug a shallow trench next to the railroad tracks and was trying to get a little sleep. I guess I had just dozed off when I heard this huge roaring sound overhead and then massive explosions somewhere down the road. Scared the fool out of me again but someone shouted that it was the cruiser Rochester offshore firing at some inland target.

We moved out the next day and captured Kimpo Air Base on my 19th birthday. Earlier, the Captain had told me that since I was only 18 I could hang back on one of the ships until I reached 19. Seems there was some UN rule that no one under 19 could engage in combat! I told him if I got hit, who was going to know and who would care and besides, I'd already been in several engagements over the past six weeks. I can only imagine what the North Koreans thought of that rule, and later the Chinese.

We were only in Inchon a brief time and then headed for Seoul, the capitol of South Korea. On the road, we passed about five or six Russian made T-34 tanks that had been knocked out. The Navy claimed their gunfire got them but upon examination, there was evidence of napalm all over them meaning our Marine Corsairs took them out. So we took bragging rights.

As we moved toward Seoul, a mile or so south of the Han River, we could see a large factory complex that was a marshaling area for the North Koreans. We had no Corsairs on station at that time so we called in the coordinates to the USS Missouri, standing offshore, and asked them to handle the job. They replied that they were moving and would be out of range but would have time to get off one salvo from one of their 16-inch gun turrets. I received their next radio message announcing, "splash," meaning the three rounds were on the way and they would land in about four seconds. What a beautiful shot - they were dead on target and blew that factory to pieces. There were bodies everywhere. Had they missed, I would have been able to adjust their fire for the next salvo if they had been able to stay in range. Several hundred North Koreans died in one of the most perfect shots I had ever seen. I have never understood how the Navy could hit such a small target from 15 plus miles on a ship that was moving and rolling. The technology of today was not available then - now it would be a simple matter.

Later, we crossed the Han River in Amtraks (armored amphibious personnel carriers) and moved north. I think that the mountain close to Seoul called Observatory Hill was our objective. We moved up to be confronted by a large wall concealing a contingent of North Koreans. They fired on us as we moved forward. We were in the open and had no target as they were pretty much protected. Fortunately, someone called in an air strike and in a few moments it was all over. Once again, our Marine Corsairs saved our bacon.

I forgot to mention that in an earlier engagement when the 5th Marines took Kimpo, we had set up our perimeter defenses for the night. We were at one end of the runway, behind some revetments. About sundown, here comes about two hundred North Korean troops almost marching in formation, right down the middle of that landing strip. They were heading for us but obviously did not know we were there. We waited until they were within 50 yards and then opened up with machine gun and small arms fire. All dropped like rag dolls. It was truly blood curdling. I don't believe one shot was fired in our direction. They met their ancestors that night. I heard later that Marguerite Higgins of Time Magazine wrote an article calling us thugs and murderers for shooting them so mercilessly. I guess it

Episode Eleven - Radio Operator

didn't occur to her that they would have gladly done the same to us. War is an ugly business.

Shortly after this incident, we got the word that we would be heading back to Inchon. We loaded up and seems like we were there for a week or so but it was probably only a matter of days until we boarded ship again. We pulled out, went around the southern tip of Korea, and headed up the east coast to Wonsan where we were supposed to disembark. The Navy had been busy sweeping mines from the harbor but we made it in safely. The night before we landed, Bob Hope and his crew had entertained the troops there.

Operation Yo-Yo was in effect while the Capitol ROK Division stormed up north from Wonsan almost to the Yalu River - like shit through a goose. Operation Yo-Yo was what we called the two weeks it took for us to get from Inchon by troop ship to Wonsan on the east coast. During the day, ships would go north carrying troops and equipment. During the night, others would be steaming south to pick up more. All the while, there were minesweepers and destroyers clearing mines from the channel and Wonsan harbor so we could land safely.

I guess that by the time we got there, the North Korean Army was pretty much whipped. The ROK Division didn't take time to clean up and secure small pockets of resistance so some of that job fell to us.

We continued up toward the Chosin reservoir, the 5th Marines to the East and the 7th Marines to the west. All single lane roads. The 1st Marines were to our rear securing our supply route. I think we were in the area 2 or 3 days and then relieved by the 32nd Infantry Regiment of the army's Seventh Infantry Division.

When the Chinese hit with their full million-man army, they were about a day late. Had they unleashed earlier, they might have annihilated us as our Regiments were spread out very thin as were most of the other units. As the 5th and 7th withdrew, one company of

55

the 7th Marines held and kept open a critical pass that was essential to our escape. A company consisted of about 200 men and most every man in that unit was either wounded or killed. But they held and we got through. We were surrounded so we didn't call it a retreat - simply attacking in another direction. I believe the Company Commander, Captain Bill Barber, the Battalion Commander, Lt. Col Davis, and a couple of other men received the Medal of Honor for their heroism in that action.

It seems to me that our Marine training was somewhat different from that of the Army units. We were always taught to fight as a team down to the smallest unit. I had the impression that Army units were not as cohesive; their individual small arms fire was not as concentrated as ours. And there was always the claim that no man would be left behind, but many were - as attested to the fact that we brought out with us a lot of individual stragglers from Army units. That was another reason I joined the Corps - I knew that a Marine would die rather than leave a buddy on the field. I don't know what the unaccounted and missing in action numbers would be from Korea but I would bet that it is much higher than that of Viet Nam - which lasted ten years. (See statistics page xxi)

Nevertheless, the cold was bitter. I had on a fur-lined parka, a field jacket, a fatigue jacket, a T-shirt and long johns and I was still bone cold. We got shoepacs finally, rubber bottoms and leather uppers but no insulation. Both my hands and both feet were eventually frozen. To this day, I have difficulty walking.

It took us about three weeks to make our way back down to the harbor. One night, during that long, grueling trip 24 of us holed up in what had been some sort of large Korean dwelling. We had a small fire going and with the flue running on the ground the length of the room, (the Korean way of heating), we were pretty cozy. Suddenly, the door behind me burst open and two or three Chinese sprayed the room with their burp guns. All but three of us died in a matter of seconds. A couple of bodies were on top of me and I lay there the rest of the night afraid to breathe. I was covered in blood but none of it was mine. The next morning, I heard some familiar GI curse words and knew I was safe. To this day, like the poker players of old, I will not sit with my back to the door.

As we moved south, I kept my radio but had to junk the batteries as they had frozen. One night, I was hunkered down in a hole, trying to sleep. A shadow fell over me as I dozed and I could see a man silhouetted on the skyline. I always had a .45 caliber pistol on my belt and without hesitation drew it, and fired. The impact must have knocked him 15 feet down the slope. Thankfully, he was a Chinese soldier and not a fellow Marine. I think that was the only occasion in which I had to use my sidearm. My primary weapon was the M-2 carbine. It was lightweight, fired semi or full automatic, and with two banana clips (so called for their shape) holding 30 rounds each and taped opposite ends together (giving 60 rounds of quick firepower), it made for a very nice weapon.

On another occasion, we got into a little scrap with a group of enemy soldiers and one came at me with a bayonet. One of my buddies shot him, but he managed to slash me slightly on the arm and I still have that scar. Eventually, I had it treated but it was just a minor scratch. However, the scars all these years later are still visible. A reminder of the past.

Those three weeks to make in back to Hamnung from the reservoir were probably the longest twenty-one days of my life. The Chinese pretty much pressured us the entire way but a perimeter defense had been set around the harbor. That and the naval gunfire gave us time to reorganize and eventually board the troop ships awaiting us. The fire from the ships offshore and the Army engineers pretty much destroyed all the useable facilities of the port so there was little if anything left for the Chinese. We were not sorry to be leaving the Chosin Reservoir area though we would have preferred a different outcome.

As I said earlier, my feet were in bad shape. I think I was the only man in my unit who had two working legs (more or less) as we

57

made our way south. Finally, when we got to the harbor I removed my boots, which required cutting the laces and prying them off very slowly. Then it took about a half-hour of soaking them in warm water before any feeling returned. A couple of layers of skin came off as well and our medic gave me some salve to put on them. He said it was the same thing that was used for diaper rash on babies, but it helped and I was grateful!

When we got back to Pusan, I was hospitalized for a short time but oddly enough, not due to combat. We were working on the docks there unloading our vehicles and equipment upon our return from Hungnam and the Chosin reservoir area. I was dead tired and one night curled up partially under a jeep and fell into a sound sleep. Unfortunately, the Army officer who had been driving it came back and took off - over both of my feet. I knew something had to be broken.

At the hospital I was X-rayed and examined and I guess was there for a couple of days. The doctors (all officers) were somewhat taken aback because when they entered the ward, I sat in bed at attention. One of them asked my why and I said, "I'm a Marine, Sir, and that's what we do." I think I was the only Marine on that hospital ship and I wanted to make the right impression.

My tour of duty in Korea was from August 1950 to October 1951. I returned home and served a total of 12 years with the Corps before accepting a medical discharge. Deep down I'm still a Marine and always will be. Semper Fi!

- TACTICAL AIR CONTROL PARTY

THE MP
WALTER WALLACE LEE

NOTE: Mrs. Lee contacted me through an ad I had run in the Orlando Sentinel news-paper seeking veterans who wanted to share their experiences through this book. Sadly, Mr. Lee had passed away in September of 2011. Mrs. Lee found notes that he had written during his tour in Korea and was kind enough to share them with me. She had never before seen them. She felt this might be a way to honor her husband and at the same time, share his memories of his service in Korea. Her daughter, Brenda Naylor, typed his notes much as Mr. Lee had written them those many long years ago.

Mr. Lee probably didn't realize it at the time but he was a participant in probably the largest retreat and sea borne evacuation in the history of our military. Our forces, including Republic of Korea units, had been driven almost to the Yalu River. Then the Chinese launched their million-man offensive and invasion into North Korea. The Marines were almost trapped in the Chosin Reservoir area but were able to fight their way out taking severe losses. Our Third and Seventh Infantry Divisions along with the South Koreans held the Chinese army at bay while falling back to Hamnung and setting up a defense of the port in preparation for the evacuation.

Naval ships were offshore laying down defensive barrages and the evacuation was under way. Approximately 100,000 military personnel, over 17,000 vehicles, 400,000 tons of cargo, and several thousand North Korean civilians were saved from what could have been a total disaster. The final act was the destruction of all of the port facilities by Army engineers and naval gunfire. Little of use was left to the enemy.

Here is Mr. Lee's story...

I entered the U.S. Army in Manchester, NH on May 4th, 1949, at the age of seventeen. From there I was sent to Fort Dix, NJ, for basic training with the 91st Battalion, 9th Infantry Division. During that time, I dislocated my shoulder and was in the hospital for a few days. Fortunately, I was given a one-week leave, which I spent at home.

I returned to the base and was put on light duty until I could get back into a new cycle and complete my basic training. I had applied for auto mechanic or refrigeration mechanic training as those jobs sounded interesting to me. But in the wiser ways of the military, I was assigned to Company C, 716th Military Police Battalion, 9th Infantry Division, First Army. During that assignment, we were constantly trained in all police as well as combat duties. We also provided the usual MP duties and patrols at Fort Dix.

From November, 1949, to December of that year, 46 of us were sent to MP School at Camp Gordon, Georgia. We were then returned to Fort Dix where we continued training and patrol duty with the 716th MP Battalion. During Christmas and New Year's, I spent most of my time on guard duty around the area.

In early 1950, I was sent to Rockingham, N.C., on maneuvers with the 82nd Airborne Division. A large forest fire broke out and one

Episode Twelve - The MP

of my duties was as messenger for the Commanding General. That excitement over, I returned to Fort Dix for more combat and MP training. That summer we were sent to Camp Edwards, Maryland, to train National Guard troops. Upon our return to Fort Dix, two MP companies were formed - the 58th and the 59th.

November of 1950, we shipped out. My company, the 58th, was to remain in Japan while the 59th was to go to Korea. Somehow the orders were inadvertently switched (or so we were told) and we of the 58th landed in Hungnam, North Korea. Not our lucky day.

Around the first of December, we were ordered over the side of the ship, down a landing net and into a waiting landing craft. There was about four inches of water sloshing around our feet, bitter cold, and we had only standard issue clothing and leather boots. We went ashore in the middle of an enemy probing attack and with no ammunition for our weapons! We were ordered back into the landing craft, returned to the ship, climbed back up the landing net and tried to get some rest. The ships PA announced the temperature at 10° below zero. I didn't argue the point.

The next morning, we were issued a belt of ammo for our M-1s. The ship pulled up to a dock so this time we were able to disembark on a gangplank. Our job was to help secure the port and its facilities. The weather was bitter cold. We found an abandoned brick building and set up headquarters, When we could sleep, three or four of us would huddle together to keep from freezing. Close by, bodies of dead civilians and enemy soldiers were being burned, as there was no time for burial. Between the cold and the odor, sleep was next to impossible.

Our unit was attached to the X Corps, 8th Army. Our job was to direct and assist in the evacuation of men, equipment, and refugees. Most of our troops including our company had boarded ships a few days before Christmas. The last of my unit, about 12 of us, helped guide some 12,000 North Korean civilians from Iwon to Hungnam and saw them aboard waiting troop transports. It was a truly horrible

61

sight. Many were starving, injured and barely able to move forward. One old woman died in my arms from exhaustion and hunger.

Another young woman gave birth to a baby right on the gangplank as she struggled to get aboard. Someone cut the umbilical cord and she kicked the infant into the freezing water and crawled her way on to the ship. Was she insane from fear and hunger? Only God would know. Their only thought was to flee North Korea. Every one of those poor souls knew that if left behind they would be slaughtered by the Chinese. All of these horrible images are burned into my brain and I wish could forever be erased. I did learn much later that approximately 100,000 refugees were saved through our efforts so that does ease the pain.

Bill Raymond and I were given the job of guarding the northwest entrance to the port. On December 24th, 1950, we were told to hold that position until we heard from Sergeant Plude, our platoon sergeant. The Navy ship, "Big Mo," the battleship Missouri, was sending 16-inch shells over our heads. Buildings were burning and exploding all around us. To this day, I think I could have reached up and touched one of those huge incoming rounds. At about 1000 hours, Sergeant Plude came up and shouted, "Run, follow me!" We made it to the beach where the last LST (Landing Ship Tank) was just pulling out with its ramp starting to go up. We barely made it. The LST was not too far out when the port went off like a huge bomb. The Army engineers had planted high explosives - those and the naval bombardment had left little of any use to the Chinese invaders.

Around Christmas of 1950, we landed in Pohang. Everyone was confused. Sergeant Plude went in search of the remainder of our company. We stayed with the LST and helped its crew unload. He returned with new orders. We were then on our way to Taegu, South Korea, where we set up our headquarters. The job was railroad security from Pusan to Seoul, the capitol. Two of our men and ten soldiers from a ROK unit would get aboard - these trains would be moving supplies and frequently our wounded. Fortunately, we had no

Episode Twelve - The MP

guerilla attacks or accidents on these trips. But I can't say they were pleasant.

In January or February of 1951, we moved back north. We rode in the back of an open truck some ninety miles in bitter, freezing weather. We did stop once for a hot coffee break. A few of our group suffered frostbite, a common hazard. We were now in Taejon, South Korea, and were quartered in a building that seemed to be a blessing. However, my friend Lawrence Cooper and I were almost immediately assigned to make a train run. We returned a day or so later only to find our building burned to the ground and two of our friends dead as a result. However, our mission was ongoing - protect a station, ride the trains, sleep in the boxcars.

We returned to Seoul and took over security of the railroad station there. A short time later, we were on the road again - to Yong Dong Po, south of Seoul and the Han River.

There we were harassed almost nightly by "Bed Check Charlie," a North Korean pilot flying an ancient open cockpit bi-plane. He would randomly toss hand grenades or small bombs over the side of his aircraft hoping to hit something of importance. I don't know of any damage to our area but this seemed to have been a common tactic of the North Koreans throughout the war.

Another incident that I well remember was going on a patrol with a captain and seven other men to find an officer and two of his men who had lost communications with their unit and were apparently lost. After several days, we finally found them - along with some dead North Korean troops. We were gone much longer than our commanding officer anticipated and we were finally listed as MIA along with the other group. Fortunately, that was not the case. We all returned safely.

Sometime later, I returned to Inchon with Bill Raymond to oversee security at the railroad station there. The Korean National Police force provided the guards. The two of us would randomly check the posts night and day. On one occasion, Bill found a guard asleep at his post. This happened two more times that same night. The fourth time, Bill reported the man to his Commanding Officer who promptly followed Bill to the still sleeping man. He took one look, pulled his pistol from its holster, and shot the man dead. Brutal beyond words. Needless to say, my friend Bill was shaken.

Not long after this episode, Bill and I returned to our company. There we along with five ROK MP's were assigned to a spur line terminating at a MASH unit. The wounded were there placed on a hospital train to begin their trip to Japan and better facilities. These were probably the more seriously wounded and unfortunately, many did not make it. We frequently helped move the litters to the train and I can still see those young faces - another scene burned forever into my memory.

We again moved, this time back to Pusan. There we were on the usual train runs, usually two or three of us but occasionally I would be alone. Guerillas were a constant threat not to mention land mines near or under the tracks. Fortunately, I had no unpleasant incidents on these trips but the danger was ever present.

In the early winter of 1951, John Zammbani, Gerry Lord, Eddy Hodreck, Nickleson, Wilson and myself were flown from Pusan to some landing strip and then by truck to Sokcho-Ri - out in the boonies.. There were 12 of us MPs and our job was to help provide security for three trucking units, an anti-aircraft battery, and an Engineer outfit.

For some reason we were separated from our supply source and for fifteen days lived on nothing but canned corned beef. However, we did have the comfort of living and sleeping in 12 man squad tents. That was better than a hole in the ground but even that had its downside. The enemy used a nasty tactic of sending in a two or three man team to slit the throat of some unwary GI asleep and snug in his zipped up sleeping bag. A twelve- man tent made a tempting target. We slept with one eye open - or took turns standing guard.

Episode Twelve - The MP

My tour was to be up in April but in late March, Zammbani and I went down to our company headquarters to check in and bring back supplies. There, I found my name on the bulletin board assigning me to a one-year involuntary extension! I was not pleased, but things were quieting down. We returned to our company headquarters in Pusan. Our job was again doing security tasks around the port and rail yard. One of my assignments was to provide security for General Ridgeway's rail car, which at the time was his "home."

Finally, my time was up. Bill Raymond and I left Korea together heading stateside. We stopped off in Japan for nine days living in tents near some of the A-bomb destruction. Some six years later, it was still evident. We finally arrived in Fort Devens, MA, in May of 1952. We were given a 30-day leave that was most welcome.

Upon my return, I was assigned to the 1117th ASU Sta. Comp. MP Detachment, Camp Edwards, MA. One week later, I was in the base hospital with sores all over my head. I was placed in isolation for several days as the doctors were stumped. They treated me with Pragmatar, shampoo, olive oil, etc. Finally, after a week or so, everything cleared up and I was released from the hospital. No one ever explained what that was all about - a parting gift from Korea I suppose.

I was honorably discharged August 16th, 1952. So many memories from those long years ago - never to be forgotten.

- WALTER WALLACE LEE

THE VOLUNTEER
AL TAYLOR

I was in a National Guard unit and knew many of the other men that I took basic training with very well. We took basic over and over again until I got sick of it. Every morning when we fell out for our first formation, the Platoon Sergeant asked if anyone wanted to volunteer for the Far East! We all knew what that meant. Everyone hoped for Japan. The dummy here volunteered. I put my hand up one morning. The sergeant looked at me and said, "Taylor, get your freakin' hand down!" He was a WWII veteran and he knew about war.

We were young, not fearless, but seeking adventure. We finally got our orders with a 30-day delay in route (leave time). Three of us went home together – we were good pals. My best friend asked me to write a letter to his future in-laws minister extolling his virtues. The family didn't like him. They didn't want him anywhere near their daughter. I wrote the letter - very flowery and complimentary and it must have been very persuasive because as of December 11th, 2011, Bruce and Margaret will celebrate their 60th wedding anniversary.

Two weeks later, we were on a train heading for California to ship out. Bruce was a real jokester. The passengers had settled down so he got to his feet and announced in a loud voice, "I just got marred a couple of weeks ago and I'm heading overseas." Loud applause and congratulations from all the passengers. Then he added, "It sure is nice to get away from the old lady." Of course, that brought down the house.

A few days later we got snowed in - Reno, Nevada! Until then we could only afford to eat candy or snacks, which we would purchase when and where the train stopped. We couldn't afford the dining car. Since being stranded was the railroad's problem, they paid for our meals in a nearby nice hotel. We ate very well for three days waiting for the storm to abate.

And, of course, we checked out the casinos. Growing up back east I remember seeing roadside signs saying, "Harold's Club or Bust," so we decided to check it out. We had very little money so we played only the nickel slots. Bruce hit a jackpot of twenty dollars or so. At about the same time, we were approached by house security that asked for our ID. We were all underage so we were promptly shown the door. As we walked down the street, Bruce counted his money (all silver dollars). I remember his saying, "You know, I really hit ole Harold a lick!" To this day, he still has two of those silver coins.

We finally made it to Camp Stoneman, California, where we shipped out. In fact, we flew by military transport. This was my very first plane flight so I looked upon it as an adventure. Until then I had never been more than three stories high. We loaded up with our weapons and gear, first stop Hawaii. We landed there about 0430 (4:30 AM) and had a nice breakfast. However, it was dark so we couldn't see a thing. But I tell everybody that I have been to Hawaii. We were then on our way to Wake Island for a refueling stop and then to Tokyo.

Everyone else seemed to have gone from Frisco to Korea or Japan by troop ship; I don't know why we were flown. Only reason I can think of is they wanted our little butts over there in a hurry. The Flying Tiger Airlines flew us; it was on lease to the government.

We eventually landed in Tokyo and then immediately shipped out for Korea landing at Inchon.

Episode Thirteen - The Volunteer

We were there only long enough to get our equipment together and then headed toward the front. It was winter and the weather was extremely cold. As we traveled, we saw many destroyed buildings and passed burned out vehicles and tanks and other abandoned equipment along the road. Now I realized what I had asked for when I raised my hand those few weeks ago.

Al Taylor at 105 mm gun position.

My unit was the 48th Field Artillery Btn., 7th Infantry Division. Our weapon, the 105mm howitzer. I had been trained on the 155mm, which was larger and not as mobile as the 105. We could pull our 105's with a truck, which was an advantage. The 155's required what we called a prime mover, a heavier type vehicle especially designed for that function.

The Seventh Infantry Division consisted of the 32nd Infantry Regiment, the 31st Infantry Regiment and the 17th Infantry Regiment.

69

Also assigned to our division were a Columbian Infantry Battalion and an Ethiopian Battalion. Our unit had to move quickly as we found ourselves firing missions for each of these units at one time or another and in various locations. We were able to move in a hurry. We could be in position and firing in a matter of minutes once we got to where we were going. On many occasions, it took us a great deal of time to get from Point A to Point B. The infantry units knew where they wanted us and that is where we went.

As time went on, I was promoted to SFC (Sergeant First Class). My platoon leader was a First Lt. and I was his platoon sergeant. Later on, I got another stripe and became a Master Sergeant. I was by then 21 years old. It was a responsible position but I didn't think much about it at the time. It was my job and I did it as well as I could and I liked what I was doing. Of course, we had the usual number of goof-offs who cursed the army, cursed the food, cursed the officers, etc. They could not comprehend that they were only making a difficult situation worse.

On occasion, one or two of us would be called upon to go up on the MLR and serve as a Forward Observer. I had that job on several occasions and would normally be there for 30 days. During that period, we never knew what might happen. The frontline units received a lot of incoming artillery fire and as an FO, I would attempt to bring our counter-battery fire back at them. Other targets of opportunity might arise or the Infantry guys might want a certain area hit so again, I would call in to our Fire Direction Center the coordinates of the target and our 105's would respond.

On one occasion, a Chinese spotter plane came in over our position and he was about to do what we were doing to them - calling back the coordinates of our guns to his artillery batteries. In short order we would be receiving incoming fire. Fortunately, we blew him out of the sky before he could relay his information. Our artillery units also used spotter planes, which was for the pilot a dangerous but effective way of finding and calling in fire on the target.

Episode Thirteen - The Volunteer

Another rather odd way of bringing our artillery fire to an enemy position or troop movement was through the use of searchlights. They were used extensively in WWII as a defense against enemy aircraft. In Korea, they were used to spot ground targets. A battery or so of the lights would be placed on a very high piece of terrain and would beam down on a Chinese held hill off in the distance. Since most of the trees and foliage had been denuded by artillery fire, the searchlights would spot any movement and our artillery would fire for effect. On other occasions, depending on the weather, the lights would be beamed at low cloud cover, which would deflect the beams downward thus illuminating the battlefield.

As for living conditions, if we were in one place long enough we built bunkers for our firing batteries, which also served as some protection for the crews. Most were sandbag structures with railroad tracks for a roof. They gave some cover but in the case of a direct hit, the outcome was not good. I suppose there were a lot of rail lines that had been destroyed so the engineers cut them into sections and brought them to where they were needed.

My 21st birthday rolled around and Tony, one of our cooks and a good friend, baked a cake for me, which I much appreciated. He was a good cook and our unit ate pretty well. No C-rations for us unless we were on the road.

I think it was about this time that a few of us got our first R and R. Tony was in the group so we looked forward to paling around in Tokyo. We flew on a huge military transport plane, which was my second time in an aircraft. It took that monster forever to get off the ground and when it did, I think we were only 15 feet in the air for ten miles - or so it seemed. I was very happy when we landed.

For some reason, we were put aboard a train and headed for Yokahama, our R and R destination. We had hoped for Tokyo but no one was complaining. We had about a week to indulge ourselves and since we had not seen a woman in over a year that was foremost on our minds. Tony hooked up with a beautiful young prostitute and immediately fell in love. I guess he was with her every night. When it came time to leave, he was in tears. So I told him, "Look Tony, you haven't seen a pretty girl in 8 eight months. You were horney - you're not in love. If you were, what are you going to do - take this beautiful little prostitute home to your mother and marry her?"

R and R ends and we are back with our battalion. As I said earlier, Tony was a cook so he really had a pretty good deal. No guard duty, no Forward Observer duty, nothing to do with the guns, plenty of good food, etc. We had been back about a week and Tony says to me, "I think I need to see the Doctor." Of course, he had the clap, GI for gonorrhea, a milder form of venereal disease. It was curable but the worst part (for Tony) was that he got thrown out of the kitchen - no handling of food with that little problem. He was immediately assigned to a firing battery - our 105's were immune to VD!

I had to give him a little dig - "Tony, do you still want to take that little girl home to meet your mother?" He was only 20 years old but he learned a hard lesson the hard way. But he was still my friend.

My Commanding Officer was a great guy, a fine officer, and a good friend. We were in reserve for a couple of days and I learned that one of my high school pals was stationed at Kimpo Air Force base several miles south of us. He was a cook in a medical unit.

I asked my CO if I could take off a few hours and visit my friend and he said without hesitation, "Sure, take my jeep and see what you can scrounge while you're down there."

I hooked up the trailer, threw in a pretty good supply of liquor, and headed for Kimpo.

I found my buddy and we had a very pleasant visit. Upon leaving, he offered me a large pile of clean sheets in exchange for a couple of bottles of bourbon. We had no beds but I figured I could do a little bartering on the way "home." Shortly after leaving Kimpo, I

Episode Thirteen - The Volunteer

spotted a large Quartermaster Depot so I pulled in to see what they might have.

An M/Sgt. approached and we discussed a little exchange. I offered the sheets and a couple of bottles of liquor - he was immediately interested. He apologized, however, saying he had nothing of value that would equal my offer. Then he snapped his fingers and said, "Wait, the cooks just turned out several gallons of ice cream but nothing with which to flavor it - except a lot of peanut butter!" He went on to say it was really pretty good. Since none of us in my battalion had tasted ice cream since we left the states, I figured it was a fair swap. The Sgt. packed several gallons in dry ice and I headed back to my unit. When I arrived, I was treated as somewhat of a hero. We enjoyed the ice cream, peanut butter and all. It seemed like a touch of home.

We were on the line about thirteen months. I think the toughest spot was Triangle Hill. All of our guns were constantly firing. Ammo boxes piled up so fast that we constantly had to move them out of our way to make room for more. There was a real threat looming but the Infantry took care of the situation. I think there were one or two occasions when we were in danger of being over-run but I don't even remember where we were. Those Infantry boys that lived in the dirt deserve all the credit we could give them.

Not long after another major battle, one of my best friends, George, was due to rotate home in a week or so. I told him to stay in our bunker, don't come out - don't take any chances. I added, "I'll take care of your duties and see that you're covered." A few days later, he asked if he could borrow fifty dollars. Most of his paycheck went home in the form of an allotment. No use for money under our conditions but I kept some on hand and was more than happy to make him the loan. "George, I'll be glad to do so - consider it a loan or gift, whatever. I don't care if you never repay me so don't worry about it."

Al Taylor with his buddy George.

He got home safely and not long after, I too, was on my way. Unfortunately, George and I lost touch, as is so often the case. He was busy raising a family and working, as was I. And my job took me all around the country. Somehow, a few years ago we made contact and started exchanging Christmas cards. Then about three years ago, I was going through some old pictures from Korea and found some of George. My wife Pat carefully packed them and mailed them to him.

Not long after I received a reply. His letter started out with, "Al, what I am about to tell you is the truth. I have known for 56 years that I owe you fifty dollars. I talked to my wife, Ruth, about sending you the money and I don't know why I never have. But you sent me these pictures and I want you to know that I found Christ and I've become a Christian."

He went on to say that he knew something was not right in his life. He said that he had again looked at the pictures I had sent and began to cry. He realized that he had not paid me the fifty dollars though it had always been in the back of his mind. George told me that things would not be right until he reimbursed me.

I called him and told him again to forget it! His wife got on the phone and said, "Albert, (which is what George always called me), you might as well accept the fifty dollars or George will never get over it." So I relented and said mail it, I will accept it.

In the course of all these conversations about that stupid loan, I learned that George and Ruth had a granddaughter who was born with cystic fibrosis. They were raising her. The check came; I deposited it and then wrote a check to the Cystic Fibrosis Foundation

Episode Thirteen - The Volunteer

in her name but in George's honor, Master Sergeant George Thompson.

The years had gone by and the child was 16 years old and near death. She was taken to Duke for a double lung transplant. The first set was not useable so she went back on the waiting list. A second set came (just in time) and the operation was completely successful. Today she is healed and about to receive her nursing degree.

I know this was a long story but in my mind it is more important than my and George's experiences in Korea. That fifty-dollar debt was so important in his life that perhaps in some way it helped him become a Christian. In addition, the fact that the fifty dollars found its way to a very worthwhile foundation gives me satisfaction. But most importantly, April, who had no childhood, can now look forward to a happy, normal life. The fifty-dollar loan went full circle.

On a much sadder note, a young 2nd Lt. had recently joined our unit shortly before my departure. He was a good officer, a good man, and we quickly became close friends. I learned that he had married his childhood sweetheart shortly before shipping out.

One morning, we had to go back to Seoul on some kind of errand. He mentioned to me that while there he wanted to hook up with a beautiful, young Korean girl. I was surprised and said, "Bill, why would you want to take a chance? You have a lovely bride awaiting your return - you could contract VD of some sort and what would that do to your marriage?"

His response was that he did not want to sleep with or become intimate with the girl. He just wanted to sit and look at a beautiful, naked female for a few minutes. I guess that in his mind that was an innocent restful interlude from the rigors of our lives. I arranged it and on the way back to our unit, he seemed much at peace.

He was a pilot flying one of our small spotter planes; his job was to find and call in artillery concentrations on Chinese positions. Thirty days after our pleasant trip to Seoul, he was shot down by

War in the Land of the Morning Calm

enemy fire and died. There are thousands of tragedies in war but that one was up front and personal. Multiply his death by thirty and you might have some idea of the loss and suffering of those he left behind - a wife, parents, brothers and sisters, aunts, uncles, cousins and friends. And how can I forget - simply put, I can't.

General Sherman said it all in three simple words during our nation's tragic conflict: "War is Hell."

- AL TAYLOR

Al Taylor, prime mover for a 155mm.

THANKSGIVING IN KOREA
EUGENIO QUEVEDO

Thursday, November 22nd, 1951. The kitchen jeep arrives in later afternoon. At the time, I am running the company ammo dump situated on a flat section downhill.

The kitchen sergeant and his helper loaded with pots and pans passes by me on the way uphill to the CP. "Hey, Sarge, where's my turkey?" I asked. "You'll be gettin' on the way down. No sense opening these pots and pans just for you," he replies his voice trailing him.

I'm hungry, starving, and can't wait to sink my teeth into that food and enjoy the traditional Thanksgiving feast relished every year by all service members of our Armed Forces.

Finally, Sarge emerges from the CP way up above me. His steps are accelerating, I don't know if because of gravity or the weight of his pots and pans—and are they empty? I shudder just to think of it.

He gets closer, I cannot wait and ask, "All right, Sarge, where is…?" Before I finish my sentence he utters, "S---, I forgot all about you. The officers liked the food so much they all had seconds, ate every bit of it. Sorry. But here, have this can of peanuts!" He handed me a large can, my Thanksgiving dinner.

"You fat bastard, you!"…My mind was spewing venom and I leave it to you to fill in the blanks! Yup! It really happened to me, the only service man that had NO TURKEY in all of Korea that Thursday, November 22nd, 1951! Don't laugh it's not funny.

Now, every Thanksgiving since I recall this anecdote and smile. I sink my teeth into my turkey and thank God that I made it back. Life is good.

THE BORINQUENEERS
EUGENIO QUEVEDO

Eugenio Quevedo - Chorwon, Korea 1951.

Ahh! The happenings of war. They were etched red hot into my brain and like it or not they are forever part of my memories. I seldom talk about myself but allow me to introduce Eugenio Quevedo to the reader, many years ago a member of the 65th Infantry Regiment from Puerto Rico.

I was born in Puerto Rico, came to the United States in late 1946, and became a resident of New York City. As I was classified 1-A at the end of WWII I was instructed by the Selective Service Draft Board to notify and register with the New York office. Soon after the invasion of South Korea by the North Korean army June 29th, 1950, I was inducted into the U.S. Army along with a couple of hundred fellow Puerto Ricans from the area.

After a rigorous 16 weeks of training at Fort Dix, N.J., we boarded trains to Fort Lawton, Washington. Then on to Camp Drake, Tokyo, then to Sasebo and finally to Pusan, Korea. There we were assigned to units of the 65th Infantry Regiment that had arrived in Korea on the 23rd of September 1950. My unit was F Company (Fox), 2nd Battalion. After several weeks working in the Command Post, I asked for and received a transfer to the MLR as a rifleman. My request was granted.

From that moment on, we were always on the go: day and night patrols (ambush, recon, etc.), LP duty, OP duty, combat and defensive missions. On the 23rd of April 1951, we were above the 38th parallel in a holding position. Fox Company sent a recon combat patrol (about platoon strength - 40 plus men) into no-man's land around noon.

A few miles forward, we observed enemy activity. We deployed and at a given signal opened fire on the North Koreans at a distance of three or four hundred yards. They were unaware of our presence but quickly recovered and hit back at us with solid rifle and mortar fire.

The soldier next to my left took a hit through his helmet killing him instantly. He had just recently joined the platoon as a replacement and his olive green fatigues were unsoiled and like new. I picked up his cap that he had on underneath his helmet - my old one was filthy. But I dropped in instantly - it was all bloody and his brains were splattered inside. He was unknown to me…

Our platoon leader, realizing that we had engaged a much larger unit, radioed for an air strike. Minutes later, three of our Saber Jets responded with their .50 caliber machine guns and rockets firing (what a show!) and strafing the enemy, circling and coming in for another attack. In a matter of moments it was over. We disengaged and carried out our one dead companion, our only casualty. Arriving back at our lines near nightfall, the last vestige of sun rays were disappearing on the horizon.

We were exhausted, took our positions, and waited - I was joined by another fellow soldier. We did not have long to rest for that night, with a beautiful golden full moon overhead, the silence was shattered with the blaring of trumpets and whistles followed by the explosions of mortars, artillery, rifle fire, burp guns and all the other weapons the enemy could amass. The gates of Hell and opened and let loose the demons of war!

To avoid being infiltrated I fired my M-l from left to right, fan like. I had two bandoliers, my cartridge belt, and four grenades. The attack intensified and we kept firing but trying not to waste ammunition. The attack continued for hours. Soon my bandoliers

Episode Fifteen - The Borinqueneers

were empty. I fed a clip from my cartridge belt but the rounds would not fire. One after the other with the same dismal results. I realized that in hitting and crawling in the dirt, the cartridges were damaged or so covered in dirt that the firing mechanism was malfunctioning. Not a good situation.

Then from out of nowhere, Sergeant First Class Ocasio comes to our foxhole and drops a couple of bandoliers of ammo and leaves. I loaded my rifle with the new ammo and my loyal Garand responded blazing away. I had christened my rifle "Virginia" carving the name on the right side of the stock. Virginia, or course, was then my sweetheart. Now, as of this writing, she is my wife of 58 very happy married years.

Rifle named Virginia - 1951

As the battle continued, we prayed for dawn to come. Finally, morning arrived amid the smell of smoke and burnt powder. The enemy had been repulsed and pulled back.

We fixed bayonets and went down the hill. There I found a wounded enemy soldier about 30 feet from our foxhole. Perhaps I had shot him. I called for our medic to attend him.

Shortly we found that SFC Ocasio and Master Sergeant Iglesias had been killed during the battle. It's my belief that SFC Ocasio, after supplying bandoliers to my position, was hit on his way back for more ammo by a burst from a Chinese burp gun. According to Lt. Chamberlain, when SFC Ocasio failed to return to the platoon CP, MSGT Iglesia went in search of him as the battle raged on. He also was killed by a blast from a burp gun, probably by the same enemy soldier.

81

Both sergeants were experienced soldiers, valiant and well liked by everyone. To this day, I still remember them and all the others who were killed, wounded or missing in action. Because of their sacrifices, we and the people of South Korea enjoy freedom. They should never be forgotten. War is Hell.

- EUGENIO QUEVEDO

FOOTNOTE: A few facts about the 65th Infantry Regiment.

- Our name, The Borinqueneers, came from the Borinquen Indians, one of the very early settlers of the island of Puerto Rico, long before Columbus and 1492.

- Over 61,000 Puerto Ricans served in the U.S. Army during the Korean War, many in the 65th Infantry.

- 48,000 joined in Puerto Rico, 13,000 came from the United States. 743 were KIA. 2,400 were WIA.

- Ten members of the 65th were awarded the Distinguished Service Cross. 256 were awarded the Silver Star and 606 were awarded the Bronze Star. The Regiment was awarded the Presidential Unit Citation, two Korean Presidential Unit Citations, and the Greek Gold Medal for Bravery.

SERGEANT RECKLESS
Robin L. Hutton

Sgt. Reckless with 75mm Recoilless Rifle. Photo courtesy of Quantico Museum Archives.

Heroes come in all shapes and sizes. The very definition of a hero is a person of distinguished courage or ability, admired for his brave deeds and noble qualities. And while we were always taught that "By their deeds, we shall know them," many times even our greatest heroes get lost in the pages of history until a lucky twist of fate brings them out into the collective once again.

That is certainly the case when it comes to one of our greatest heroes from the Korean War – a forgotten war hero in a forgotten war. Believe it or not, this hero is a horse – a forgotten warhorse named Reckless.

Reckless was a small red Mongolian mare with a white blaze and three white stocking feet that became the greatest war hero horse in American history. Now, before you dismiss that statement as hyperbole, in 1997 LIFE Magazine published a special Collector's Edition of our greatest heroes entitled "Celebrating our Heroes" where Reckless is listed alongside such a notable heroes as George Washington, Thomas Jefferson, Abraham Lincoln, Mother Teresa, Eleanor Roosevelt, Martin Luther King, and John Wayne – just to name a few. That is pretty good company!

Reckless became an American icon in 1954 when a story ran in the Saturday Evening Post that detailed her heroics during the Korean War – heroics so great that she was officially promoted twice to the rank of Staff Sergeant in the U.S. Marine Corps, with the Commandant of the Marine Corps doing the honors at her last promotion. This honor has never before, or since, been bestowed upon an animal.

It wasn't just her heroics that made her so popular - beloved not only by the Marines, but also by people of all ages... It was her endearing personality and sense of humor that captured the heart and soul of the entire nation, and her antics became as legendary as her heroics. She was as famous as Lassie, Rin Tin Tin, and Mr. Ed – and yet today people are only starting to rediscover her. In fact, sadly, most U.S. Marines today have never heard of Reckless – even those stationed at Camp Pendleton, where she spent the last fourteen years of her life! Thankfully, this is changing.

Reckless' heroic story with the Marines began during the Korean War on October 26, 1952 – a war fought in the most horrible conditions of freezing cold winters, and impossible mountain terrain. Lt. Eric Pedersen, commanding officer of the 5th Marines, Anti-Tank Division, Recoilless Rifle Platoon, bought her from a young Korean boy, Kim Huk Moon, for $250.00, because he needed an ammunitions carrier to help carry the heavy artillery up the steep mountains where the jeeps could not travel. Young Kim sold his beloved "Flame" (Korean name, Ah-Chim-Hai, or "Flame in the Morning") to the Marine because Kim desperately needed the money to buy an artificial leg for his sister, Chung Soon, who lost hers in a landmine accident.

The Marines named her "Reckless" because she would be carrying the gun ammunition for the - Recoilless Rifle - it was so dangerous it was also called a 'reckless' rifle... Partly from a contraction of its true name and partly from the fact that one has to be a little on the reckless side to associate with such a weapon. (You could not stand behind it without getting severely injured because of the dangerous and horrific back blast, and so it was impossible to conceal the firing position. The enemy knew immediately where to respond with their counteraction.)

The rounds were heavy – 24 pounds apiece – and most carriers could only handle 2 to 3, sometimes 4, rounds a trip. Reckless would catty 6 rounds per load, yet if necessary in the heat of battle, she could be strapped down with up to 10 rounds of ammunition per trip. That's an incredible amount of weight when you consider her small frame of 900 pounds and only 14.1 hands high.

Reckless took to the Marines like a duck to water. She had incredible intelligence. Platoon Sgt. Joseph Latham was in charge of putting her through "hoof" camp. He taught her how to get in and out of a trailer, and even how to adjust herself in the trailer since it was only 36" x 72". He found that she only needed to be shown something once or twice, for instance getting down in the bunker when incoming shells hit, or stepping over communication and barbed wire – and never had to be shown it again. Or, she could be led once or twice across open rice paddies and up treacherous mountain terrain from the Ammunition Supply Point to the guns on the front line, and she could then make the trip by herself to and from the guns.

Joe Latham & Reckless
Photo courtesy of Nancy Latham Parker.

Never in his fourteen years of being in the Marine Corps had Latham worked so hard, nor been more proud, of any recruit.

Late November 1952 was Reckless' "baptism of fire." Some Marines were worried about how Reckless would perform because it is a well-known fact horses generally do not like incredibly loud noises or a lot of commotion. But Reckless came through it with flying colors, and no one ever doubted her again. Pedersen earned back more than his investment in her very first mission, and she became an extremely valuable member of the platoon. There were quite a few firing missions for the rest of December, but it wasn't until the new year that Reckless' work really began.

Colonel Lew Walt, new commander of the 5th Marines, had devised a series of daylight raids against the Chinese in the hopes of capturing prisoners and gaining intelligence on the enemy.

"Raid Tex" took place on January 31st, 1953, north of an area known as Outpost Berlin. This would be the first time that Reckless would carry ammunition from daybreak to sunset. Reckless made close to 15 trips from the Ammunition Supply Point to the firing line, and carried more than 2,000 pounds of explosives on her back

Incredibly most of these trips she made by herself, after having been shown the route only once or twice. "I took her up near the guns," Latham said, "checked the pack-straps to make sure the ammo would ride securely, and pointed her in the direction of the gun. From then on she worked like a charm."

The next raid was "Operation Charlie" on February 25th, 1953, a raid led to reclaim Outpost Detroit, which had been lost to the enemy in October 1952. This would prove to be Reckless' most difficult assignment to date. Carrying 6 rounds of ammunition a trip, she made 24 trips back and forth to the firing sites. This totaled 144 rounds of ammunition (3,500 pounds), and an estimated distance of over 20 miles up and down the mountainous terrain. She was exhausted by the end of the day as she walked back to her bunker with her comrades in battle. After a bucket of warm bran mash, and a good rubdown by Lt. Pedersen, Latham, and PFC Monroe Coleman (another one of her handlers), Reckless was asleep before they left the pasture.

Yet her finest hour was still to come – in the Battle for Outpost Vegas in March of 1953. At the time of this five-day battle it was written that, "The savagery of the battle for the so-called Nevada

Complex has never been equaled in Marine Corps history." This particular battle "was to bring a cannonading and bombing seldom experienced in warfare... twenty-eight tons of bombs and hundreds of the largest shells turned the crest of Vegas into a smoking, death-pocked rubble", and Reckless was in the middle of all of it.

Enemy soldiers could see her as she made her way across the deadly "no-man's land" rice paddies and up the steep 45° mountain trails that led to the firing sites. "It's difficult to describe the elation and the boost in morale that little white-faced mare gave Marines as she outfoxed the enemy bringing vitally needed ammunition up the mountain," Sgt. Maj. James E. Bobbitt recalled.

Sgt. Harold Wadley, a Demolition Specialist (Sapper) and Anti-tank Assault with Able Company, Third Battalion, 5th Marines, along with two other Marines, Cpl. Allen Kelley and Lt. Milton Drummond, blew out the man-made protective caves for the wounded on Reno and Vegas. He was one of only two men who made it off of Outpost Vegas alive before the attack began. (The other man was Pvt. James A. Larkin, an artilleryman who was part of a forward observer team responsible for directing artillery support.) Wadley remembers the day as if it were yesterday. "The battle was indescribable. It was horrific. I still don't know how the mare lived through it."

Cpl. Chuck Batherson watched Reckless through binoculars at one point during the battle. "She was getting hailed all over the place and she was jumping all around. I'm watching her jump all over the place and we were catching all kinds of hell."

Wadley watched as Reckless would make a trip up the hill carrying her rounds of ammunition, and on the return trip, she would carry out the wounded. "They would tie a wounded Marine across her packsaddle," Wadley said, "and she would carry them out of there with all of this artillery and mortars coming in. The guys down at the bottom would unload the wounded off of her and tie gun ammo on her, and she would turn around right on her own and head right back up to the guns. She was always moving, an unforgettable sight in that skyline in the flare light."

On one trip, Reckless shielded four Marines who were going up to the front line. They threw their flak jackets over her for protection, risking their own lives. "You talk of the Fourth of July!" recalled Wadley. "The different colors of the tracers in the night were coming in and going out so fast a lot of them would collide in mid-air over us. The rounds were hitting each other up there and causing aerial bursts like fireworks. The counter mortar radar (team) that tracks the incoming rounds so they can return the fire – they said there were so many rounds it just blurred their screen device and they couldn't tell anything except it was all coming in their direction."

But Reckless never stopped. She kept the guns so well supplied that one of them crystallized and was forced out of commission. "I can still remember the flare light and seeing that little Mongolian mare heading up that slope without anybody leading her and going up to that gun pit," Wadley said. "There was an angel riding that little mare's back every time she went up and down Vegas – no doubt about it."

During this battle, Reckless made 51 trips from the Ammunition Supply Point to the firing sites, 95% of the time by herself. She carried 386 rounds of ammunition (over 9,000 pounds – almost FIVE TONS!), walked over 35 miles through open rice paddies and up steep mountains with enemy fire coming in at the rate of 500 rounds per minute. She was wounded twice, but that did not stop or slow her down. Reckless has a job to do – and she would not stop until it was completed.

What Reckless in this battle not only earned her the respect of all that served with her, but it got her promoted to Sergeant. Her heroics defined the word "Marine."

When the Marines went on Reserve, Reckless' work didn't stop. While she did not have to carry her heavy ammunition, she would carry things like grenades, rations, sleeping bags, and small arms ammunition. She also helped string communication wire by strapping the wire to her pack and then she would walk along the hillside. "She could string more (communication) wire in one day than ten Marines," one reviewer would write.

Sgt. Reckless and her crew.
Photo courtesy of Quantico Museum Archives.

It was not only Reckless' heroics that endeared the Marines to her; it was her incredible antics off the battlefield. You would not believe her antics when she was being ignored, or if she was hungry, let's just say you never wanted to leave your food unattended. Her appetite became legendary – especially when she ate a clip of ammunition! This horse had a mind of her own, not to mention being very determined.

Navy Corpsman Robert "Doc" Rogers of Baker 1-5 Infantry Company recalled the time he bought cookies in the PX and had them stashed away in his tent. "We went out for the day and when I got back, it looked like a bomb had hit that place! The blankets were off of my bunk, and everything was just all torn up in there. Reckless went into the tent, tore the place apart, and found those cookies. She ate every last bit of them – the wrapper included!"

Reckless had a voracious appetite. She would eat anything and everything – but especially scrambled eggs and pancakes in the morning with her morning cup of coffee. She also loved cake, Hershey bars, candy from the C rations, and Coca Cola – even poker chips, blankets, and hats when she was being ignored – or if she was trying to just prove a point. But her very favorite was just sharing a beer with her Marines after a hard day's work.

When the war was over, and her comrades returned stateside, Reckless was left behind in Korea. It wasn't until an article appeared in the Saturday Evening Post in April 1954, that a national outcry finally got her home.

When she finally arrived to the United States in November of 1954, she created such fan fair on the docks of San Francisco that one veteran newsman observed, "She has more cameras and reporters to meet her than Vice-President Nixon had a week ago when he came to town."

Then Governor of California, Goodwin J. Knight, had issued a proclamation welcoming her to California. "Californians are proud to join with our United States Marines in welcoming Sergeant Reckless home from Korea... I am proud California has been chosen as home for this heroic animal."

Reckless fittingly touched "hoof" on November 10th, 1954 – the U.S. Marine Corps birthday. That evening she was the guest of honor at the 179th USMC birthday celebration in San Francisco, where she walked into the banquet hall to the thunderous applause of over 400 people, and flash bulbs "popped like mortar shells" as everyone tried to get a picture of her. In true form, Reckless spied one of the anniversary cakes, and before Lt. Pedersen could restrain her, was up to her nostrils in it. It was a fitting tribute to this incredible hero.

Reckless was stationed at Camp Pendleton, and there she would live out her days – and what great days those would be. She would be paraded out for regimental parades, change of command, reunions, and retirement ceremonies – just about any celebration the Marines could imagine. There were standing orders never to put anything on her back other than her blankets, and if she outranked a Marine, that Marine could not give her orders!

She had three colts: Fearless (1957), Dauntless (1959), and Chesty (1964), plus a little filly that died at a month old from unknown causes. All of her offspring are buried in the Rodeo Grounds at Camp Pendleton.

Reckless was promoted twice to Staff Sergeant at Camp Pendleton. Commanding Officer of the 5th Marines, Col. Richard Rothwell, did the honors the first time on June 15th, 1957. "There was a full regimental parade and she was presented her promotion at the parade," Col. Rothwell remembered fondly. Her colt Fearless was even in attendance and promoted to Private First Class.

Her final promotion came when the rank structure changed and two new pay grades were added, therefore qualifying Reckless for another promotion. On August 31st, 1959, Commandant Randolph McCall Pate did the honors, which included a nineteen-gun salute and a parade of 1,700 Marines that marched in formation in Reckless' honor. This time Fearless and her latest cold, Dauntless, were both in attendance.

On November 10th, 1960, she retired with full Military honors. In lieu of retirement pay, she was provided with food and shelter, according to Marine Corps documents. Her Military Decorations included two Purple Hearts, Good Conduct Medal, Presidential Unit Citation with star, National Defense Service Medal, Korean Service Medal, United Nations Service Medal and Republic of Korea

Presidential Unit Citation, all of which she proudly wore on her red and gold blanket.

Sadly, on May 13th, 1968, Reckless passed away after severely injuring herself on a barbed wire fence. She was 20 years young. A headstone still stands in her memory at the entrance of the Stepp Stables at Camp Pendleton. But for all of us who have come to know this wonderful heroic horse, she will live in our hearts forever.

Robert "Doc" Rogers said it best: "May her memory live as long as we have the Marine Corps."

Amen to that... One thing is for sure, there has never been a horse like Reckless, and her story deserves its place in history.

NOTE: I don't know why I had never heard the heart-warming story of Sgt. Reckless, but when I by chance ran across it on the internet; I called Robin and asked if she would submit the story for this book. She was kind enough to do so and I am much indebted. I hope you enjoyed it as much as I did.

To learn more about Reckless, please go to www.SgtReckless.com. You can also join her Official Fan Club on Facebook, and you can view her video on YouTube at http://www.youtube.com/watch?v=YIo3ZfA9da0. For any other questions about Reckless, you can email us at SgtReckless@yahoo.com.

While there is the memorial headstone at Camp Pendleton, Reckless is actually buried in an unmarked grave behind the stables office building. We feel she deserves so much more and want to change that. Plans are in the works for two memorial statues: one to be placed near Washington, DC. (Possibly the national USMC Museum at Quantico); and the second will be a more fitting statue and grave marker at Camp Pendleton. Please visit her website for The Sgt. Reckless Memorial Fund to learn how you can help.

- Robin L. Hutton

SQUAD LEADER, WEAPONS PLATOON
Charlie Morgan

I was born in Forsyth County, Georgia, about 50 miles north of Atlanta. My father was a hardscrabble dirt farmer as was my wife's father. You've heard people say that they were poor but didn't know it. I can tell you for a fact that we were truly poor and we knew it.

Our home consisted of three rooms shared by my parents and brothers and sisters. We had no electricity, no running water, no heat but a fireplace, and of course an outdoor privy.

We all had chores to perform. Mine included shooting the occasional squirrel or rabbit to put meat on the table.

I attended school in a two-room schoolhouse, which was a pretty good walk. I made it to the ninth grade and then the schools were consolidated and we lived too far away for me to attend. Nor did I have money for the little incidental expenses that came along - school supplies, lunch money etc., so I dropped out before finishing the ninth grade.

By age 15, I was pretty much supporting myself. I worked running a cotton gin, then later got a job at a sawmill. Next, to the Atlanta Paper Company operating a print machine. I believe my last civilian job was with the National Biscuit Company before my life took a dramatic turn.

The Korean War intervened and I was drafted. First stop as a young GI: Fort Polk, Louisiana for sixteen weeks of basic infantry training. Next on to Hokkaido, Japan and another nine months of training. My job was to learn the basics of a weapons platoon, part of a rifle company. This consisted of learning to use the 60mm mortar and the 57mm recoilless rifle along with regular infantry tactics.

We shipped out for Korea on Christmas Eve in 1951, to join the 45th Infantry Division, an Oklahoma National Guard outfit. We made port at Inchon, came off the ship down rope ladders and on to landing barges to take us ashore. There we boarded an ancient train to take us to Uijongbu, very near the 38th parallel, our destination. It was bitter cold. I remember we trotted (as best we could) up and down the aisle to keep from freezing to death.

We checked in to Division Headquarters a couple of miles behind the MLR to receive supplies, winter clothing, weapons, etc. A few days later, we were trucked up to our positions near Old Baldy to relieve the 1st Cavalry Division. The cold penetrated every pore of a man's body.

I was assigned to the weapons platoon of our company as squad leader of a 57mm recoilless rifle team consisting of gunner, assistant gunner, loader, ammo bearers, and myself. We were thoroughly trained, and I had great confidence in my men and our weapon. The 57mm was highly portable and quite powerful for its day.

Our unit later moved to an area known as the T Bone and Alligator Jaw. All the positions, mountains, hills, etc., were given colorful and descriptive names. For example, Tom, Dick, and Harry was three large outposts held by our units in another area of the combat zone. Such places were also designated by their height as in Hill 412. Back at T-bone, it was Easter Sunday. We were relaxing a bit and standing around in the chow line waiting for what we hoped would be a nice meal. We were behind the MLR but Chinese artillery and mortar fire found us. A couple of rounds landed directly on the food line resulting in five KIA and fourteen wounded. It turned out to be a very unhappy Easter.

Sometime later, my platoon was sent out on a combat patrol. Five of my men and I were ordered to stay behind and hopefully keep secure our positions on the MLR. Needless to say, we were strung out pretty thin. Unfortunately, a Chinese unit ambushed our patrol and an enemy grenade killed one of my best friends. He was brought in with half of his face missing - but at least he died instantly. We had been buddies since our first day in the Army. I was chosen to write the letter of condolence to his family. That was the

Episode Seventeen - Squad Leader, Weapons Platoon

hardest task ever given me. To this day, I can't speak of him without tears coming to my eyes.

Later, in another area known as Poke Eye Ridge, my company was to occupy and improve a position in a valley facing the Chinese. There were half finished bunkers in the area and we worked to improve them during the day. Usually, the Chinese artillery was pretty quiet during those hours. I suppose they were a bit afraid of our counter-battery fire. So we worked in relative peace.

At night, we moved back to our positions on the MLR and the Chinese moved into the same bunkers that we had worked on during the day. A really odd situation but our goal was to complete the repairs and then occupy the bunkers and the area 24/7.

On one occasion, we were working like demons and the Chinese decided to risk dropping a few artillery rounds on the area. My platoon leader and platoon sergeant were standing in front of one of the bunkers with one of my men directly behind them. A shell dropped in close to the three knocking the platoon leader and sergeant to the ground, stunned but uninjured. The man in back of them was killed. We put his body on a stretcher and carried him to the rear. Luck of the draw. Shortly after, we moved to another area so I don't know what became of all our hard work.

We were in battalion reserve for a short period and then moved back up to the MLR in the T Bone area. Dagmar (one of the landmarks) was to our front and again our bunkers were in the middle of the valley wide open to enemy artillery. On one occasion, I was sent back to the company CP to pick up mail, supplies, etc.; I wasn't in a hurry, just walking along. Then I heard an odd splat like sound off to my right. I kept moving and then heard it again, this time accompanied by a furrow of dirt being plowed up just a few feet away. I realized I was the target of the day for the local sniper. Needless to say, my leisurely stroll ended and I covered the last couple of hundred yards in record time.

A few days later, we loaded up and moved to what we hoped would be a rest area with hot food and showers. We'd been told a field kitchen was awaiting our arrival. As we pulled in to our new location, a small helicopter landed and a two star general and his aide hopped out and proceeded to walk about. Apparently, a Chinese artillery FO spotted the chopper and called in a few rounds. One hit near the chow line with considerable damage to what appeared to have been a nicely prepared meal. Some large cook pots were blown down the hill but, thankfully, they were the only casualties.

Meanwhile, the general continued his inspection, or whatever, as though nothing adverse was occurring. I'm sure his pilot was anxiously awaiting the general's return. Finally, he and his aide boarded the chopper and off they went. I don't know who he was but he was either the bravest or the dumbest individual in the area.

Not long after, I came down with hemorrhagic fever and was evacuated to a field hospital well to the rear. Several men died of the disease while I was there. I was fortunate and recovered in fairly short order. I do remember that one part of the treatment was to limit the patient's intake of food and liquid. I often wondered about that but for whatever reason, I was able to rejoin my unit.

We were in reserve at that time. Meanwhile, the Second Infantry Division had taken heavy casualties on Heartbreak Ridge. I rotated home shortly after (due I guess to the hemorrhagic fever bout) but later learned that my division had relieved the Second and had also taken heavy casualties. In all, I consider myself very fortunate but will never forget those who didn't make it home. I spent only seven months in Korea but those seven months will forever remain in my memory.

- CHARLIE MORGAN

GRAVES REGISTRATION
John E. Moore

I forgot about Korea for about 48 years or so and then it started coming back to me. The way it returned was the strange part - it was during a holiday, Christmas I believe. I awoke with this uncontrollable feeling, like a boy in summer camp for the first time. I was 'homesick.' I wanted to go back over there and see all the 'boys', my buddies.

I made the mistake of telling my daughter of my problem. She reminded me that if I could go back, none of them would be there. I knew that but it did not stop my emotional mental problem. It only lasted a short time. It helped when I got out my yellow legal pad and started making notes of events as they came back to me. Here is one of those memories:

I don't remember where we were going or why but three of us were in a Jeep and heading south. I think we were going back to Regimental Supply to pick up needed items for our Battalion Aide Station of which I was a member. This was in spring of 1952 and the weather was warm.

Suddenly, we found the road blocked. One of our trucks was on a small bridge and on fire. There was nothing we could do to help so we decided to detour through a rice paddy. There was a pretty good size ditch so Bob, who was driving, nosed the Jeep in to it. Jim and I went to the front of the vehicle and told him to gun it as we lifted the front end up to road level. Now the rear of the Jeep was in the ditch so we started to lift it up as Bob prepared to gun it again.

At the same moment, I glanced to my left and there, only six feet from me, were the bleached bones of a GI. There was no doubt that he was an American as the fabric of his uniform was still in fairly good condition. I had seen bodies of South Korean farmers who had stepped on a Chinese mine while trying to tend their crop. I suppose this was one way the enemy had of reducing the rice production and thus making more hardship for the South Korean people.

I think all three of us were holding our breaths (waiting for another hidden mine to explode) as we slogged around in the muck preparing for the final lift of the Jeep, which was successful. We were back on the road and I made note of our location. When we arrived at the aide station, I looked up the coordinates and called Graves Registration with that information so they could retrieve the body.

Now, all these years later, I wonder if it was located and sent home for a proper burial. Or was he never found and a mother or a wife still wonders about the fate of her husband or a son? Those are the memories that never leave us - may he rest in peace.

- JOHN E. MOORE

A HARD DAYS' NIGHT
Bill Ingbretsen

The following is a letter of December 19th, 1992, which I wrote to my family after almost forty years of virtual silence. I had decided it was time to tell them of my most dangerous night in Korea. Over the years, I made slight hints about my time on the frontlines. Now, those many years later, I thought it time to tell them "the rest of the story" as Paul Harvey used to say in his radio broadcasts.

I hoped this might help them to understand my occasional lapses into nightmares, depression, and other erratic behavior. At the same time, I felt ambivalent about revealing my combat experiences as I know there are many veterans out there who endured much more dangerous situations on the front lines than I did.

At any rate, Jim encouraged me to release my letter for use in his publication, "War in the Land of the Morning Calm." Following is that letter:

My Dear Family,

We landed in Inchon, Korea, on July 4th, 1952, and were assigned to the Third Reconnaissance Company of the Third Infantry Division. That night we were stationed next to a British Artillery outfit that was taking incoming rounds from the "Gooks," the standard derogatory word for the Chinese and North Koreans facing us. Fortunately, none of their rounds hit our positions for which we were most grateful; but we had our baptism of fire rather quickly!

The next day we moved out never to see or be with the Third Division, our parent unit. In most combat situations, this separation would rarely happen. A Reconnaissance (or Recon) unit is the eyes and ears of the Division. But we were deployed and assigned to many sections of the MLR all across areas of North and South Korea.

As those eyes and ears, a Recon company was sometimes the first unit to engage the enemy. However, we were required to avoid firefights or combat with them unless absolutely necessary. Our responsibility was to infiltrate into and behind their lines to gain knowledge of the enemy's location and troop, weapon, and equipment strength. Avoiding them was not always successful, as they would sometimes ambush us in a surprise attack.

Because we were a special Recon outfit, we were deployed among various U.S. Army divisions, the 1st Marine Division, and Turkish and Greek troops. In addition to our duties such as recon patrols, we often had to maintain and hold a section of the MLR. There, we might have bunkers and trenches for our "living quarters;" most of the time we did not.

Our outfit was in Korea during the second half of the conflict but we were never involved in a mass attack by thousands of "Gooks". Most of what I observed was both sides jockeying for areas of strategic or tactical importance - each side wanted to be in the most advantageous position when the truce was signed. That caused some severe battles that could be anything from random probes to mass assaults. It was of course, a dangerous situation.

Attacks on key positions were well planned and calculated. We could count on them recurring in various areas as both sides traded territory back and forth. The enemy now had many more well-trained and seasoned soldiers and the Chinese and Russians were throwing in more and better weapons and equipment.

The situation was very fluid and created the circumstances that almost cost me my life on February 9th, 1953, just five months before the cessation of hostilities. Dusk was settling in as our sergeant briefed us for another night patrol into enemy lines across the valley. G-2 (Intelligence) needed information about the "Gooks" once again.

We moved out along a narrow path littered by communication wire, which ended up at our LP. The guy on duty at the LP called at frequent intervals to the Company CP to check in. If the Company CP didn't hear from him, either the wire was cut or the man on the

Episode Nineteen - A Hard Days' Night

phone was dead. That could indicate that the Chinese were on the move so prompt action was taken to check out the situation.

On each side of our path as we made our way toward the LP was a minefield covered with various types of barbed wire designed to force the attackers into the mines. Needless to say, we watched out steps. As we approached the LP, we were challenged by the password, "Joe." We countersigned with, "DiMaggio." Not very imaginative but we were happy to find our man alive and well.

Soon dusk had turned to dark and we were walking more cautiously as we were entering "No Man's Land," that uncontested area between our MLR and the enemy's. We were in the Chorwon Valley, a crucial invasion route to the south. Our steps were more cautious as our eyes were trying to adjust to the darkness. As our night vision became better, we picked up the pace, which unfortunately, also increased the noise level of our passage.

This concerned me because our enemy was usually much quieter than we were. They could sit for days with a bag of rice and you would never know they were close by. One way to search them out was with a German shepherd scout dog as the enemy's scent was so much different from ours. We kept on moving into and across the valley toward the mountain range opposite us.

After a couple of hours, we halted and our sergeant admitted that we were off course and lost. Not only were we noisy but also now confusion had raised its ugly head. Shortly after, we heard other voices and footsteps approaching. I knew it was not the enemy - this group was as loud as we had been. Much too loud!

Fortunately, I was correct - these guys were members of a rifle squad from one of our units out on a routine combat patrol hoping to engage the enemy. A 2nd Lieutenant led the twelve-man squad and our team consisted of only five or six men, as we were out to accumulate information about the enemy, not to engage in a firefight. We were led by our sergeant. He and the Lt. discussed matters for a few moments. Then we moved out, tagging along behind the rifle squad.

Once under way, I knew we were in real trouble. The noise we were making was almost deafening on that cold, quiet February night. It got louder when we marched into a dried up riverbed, which was deep enough that our heads were about one to two feet below the line of the riverbank. We were slipping and stumbling on the stones and rocks when suddenly we heard screams and gunfire. As I looked back over my shoulder the Chinese were coming at us from the top of the bank less than ten feet away! They were notorious for their ability to set up an ambush or a surprise attack. We were in trouble.

The immediate shock of the attack seemed to freeze every movement of our bodies for seconds - but then we spun around firing our weapons against the onslaught. Their attack was fast and deadly. They disappeared into the darkness leaving many dead of our combined eighteen-man patrol.

Now, as you can imagine, there was mass confusion on our part. I've never figured out how I came to take over the remnants of our group. I was only a PFC (private first class) but I rounded up the survivors and headed back for our lines. As I had been assigned to LP duty many nights, I was familiar with the mountain ridges. I listened for the bark of the German shepherd knowing one was with our unit on the MLR. We kept moving.

Sometime later, I knew we were headed in the right direction and was very excited that we would soon be back with our buddies and the safety of a bunker. Minutes later, we bumped into the barbed wire that we had left many hours ago. We were home - almost. Suddenly, we heard the screams and the ripping sound of the Russian Burp guns as we were bushwhacked once again!

We hit the dirt - there was no place to go - surrounded and trapped by our own barbed wire. The enemy was virtually on top of us. We didn't have a chance to return fire or escape. They ran their bullets up and down our bodies, as we lay helpless on the ground. My buddy Goldsmith was hit and his cries for his mother rang in my ears as he lay next to me dying. Horrible and terrifying.

Somehow, I had not been shot although I felt something smack my boot. At first, I thought I was hit by gunfire but it was not a bullet, rather an enemy soldier kicking my foot to see if I was alive. As the "gook" stood between my legs, I expected his bayonet in my back at any moment. I was not going to allow myself to be captured so I stopped breathing and played dead. Better, I thought, to die rather than be captured and tortured by the North Koreans or the Chinese.

It was common practice for the "Gooks" to do a body count when they over-ran one of our patrols. This was concluded by bayoneting the fallen to make certain all were dead. Why that didn't happen to me, I'll never know. I just considered it a miracle that I was spared. The "Gooks" would then proceed to rip off watches, jackets, grenades and anything of use as well as looking for any paperwork that might prove useful to their intelligence people. A U.S. Air Force retired medic confirmed this rite in a conversation with me some time back. He had air-evacuated many of our dead with such wounds evident.

In short order, it was all over - the crying and moaning finally ceased. I guess I was in a state of shock for a few moments. Finding no one else alive and the enemy gone, I proceeded to check myself over and found to my astonishment that once again there was not a scratch on me! The sun would soon be rising so I needed to move. Suffice it to say that the barbed wire and minefield would not deter me from getting back to our line.

I had no choice but to slide on my back and move under two rows of accordion and apron wire which was time consuming and dangerous. I feared that I would detonate a hidden mine. But I was certain of one thing, I was not going to stand up and make myself a target again that night for the "Gooks"'

I had to leave my carbine and grenades behind. The barbed wire was too close to the ground to attempt to bring them with me. I literally had to slide inch-by-inch moving and picking the barbed wire from my face and off of my clothes as I progressed. To get through this obstacle took about an hour but I finally made it.

Now I had one more danger to fear. Would one of our machine gun positions think I was an infiltrating gook and shoot me by mistake? Fortunately, I was not detected and made it to our trenches just as the sun was rising on the morning of February 10th, 1953.

I immediately reported to our Command Post. Within an hour, I was rushed to G-2 (Intelligence) at Division Headquarters and was debriefed by General Dwight Eisenhower's son John and other officers. Major Eisenhower was extremely considerate. After describing the event in detail, I was ordered to return to my unit and was then sent out with one other man to try and find the bodies of my dead friends - in broad daylight, which I didn't think was very smart. Unfortunately, we were not successful.

So February 9th, 1953, was my "Hardest Days' Night" during my tour of duty in Korea. A night I will never forget though I wish I could forever erase it from my memory. Many men died in that war, why I was not one of them will forever be a mystery in my mind.

Merry, Merry Christmas 1992
And a wonderful New Year to all my loved ones.
Love, Dad (Pops and Pop-Pop)

So concluded my letter to my family.

FOOTNOTE: In the spring of 1954, I almost died as the result of a very bad automobile accident. The irony of it all; I made it out of Korea only to face a more dangerous incident at home. Go figure... such is life!

- BILL INGBRETSEN

THE B-26 MARAUDER PILOT
AL VAN AMAN

I was attending school at Glendale College, near Los Angeles, California. The draft was in full swing and I was not really desirous of being an Army grunt. I signed up with a nearby Naval Reserve Unit. We attended training meetings and weekends at sea on a destroyer - where I managed to get deathly seasick.

Then I transferred to San Jose College and spent two years there finishing my education. I was too far from the Navy base to continue my service with the Reserve Unit so I just dropped out.

I found out that the Air Force was looking for pilots and I took the preliminary exam and passed. Shortly after, I took the physical and checked out OK. A few days later, I got my draft notice so I volunteered and joined the Air Force. The next day I was on a train with other recruits to Lackland Air Force Base near San Antonio, Texas, for our initial training.

Our next stop was Langley, Virginia for gunnery and bombing instruction and then on to Reno, Nevada, for survival and evasion training. Part of that ordeal was to be put in the wilderness with one can of pemmican (a concentrated mixture of dried beef, suet, dried fruit, etc.) and a canteen of water. Mixed with water, the pemmican wasn't bad. It was terribly cold with much snow. Fortunately, I had spent many summers exploring the California deserts and mountains so I was in pretty good shape. Our assignment was to avoid the cadre and make our way back to base without being captured. That was a three-day event but we made it safely.

Somewhere along the way during my training, the Commanding Officer called me to his office and said, "What are you doing here?" "Sir," I replied, "I hope soon to be a pilot and engage the enemy!" The CO then asked if I happened to know that I was also in the Navy. Well, yes, it did come back to me. He told me not to worry; he'd take care of it. So that was the end of my short Navy career. I guess I was lucky I didn't get court-martialed.

Our flight training consisted of 6 months basic training in the old Stearman bi-plane and then on to six months advanced training in the B-26 medium bomber, the same type aircraft that saw much combat in WWII. It was a very fast plane topping out at near 400 mph and carried a bomb load of 4000 pounds. There were several different configurations to the aircraft and the one we flew in Korea had a three-man crew - a pilot, a navigator, and a gunner.

Our bomber was armed with four .50 caliber machine guns in the nose, three in each wing, and four in the tail - fourteen very powerful and rapid firing weapons. Normally, we carried 8 five hundred pound bombs on our missions. By the time we got to Korea, we were well trained and ready.

Our squadron (about 20 aircraft) was stationed at Kunsan very close to the southern tip on the Korean peninsula. It looked very much like something out of WWII - tents, Quonset huts, and runways. Our living conditions were not at all bad. The food was decent and we had a couple of Korean girls to do our laundry and clean our living quarters. The only problem was that they insisted on cooking their kim-chi (traditional Korean food) in our quarters and the odor was awful.

Any time we were fortunate enough to get an R and R to Japan, the girls begged us to bring them a bolt or two of silk. And we did of course as they certainly helped make our lives more comfortable. I suppose they made kimonos (maybe to sell) or something of that sort. They were always most appreciative and for us, it was a small thing.

We would normally fly three or more missions a week, always at night. The North Koreans did not fly in darkness or in bad weather so we worried very little about being intercepted. Our briefing before a mission was "brief" consisting of anticipated weather conditions, time, distance and heading to the target. We had neither radar nor any

Episode Twenty - The B-26 Marauder Pilot

of the advanced equipment of today. We had an Auto-Direction Finder (ADF); we knew the distance and our speed so we calculated about when we could expect to arrive over the target area. Unfortunately, considerable wind would cause problems in our calculations. We were pretty much flying by dead reckoning (and the seat of our pants, as the old saying goes).

We would normally cruise at about 20,000 feet and when we decided we were over the target area, I'd take us down to eight or nine thousand feet - that was a little nerve-racking as Korea is very mountainous and in a collision with one of them, we'd have come out second best. We flew the valleys since we were looking for lights on the ground indicating a truck convoy or a troop or supply train. If we saw lights we dropped the bombs, banked sharply and looked for (and hoped for) secondary explosions.

These missions normally lasted three to five hours depending on the distance to the target area. Of course, the interior of the aircraft was freezing cold but we did have electrically heated flying suits. We rarely received any anti-aircraft fire but needless to say, we were always happy to return to base in one piece.

A couple of interesting events did occur on the ground. Occasionally, some unfriendly would get in a concealed position on one of the nearby hills and start popping away with a rifle. He was too far away to do any damage and I don't believe any of our security guys ever bothered to go after him. He was a lousy shot.

The other enemy effort was even more bizarre. Occasionally at night, an old antique bi-plane would fly over and the pilot would hand-toss three or four lightweight bombs or grenades over the side. We called him Bed-Check Charlie. He never damaged anything but I guess he was doing his part to defeat the Ugly Americans. Since he flew only during hours of darkness, we never discovered his landing strip. Probably some old road where he could conceal his plane with bushes, etc. during the day. We could not be help but admire his dedication!

I did have another job when on the ground. I was assigned as Liaison Officer to the Neutral Nations Inspection Team! The team was made up of a couple of Italians, two Poles and a pair of Dutchmen. My job was to keep their noses out of our business. Their job was to make sure we followed the proper rules of engagement and that we had no more aircraft that we were supposed to - whatever that meant. But they would actually go to our flight line and count the number of our B-26s! I wondered if they had a team with the North Koreans and Chinese doing the same. I would not have bet on it.

Eventually, the war ended after much death and destruction on both sides. It was an experience I'll never forget. Unfortunately, it seemed a very short time before we found ourselves involved in the Viet Nam conflict. As I was now a career Air Force officer, I saw combat in that arena as well. I look back on my life with many memories, some good, and some bad but with no regrets. I am proud to have served.

- AL VAN AMAN

THE BIRD COLONEL
Bob Moore

A bird colonel (Army slang) is pretty high up the chain of command - just one step below a Brigadier General. The nickname comes from the insignia he wears designating his rank as a Colonel - a silver eagle with spread wings.

Sandbag Castle - January - March 1953.

We were on the MLR in an area known as Sandbag Castle. This position was in close proximity to the Chinese lines with only a hundred yards or so separating us. On this particular day, things were relatively quiet. The Chinese would lob an occasional mortar round in our direction and we would return the favor. There wasn't much action during daylight hours.

We were going about our business - we had received a shipment of hand grenades (a small explosive device easily thrown) and were busy unpacking and storing them for future use. Our Company Commander was pitching in and we were hard at work. We used a lot of grenades, as the Chinese would probe our line during the night. We had a great deal of barbed wire in front of our positions and we could hear them trying to work their way through. So we tossed grenades at them until they got discouraged and left us in peace. We might give them a burst of machine gun fire to hurry them along.

A few minutes into our job of busting open crates, etc., we look up and here comes a bird Colonel with some sort of entourage - maybe some PR people doing an article on the hazards of combat. The Colonel was immaculate in his pressed and clean uniform, freshly shaved, hair trimmed - right out of Central Casting, Hollywood.

He immediately began berating our Company Commander (whom we much admired) for our sloppy appearances - dirty, bedraggled, unshaven, filthy uniforms - certainly not ready for a parade. We probably had not had a shower or bath in weeks Then he said, "Why are you ripping open those crates of grenades; you can't stack them neatly. And you have them scattered all about, etc. etc." The Colonel was obviously playing to his audience with their cameras and note pads.

Our CO replied, "Sir, we tear the crates open so we can get to the grenades quickly. And they are sorted out into piles as they are bound for different positions in my area of responsibility. We find them very useful."

The Colonel responded that he wanted the area policed up, the clutter gone, the men cleaned up and looking like soldiers – and on and on. Our CO replied with a respectful "Yes, Sir," and a snappy salute. The Colonel departed, head up, chest out, convinced I'm sure that he had impressed the group attending him. We were kind of hoping the Chinese would drop a couple of mortar rounds in the area to hasten him along.

Once the Colonel was gone, our CO turned to us and with a stern voice said, "OK, you heard the man - get to it and no slacking off!" Then he paused and asked, "You guys did hear what the Colonel said, did you not?" Another pause and his next statement sent us into hysterics: "Well, I didn't hear a damned thing from that pompous SOB, so let's get back to ripping these crates and get this stuff up on line." To say that we admired him would be somewhat of an understatement - he was a leader, which in the Infantry is a true compliment. He was also one of the few black officers in the Regiment.

The Army began the process of full integration in 1946, only four years before the outbreak of the Korean War. At that time, there were probably very few black enlisted men and fewer black officers. But in combat one learns very quickly that the color of a man's skin, or whether from the North or the South, or regardless of ethnic background - Pole, Jew, Turk, etc., or his religion (or lack thereof) matters not. What matters is his character. Our Company Commander had it.

- BOB MOORE

THE BLADE MAN
WILLIAM JAMES CARTER

NOTE: I ran into Todd Carter, James Carter's son, quite by accident. In the course of our conversation, Todd told me that his Dad had served in Japan and Korea during the early stages of the war. In fact, he said that after his father passed away in 2004, he found the carbine bayonet that his father had carried in Korea. There were seven notches on the scabbard. That aroused my curiosity and I asked Todd if his Dad ever spoke to him of Korea. Yes, occasionally, and these are his recollections of those conversations with his father:

My father joined the U.S. Air Force in January of 1950. He took his basic training in Denver, Colorado, and then shipped out for a 12-month tour in Korea. He told me that the boat trip lasted somewhere around 23 days and convinced him he would never want to be in the Navy. And who in their right mind would want to chip paint day after day?

They landed in Japan and his goal was to be a tail gunner on a B-29 bomber. I have no idea why other than the fact that I think he just wanted to fly. But he was too tall (at 6'2") and was turned down. But is so happened that the 82nd Airborne Division had a training group there and he volunteered for that. I don't know the connection between the 82nd and the Air Force - might have been some special assignment, base security, etc. He did say the Air Force was training him in some radar stuff and he was bored with it. So he might have just resigned from the AF, joined the Army, and took the airborne training. He never really explained all of that.

At any rate, he said the training was extremely tough including night jumps, extreme physical exercises, etc. Push-ups he hated - said it was tough on his long frame! But as he put it, "Wherever we went, we were treated with respect. Everyone knew we were bad asses! We were even allowed to go to the front of the chow line!"

113

He shipped out for Korea and some of the paper work that I found indicated that he was with the 7th Fighter Squadron, 49th Fighter Bomber Wing, "The Screaming Demons." It also mentioned that he was a Ranger. Not knowing anything about the military, I didn't understand any of this and the two of us never really talked about it. Airborne and a Ranger? I don't know. One thing for certain, he was very proud of his jump badge that I have displayed along with a couple of his other items in my den.

He did tell me that on one occasion, he was on a flight somewhere and the plane took a hit. Dad took some shrapnel in the chest for which he later received the Purple Heart. For whatever reason, he felt he didn't 'earn' the award and later threw it away. He did receive some serious damage to his fingers in another flying incident. The cockpit was slammed on his hand and he almost lost three fingers. In fact, the medics wanted to amputate them but he refused their offer! He kept his fingers and they healed reasonably well.

That might have been the time that one of the fighter-bomber pilots asked Dad if he'd like to take a 'ride.' Of course, he jumped at the opportunity. As soon as they gained altitude, the pilot started a lot of high-speed maneuvers - dives, rolls, loops, etc. Dad loved it, but when they landed the pilot said, "Jim, you better check your drawers when you get back to your barracks." Sure enough, he'd messed his pants - his body wasn't accustomed to pulling all those "G's."

Another incident that he vividly recalled was an attack by the Chinese and North Koreans. He said they almost drove our forces into the ocean with so many of the enemy attacking that they looked like a mass of ants coming down out of the hills. The odds were 100 to one in their favor. He thought his unit was about to be wiped out but then the cavalry came to the rescue - in the form of Marine, Navy and USAF fighter bombers making strafing runs and dropping bombs and napalm. And reinforcements on the ground. The enemy assault was finally stopped.

Episode Twenty-two - The Blade Man

Somewhere during that period, he recounted another experience that stayed with him forever. He was pulling guard duty around the base, maybe at Taegu, where the 49th Fighter Bomber Wing was stationed. He was on duty several nights partnered with a young South Korean soldier. It was bitter cold and the Korean would ball up and fall asleep. On one of those nights, Dad kept waking the kid to keep him on his feet. Unfortunately, the Korean soldier's commanding officer came by while the boy was sleeping. The officer pulled out his pistol and shot the young soldier in the head killing him instantly. The officer smiled and my father clobbered him.

Dad was a God fearing man and over the years told me that he was afraid that God would not forgive him for the things he had done. His mother suffered a long, uncomfortable death and he didn't understand why God would let such a gentle, sweet person suffer so much. He was angry with God for that. And as he put it, "I can only imagine what God has in store for me for all the bad stuff I've done." I tried to reason with him and to tell him that he was in a war and killing was a part of it. I told him he wasn't slaying innocent people and his reply was, "Yes, I did." He was bothered by it all. He felt he could not be forgiven. Over the years, we talked about those things and I tried to convince him to go to church and find healing. He'd just say, "That's not for me, son."

Apparently, what started his lack of compassion was the fact that he and a good buddy had captured a young Chinese soldier and showed him mercy since their captive was nothing but a kid. Unfortunately, the boy had booby-trapped himself and exploded a grenade right next to my father's friend. His buddy lost a leg. The Chinese boy died. After that, my dad said he never took a prisoner, civilian or military, women, or children. As he put it, "I did more than I had to do." He knew he was going beyond his training and duty. He figured the more of "them" he killed the sooner he'd get home.

Some of his buddies said he was beginning to take pleasure in the killing. Dad said, "No," he didn't like it – but as he put it, "I

115

damn well didn't want to die." Not long after he passed away at age 73, I was going through his belongings and found the bayonet (mentioned above) hidden away and wrapped up in an old army blanket. I had never before seen it. Scratched on the scabbard you can see his initials and the nickname his buddies gave him, "Blade Man." And the seven notches. I often wonder what that weapon would recount if only it could talk. Perhaps better I don't know.

Dad told me that when he finally shipped out from Korea and headed back home on one of those big, old troop ships, they hit a typhoon a few days out. The ship was rockin' and rollin' and everyone was ordered to go below. He said no way was he going down into the bowels of that ship and drown like a rat if it capsized. So he stayed on deck and held on for dear life. Eventually, they made it home.

He finished out his tour of duty at Connelly AFB in Waco, Texas. He was honorably discharged on December 15th, 1954, and returned home to Dawsonville, Georgia, his birthplace. Years later, I guess I was around fourteen; the two of us went deer hunting on a cold, wet, November morning. We climbed into our separate deer stands several yards apart. He didn't much like deer hunting but went along to keep me company.

We had been in our stands for an hour and the cold was penetrating. Then I smelled smoke close by. Curious, I came down out of the tree and walked over toward my dad's stand. There he was, sitting on the ground, leaning back against the tree, boots off, and feet close to a very hot campfire. I said, "Dad, how the heck we gonna get a deer with all that smoke blowin' around?" His reply, "Son, I near froze to death in Korea and got some frost bit toes to show for it - I vowed I'd never be cold again. You go on up-wind and get your deer, I'll just sit here and enjoy my fire.", and so he did. Korea was never far from his mind.

He passed away eight years ago. He had a heart condition and it finally caught up with him. We were together waiting for him to go in to the operating room for open-heart surgery. Again he spoke of the sins he had committed during combat and was afraid that God would now punish him. "Dad, you've always been a God fearing man. Ask him now for forgiveness. From your heart." Silence and a few moments or so later a peaceful smile came upon his face unlike any I had ever seen. He looked at me and said, "Thank you, son." He was wheeled into the emergency room and died a few hours later.

I like to think that God did forgive him…

- WILLIAM JAMES CARTER

145TH FIELD ARTILLERY BATTALION
Robert Warilow

NOTE FROM THE AUTHOR: While seeking out fellow Korean War veterans to aid in this endeavor I had the good fortune to meet Rob and his wife Tina. He is writing a book about their lives. Only a small portion of his coming publication concerns his experiences as a Medic in Korea but he was gracious enough to allow me to condense those two chapters of his life. Here is his story:

Like most Korean veterans, I was brought into this world during the Great Depression. I was too young to have many memories of that era but I do know that unlike many others, we had a comfortable life. My father was a foreman in a plant that produced varnish. Though many men were laid off, his job remained stable and he had a steady income during those uncertain years. We were very fortunate.

One night, he brought home a set of encyclopedias, a gift from the plant manager. I recall being entranced by those books - every night I would sprawl on the floor and read, absorb, and learn. They were the TV (not yet invented) of my life and I learned among other things that I could teach myself. The experience instilled in me a thirst for knowledge and education that influenced my entire life.

Years later, as a teenager I studied at the University of Michigan. In my third year, I finally wondered why I was in college. I was entering my senior year at the ripe old age of twenty so my entire college career was spent competing with veterans of WWII. They had matured through serious and sometimes dangerous times and were determined to improve their lives through a college education. Though academically I could compete, I found that the maturity that those young men had, I lacked. So I decided to drop out, work for a year or so, and then resume my education.

Then my life took a rather dramatic turn. Uncle Sam had other plans for me - I received greetings from President Truman informing me that I had been "selected" to serve in the U.S. military. I chose to enlist instead as I was advised that by serving an additional year I would possibly receive additional benefits.

Soon I was on a bus to Fort Knox, Kentucky and then by train to Fort Hood, Texas. I was assigned along with many others from the Midwest to serve with the 145th Field Artillery Battalion, a National Guard unit from Utah. It was recently reactivated to serve in Korea.

After basic training, the battalion was moved to Fort Sill, Oklahoma, to learn the more complex procedures of artillery missions. By that time, I realized that killing another human being was an occupation uncharacteristic of me. As luck would have it, the battalion needed medics and I was given the opportunity to take one of those slots. That was for me - now I would be able to save lives, not take them. We were trained by one of the battalion doctors in what might be considered a cram course.

While undergoing this training, I was promoted to the rank of Corporal. My three years of college gave me some advantages over my counter-parts. I had good clerical and organizational skills, could speak and write well, and above all enjoyed being a medic. Our battalion doctor recognized this and promoted me to Staff Sergeant. God knew but I did not, that my "paperwork" skills would later save my life.

Training over, we soon found ourselves on a troop ship arriving in Pusan, Korea. We debarked and headed north with our tractor-drawn guns, personnel and all the other equipment and supplies necessary to complete our missions. Soon we were north of the 38th parallel and in enemy country. Our guns were emplaced and South Korean workers were busy digging ammo bunkers, living bunkers, etc. Things were looking pretty comfortable but it was not long before we started receiving incoming artillery from our Chinese counterparts.

Episode Twenty-three - The 145th FAB

My very first night on the line, however, proved to be anything but comfortable. I was in our squad tent when someone outside started screaming, "Medic, medic!" I grabbed my bag and hit the deck running. It seems that one of the gun crews was firing a mission and for some unknown reason, when the gunner pulled the lanyard (which fires the weapon) nothing happened. He bent down and toward the weapon and either purposely or accidentally pulled the lanyard a second time. The big gun fired that time and the breech-end of the weapon slammed against the side of his head killing him instantly. There was nothing I could do. Such was my baptism to war.

Soon after that incident, Lieutenant Taylor, our doctor and commanding officer of the medical unit, informed us that a mission was to take place whereby one of our 155mm "Long Toms" would be towed to the MLR for purposes of putting direct fire into Chinese bunkers. Tank guns and smaller artillery pieces were not proving very successful in destroying their well-entrenched positions. One medic would accompany the gun crew and the lieutenant selected me. I saluted and said, "Yes, Sir!"

Just before we moved out, Lt. Taylor approached me and said, "Sergeant, I've changed my mind - we are too far behind in forwarding casualty reports, requests for replacements, etc. to Headquarters in addition to tending our sick and wounded. I'm sending Corporal Farley in your place." Again I saluted and said, "Yes, Sir."

By way of explanation, a 155mm field gun is a very large piece of equipment designed to fire a projectile 6" in diameter weighing approximately 42 pounds a distance of 25,000 yards (14 miles). Ours were not mounted on an armored tracked vehicle but were towed into place by a very heavy-duty tractor. Normally, we were in a firing position far to the rear of the MLR. The 155mm was not designed as a direct fire weapon nor did the crew have any protection from flying shrapnel other than a steel shield to the front. This shortcoming proved disastrous to the mission.

Our crew was on the way, the big gun being towed to the MLR and placed in its firing position. As said before, I was left behind. The crew began firing on the visible enemy emplacements and bunkers with some success. However, the Chinese took little time in returning fire and one of their rounds landed close enough to damage our cannon and wound several of the crew. Unfortunately, my friend Bill Farley (my replacement on this mission) was wounded and later evacuated to the States with a Purple Heart.

Our gun was damaged to the point that it had to be towed back to the rear area for repairs. Another gun and crew was selected and again Lt. Taylor informed me that I would be the medic on the new mission. And once more I said, "Yes, Sir!" I proceeded to get my gear together when the Lieutenant again changed his mind for the same reasons as before. He said, "I'll send up one of the new replacements who just came in from stateside." "Yes, Sir," I replied.

The crew went back in to position on the MLR and began firing its missions. This time the Chinese mortar crews were right on target making a direct hit on our gun killing the entire crew - including the new man who had replaced me. He had been with us only two weeks. I felt terrible pain in that my friend Farley had been wounded and the

Episode Twenty-three - The 145th FAB

man who had replaced me died. As I said earlier, God protected me - "There but for the grace of God, go I."

It was not long after this episode that on a quiet Sunday afternoon several of us set out to explore some of the foothills outside our battalion area - and also out of the zone where Chinese artillery normally impacted. My good buddy, Alvin, came along - a very likeable young man with a pronounced speech impediment. I never heard him utter a sentence without stammering - but none of us really noticed it or ever mentioned it.

As we meandered about, we discovered an abandoned North Korean bunker. It was well constructed in an L-shape configuration with a small entrance and then a ninety-degree turn into the main room. Thus, if shrapnel were to be flying about it would harmlessly hit the sandbagged entrance wall and not the interior

I said to Alvin, "Let's take a look inside." He replied, "Th-th-that's fi-fi-fine with m-m-me." The entrance was only waist high - I asked Alvin if he was ready. "Re-re-ready," he responded. As we entered the main room, I spotted a small beautiful black table of Oriental design against the far wall. "Al, I'm going to get that table and ship it home as a souvenir."

As I moved toward the little table, Alvin shouted, "Look out for that trip wire!" The wire ran across the room and was attached to a hand grenade anchored on the opposite wall. One more step and Al and I would have both died an ignominious death. I believe that God once more intervened to save our lives. That was the first and only time I ever heard Alvin make a statement without a bit of stammer. "Thank you Alvin, Thank you, God!"

Shortly before I was due to rotate home, a man from an adjacent unit went into that same area to do as we did - just explore and relax on a quiet and beautiful day. Unfortunately, he stepped on an old Chinese anti-personnel mine and lost both legs. I don't know whether or not he lived - he suffered a horrendous loss of blood. One can't

123

help but wonder why the gods of war select some to live and some to die.

Finally, I returned home, was honorably discharged, resumed my education, married, helped raise our family and in short, I can honestly say I've had a good life. My continued interest in education led my wife and me to the teaching profession. Our studies and our careers eventually took us to Europe where we lived in the Netherlands (home of my wife), Belgium, and Yugoslavia. We were in Yugoslavia for six interesting years. We were fortunate in that we were able to rent a very beautiful home at a very reasonable price. There was one minor problem - the owner was a devout Communist - we are serious Christians. That made for some interesting conversations.

But all of that is in my book, entitled "Up the Hill and Into the Wind." Hopefully, it will be in publication soon. You'll find it primarily in Christian bookstores as so much of my life was protected and guided by Him. I am thankful - and God Bless.

- ROBERT WARILOW

190 PROOF
Walter Adams

One lovely day in Chosin (temperature about 30 ° below zero), I noticed a GI walking about with no parka, just a wool shirt over the upper part of his body. He looked so warm that I could envision blue birds on his shoulder and a beautiful bikini clad babe on each arm. I caught up with him and asked, "What is your secret, it's freezing out here and you look like a Palm Beach tourist?" He opened his shirt and showed me an ammo bandolier around his waist filled with pocket hand warmers in every pouch. No wonder he was warm and cozy.

I rushed back to my bunker and immediately got off a letter to my wife asking her to send me hand warmers ASAP. A couple of weeks later a large package arrived and I ripped it open. My sweet wife had not sent a few small hand warmers but the largest, best, single warmer that money could buy. It was so large it required an entire can of cigarette lighter fluid. But lighter fluid was not available so I availed myself of the next best thing - 190 proof alcohol conned from our medic tent. It was used for cleaning medical instruments, wounds, infections, etc. And perfect for my needs.

I fired that baby up and made a sling for it around my waist; put on my parka with hood, wool scarf around my neck and covering my nose, and zipped the parka closed. Warm as the proverbial toast. After about an hour, I was beginning to feel no pain; in fact, Korea was not such a bad place after all. About then, one of my buddies came along and said, "What's with you? You're staggering around like a drunk!" As it turned out, I was. Breathing the fumes from that 190 proof firewater did a number on me. I made my way back to our bunker and collapsed. Cheap drunk but what a hangover. Never again.

My giant hand warmer worked great in my sleeping bag. Often, my clothes would be covered in snow and ice. To strip down and crawl into that big, warm sack was sheer pleasure. Those arctic bags were in three parts - the inner most was a down filled quilted bag, the next one was wool, and the outside material was waterproof and zipped tightly shut.

One night I came in from the freezing weather to find all my mates sound asleep. I did my usual drill - fired up the hand warmer, got out of my snow and ice covered clothes and slipped into my cocoon. Sometime later, I managed to kick the cover off my hot warmer. When my foot made contact, I yelped and jerked my foot away, which flipped the warmer up, on my bare leg. That, of course, produced more kicking and hollering and in my effort to escape the bag and the hot warmer I somehow managed to sit on it - which must have singed my butt producing more bedlam.

All my buddies by now were on their feet, armed with weapons pointing in every direction, looking for what surely must have been Chinese infiltrators. Somehow, we managed not to shoot one another and I proceeded to the Medics for treatment of my burned, raw, and sore rear. When they heard my story, they went into hysterics. Not sensitive at all to my grievous wounds though they were kind enough to apply some salve. One wise guy said he would write me up for the Order of the Purple Butt. I made my way back to my bunker only to be met with more derision from my erst-while friends. Needless to say, I was a bit more cautious with my bag warmer after that episode.

Walter Adams with M3 45 cal. - 30 degrees below.

NO PURPLE HEART TODAY
Joe Jones

It was a beautiful summer afternoon. Not much going on. We were standing around on our mountain jawboning, fooling around, soaking up the rays as the kids nowadays would say. I suppose the Chinks were doing the same on their mountain opposite us and just across the valley. More than likely though they were sitting it out in one of their mountain cave-tunnel complexes playing Chinese Checkers or something. Of course, I don't really know what they did for entertainment when they weren't shooting at us - but all was quiet which was a nice change.

Our platoon sergeant strolled by. He was a good guy and we liked him. One of my Arkansas buddies said, "Hey, Sarge, see that ole GI helmet down that'eer slope? Five 'ell getcha ten you kaan't hit it!" Immediately side bets were made and money changed hands.

The Sergeant looked around, saw all his boys watching, and said, "You're on." The old helmet was about 30 feet down the ridge and presented a pretty small target for a pistol shot. But the Sarge pulled out his .45 Colt, took aim, pulled the trigger and wham, he rang the bell. A great shot but unfortunately, there was a large rock embedded in the ground in back of the helmet. And the inside of the helmet was facing us. Sarge's shot was right on - it hit the lower lip of that old steel pot, zoomed around the back of the helmet doing a 180° turn on its journey and headed right back at us! All of course in a split second.

It hit one of my pals who was standing right next to the Sarge. It slammed into his left shoulder and knocked him flat on his arse - bam! He didn't even holler though it must have hurt since the bullet lodged in his shoulder. Sarge called the Battalion Medics who sent up a jeep and my squad mate was promptly evacuated to the rear. We don't know what happened after that but he didn't return to our company. If he was given a choice, I suspect he asked to go somewhere else! Couldn't blame him.

Nothing more was said about the incident but I expect our Sergeant informed our CO. Just one of those things and that was that. We all hoped that the CO kind of embellished the story a bit and got the kid the Purple Heart or the Good Conduct Metal or something! I don't think the Army has an award for getting shot by your own Sergeant but my buddy sure deserved some kind of recognition - at least a seven day R& R to Japan.

In all the excitement, I think all the bets and side bets were forgotten and we started looking around for a less hazardous form of entertainment on that beautiful June day. Like us, the Chinese had some pretty powerful binocs and scopes. I wonder if they saw what happened - probably said, "Crazy Americans!"

- JOE JONES

FORT RUCKER STORY
Bill Williamson

My tour of duty at Fort Rucker was pretty awful, dull beyond imagination. The 47th was a training division turning out one eight-week cycle of recruits after another. We company grade officers did most of the instructing. One day word came down from Headquarters that the General wanted the division to pass in review, and we had better look good. So for about two weeks, we did nothing but train that cycle of recruits in close-order drill, manual of arms, etc., and all other training stopped.

One fine morning one of the staff officers from Division Headquarters came down to see how we were progressing. My CO ordered me to report to the inspecting Colonel on his behalf, which I did. As the Colonel removed himself from his Jeep, (his driver standing at attention) I saluted sharply and said, "Sir, Lt. Williamson reporting, and I'm at your service Sir!"

The Colonel asked me how things were going. My reply, "Not good, Sir." He was somewhat taken aback and said, "Explain, Lt." I replied, "Sir, we've lost two weeks of essential training simply to have our unit look good for a parade. These men will be in Korea shortly and they will not be prepared for combat in my opinion." He looked at me somewhat oddly so I figured I'd be on MY way to Korea in a few days. Nothing happened however, except that I spent another six months at Fort Rucker, I guess that was my punishment!

During that time, we spent many hours on the various weapons ranges training one cycle of recruits after another. During one period of time, the weather became quite chilly, and being on one of the weapons ranges for hours on end became uncomfortable. Several of us developed hacking coughs, sneezing, and so on. I thought of one of our thirty-year corporals who was an alcoholic. He drank anything including after-shave lotion, but his favorite was GI Gin. GI Gin was a cold remedy consisting of alcohol and codeine. This gave me a brilliant idea...

I went to our aide station and told the young medic on duty that I needed a sizeable quantity of 'cough syrup' for our company recruits. He readily complied with a couple of quarts! The next day, cold and dreary, and back on the rifle range I shared my booty with my fellow officers. We stayed warm that entire day but I do believe I passed out cold when we finally returned to our quarters late that evening. Fortunately, none of our superiors ever heard of that little episode or I would have probably been busting rocks at Fort Leavenworth (Army lock-up) for an extended period of time.

I was lucky that day, and I never had much of a taste for alcohol after that.

- BILL WILLIAMSON

DEAR JOHN
Bill Williamson

No war story would be complete without the proverbial and universal "dear john" letter. I got mine two weeks after arriving in Korea. I remember it very well. The postal service from the states was quite good and regardless of where we were, the mail caught up with us regularly. I was in my platoon position facing the Chinese held mountains - just standing there surveying our world. It was a beautiful warm day. The company clerk was making the rounds and handed me a letter with a "Here's yours, Lieutenant."

I knew who it was from and what it would say: "Dear One, I'm sorry but I'm getting married in three weeks to the man with whom I was engaged before I met you, etc."... I tore it to pieces and tossed it into the wind. Though I knew it was coming, it still hurt.

Her name was Fran. She was a little doll, petite and pretty, vivacious, smart, funny, personable. We met on a blind date arranged by one of her friends - six young soldiers and six pretty girls. My five buddies and I were going through Officers Candidate School at Fort Benning, Georgia. All of the girls were from Columbus, home to Fort Benning.

I don't know how we paired off but Fran was my date and we went to a very nice restaurant for the evening. We were a compatible group - the girls were all college students in their late teens; we were young guys in our early twenties. Fran, as I said, was very pretty but for one thing - she had a congenital birth defect that gave her nose a perfect "S" shape. I found it a little disconcerting at first but before the evening was over, I thought that cute little curved pug nose was perfectly normal. I never noticed it again. I was, as they used to say in the dime store novels, smitten.

We dated as frequently as possible - dinner and dances, drives in the country, meeting with relatives, (her parents were very fond of me) late nights together - all the romantic and fun things that young people do when attracted to one another. It was two or three weeks into our romance that she told me that she had been engaged to an Air Force pilot. It seems that she broke it off because her parents disliked the man. I got the impression that she was not over that relationship which made me all the more determined to win her heart.

We were separated by my finishing training and being sent to Fort Rucker, Alabama, my first duty assignment with the 47th Infantry Division. She returned to college in New York. But we talked "long-distance" and exchanged letters. On one occasion, I had a four-day weekend and drove straight through to New York City to see her! We went to dinner at one of the big hotels (top floor) and dined and danced to the orchestra of one of the big bands - I don't remember which one - Woody Herman, perhaps. The next morning I headed back to Fort Rucker, tired but happy.

We saw each other off and on and eventually I received my orders for Korea. We had talked lightly of marriage but now the subject took on more meaning. She was home for a couple of weeks - we took a short trip to Florida. I wanted to ask her to marry me. I think there is an innate desire within us to want to leave someone behind (other than our own family) who will remember and grieve for us should we not return. At the risk of sounding morbid, I truly did not expect to make it back from Korea. So it seemed unfair on my part to even think of marriage under such circumstances. As for her, she let me know that if I came home to her badly wounded, she didn't think she could handle that situation. I knew then that she did not truly love me.

So when the letter came, I was not surprised. And thankfully, I had other things to think about at the time. My job as a rifle platoon leader put my men and me in harms' way so my thoughts of her faded pretty quickly. When I returned home, I stopped by to see her. I didn't meet her husband but I did meet their first baby. We chatted a bit; I bid her goodnight and never saw her again.

Not long after, I married Patti - my first sweetheart upon my return from Korea in 1947. We had dated off and on for seven years. She was in the Canal Zone while I was on my second tour in Korea.

Episode Twenty-seven - Dear John

We came back to the states about the same time and married within three months of our joint return and reunion. It was a happy marriage and the years went by too quickly, 52 to be exact. She died of a stroke in 2006. It was devastating but fortunately, our three daughters (whom I love very dearly) were there to get me through a very difficult period of my life.

And now the end of this story. Two years or so after Patti's death, my little sister asked me to be her date at her 50th high school reunion in Columbus, Georgia. I agreed to go, somewhat reluctantly. We had not been there ten minutes when a gentleman walked up and said to me, "I know who you are." I was somewhat surprised as I had never seen him in my life but he went on to explain that he was Fran's cousin.

He told me that her parents and the rest of the family did everything they could to encourage her to marry me - even to the extent of allowing her to go with me to Florida on my last leave before Korea. In those days, that was quite a stretch - not something that polite society looked upon with favor. He continued the story she married the pilot. They had three children. But apparently, their marriage was not the greatest. She died in her early 60's. There are times, even now and in the past that I wonder about all of this. One cannot but help playing the game of "what ifs."

If there is a moral to this story, I don't know what it might be. I suppose it would be safe to say that life takes its peculiar twists and turns. At times, we might be in control of our destiny but for the most part, we are like a leaf drifting in the current of life. But those currents have been good to me. I left the service a year after our marriage - with some regrets. And Patti and I had a great life - three wonderful daughters, three wonderful granddaughters, and lately the addition of a great granddaughter. Life goes on... life is good.

- BILL WILLIAMSON

DETECTIVE STORY
Jim Campbell

I'm sure you've all read a detective story or seen a movie whereby the bad guy is out to get the hero. The hero knows that he must therefore never take the same route when going home or to work or wherever his destination might be. This, of course, confuses his enemy and the hero always arrives safely.

I should have remembered all of that because in a millisecond, my life almost ended. Our company occupied a very high mountain and ridgeline, our portion of the MLR. We were dug in as much as possible but since we were sitting on one huge solid rock, we had very little protection.

My command post was a small bunker blasted into the reverse slope of the ridge. Inside, we had a bunk made of old communication wire, a table, a Coleman lantern, and most importantly, our EE8 phone, which was connected to my two Listening Posts 30 yards to my front, to my company commanders CP, and to the other platoons of the company. The EE8 phone was about as basic as two tin cans tied together with string that we played with as kids. But it had quite a range. It was important that either my platoon sergeant or I manned it - particularly at night.

At first light, I made it a point to check on my guys. And I always crested the ridgeline at exactly the same spot and about the same time early every morning. I was silhouetted for only a second or so but apparently, a Chinese gunner was waiting. I didn't hear the round that he fired but it was probably one of their 76mm mountain guns. But I do remember the crack or the whoosh and the shock wave as it went by my head. I distinctly felt it. Of course, it happened so quickly, I had no time to feel any fear. I went on about my business but I've got to give that gunner credit - he was good. I wish I had thought to shoot him the bird. I believe Winston Churchill made this statement: "Nothing in life is so invigorating as to be shot at without result."

I have to admit also that we were pretty careless. At night, we took cover as best we could because the Chinese pounded us with mortar and artillery fire. It wasn't uncommon to be on the receiving end of several hundred rounds. But during daylight hours, things were pretty quiet and we caught a nap or strolled around on our ridge like a bunch of kids looking for something to entertain us. They knew and we knew that if they fired during the day, our artillery would quickly locate their position and make their lives miserable.

But sometimes they just couldn't resist. For example, they knew that around 1800 hours (six in the evening) our guys would get back on the reverse slope somewhat out of their sight and break out the C-rations. They might light up a couple of small fires to try and heat the canned spaghetti or whatever other delicacies the rations provided.

The Chinese positions were even higher than ours were, so I guess their artillery forward observers could see us pretty well. Sure enough, we'd get a few incoming mortar rounds close enough to upset our delicious meals and we'd have to take cover until they got tired of the game. I'm sure they got a big kick out of all of this.

As a matter of information, when a mortar is fired the shell is dropped down the mortar tube. An explosion of the propellant takes place and the mortar round is on the way to the target. Depending on the distance to that target, it takes a few seconds for the round to reach its objective. If the wind was coming at us, we could sometimes hear the initial explosion of the round leaving and knew that trouble was coming our way. And we'd automatically duck for cover.

On another occasion, I was looking down to my left where our adjacent company was located. They were pretty much at the bottom of our mountain in a very low and exposed area. Being in a defensive situation, one of the tanks from our division tank battalion was assigned to their area. It was a bright sunny day and the tank crew had their shirts off, sprawled out on the ground next to their steel monster taking in the sun like New York tourists in the Bahamas.

Episode Twenty-eight - Detective Story

The Chinese couldn't resist. They lobbed four quick mortar rounds at that crew and every one landed within 20 or so yards of the target. It was almost funny - when the first round hit, three of the guys were on top of that tank in a second and literally dove down the hatch. The other two disappeared under the tank. No casualties. The Chinese gunners must have had time at some point to pre-register their fire to have been so accurate on those first shots. That tank crew was lucky.

I had a similar experience. We were in a new position on the MLR in a small, fairly well protected valley. But once again, the Chinese were on the high ground and had a good view of our position. One afternoon, a buddy wanted to try out his new Canon 35mm camera, which he had purchased on his way over. We were goofing around and I guess a Chinese FO was watching. I was sitting on a big chunk of rock, my friend was sighting on me and adjusting his camera and about a second after he snapped the shutter, a mortar round hit the ground thirty yards in back of me. Fortunately, it must have been one of the small 60mm jobs as no damage was done. I think that picture is on the cover of this book.

I know the Chinese FO enjoyed that and again I was amazed at the accuracy of that one round. Had they unleashed a half dozen, we'd probably not have seen the result of our picture taking session. I still have that photo - Papa San Mountain is in the background and I often wonder what the picture would have looked like had my buddy clicked the shutter just a second later. Another day in Paradise and close to our last day.

- JIM CAMPBELL

MEDAL OF HONOR
JOHN B. MEYERS

I was born on January 29th, 1928, in Iron Mountain, Michigan. That's in the Upper Peninsula. I was a "Depression Baby," the cataclysmic event that started a year later affecting the lives of hundreds of thousands of families including mine.

We had moved to Quinnesec, Michigan, and my father was the foreman of the Ford Motor Company wood yard. One of my earliest recollections is of sitting on his lap and helping him drive his Model T Ford. Times were tough. Dad was laid off and we were having some major financial difficulties.

We were living in an old dilapidated house - it probably had fifteen rooms. We didn't use the upstairs at all is it was full of old picture frames, hundreds of them! It got so cold there in the winter that we burned those frames in our one downstairs fireplace. Some of them were very ornate and must have been of some value but to us they were firewood - and warmth.

Shortly thereafter, we moved across the Menominee River to Niagara, Wisconsin. Our home there was part of an old burned out nightclub complex. It had been full of slot machines during its heyday. My aunt would come over when she needed grocery money and rake through the ruins and ashes looking for nickels, dimes, and quarters.

Things were not improving and on some occasions, our dinner consisted of bread and milk with a little sugar in it. We were on food stamps, courtesy of the WPA (Works Progress Administration). But we still had our pride and were somewhat embarrassed to go to the

139

store with those stamps to help buy our groceries. We had a wagon that we loaded fast after exiting the store very quickly.

My Dad had been doing pick and shovel work with the WPA but later got a job selling insurance for Metropolitan Life. He found many of his clients in bars and cafes. I guess it was easier to sell a policy if a prospect had consumed a few drinks. He soon became a "Million Dollar" salesman!

Times were still tough and now we were living in part of an old jail in Niagara. The Sheriff's living quarters had been upstairs before he was moved to the new jail. I had two brothers and four sisters and with Mom and Dad, the place was quite crowded. But we managed. I had a job delivering milk for my uncle who owned a small dairy farm. It required my getting up at four o'clock every morning. And Dad was hired by the Kimberly-Clark paper mill in Niagara - always searching for a better way to support the family.

In 1937, we moved to Niagara Falls, New York. Dad got an interim job selling silverware door to door and was paid $24.00 a week. Times were still tough. Mom helped out by baking Parkerhouse rolls and we kids went down the street selling them for twenty cents a dozen. They sold better than hotcakes!

I was in Pacific Avenue grammar school by now and time went by. Dad got a job at the Isco Chemical Company, one of many such companies in Niagara Falls. He was the night shift superintendent. I remember that he had no car and would walk the railroad tracks every night that led to his job. One of the unions put on an organizing campaign in his company and he was opposed to it. However, the union won the election and that caused Dad to lose his position. But I always had a job - I sold newspapers, set pins in a bowling alley, worked in a grocery store stocking shelves, mowed lawns, and did anything else that would help the family finances.

Finally, I made it to La Salle High School. I was small for my age but I went out for the football team anyway. I was playing

140

quarterback in an intra-squad game and doing pretty well. We scored a touchdown but the coach pulled me from the team. I was not happy and asked the coach, "Why?" He said, "I was afraid you'd get killed out there!" That was the end of my football career.

My Dad smoked three packs of Camels a day and eventually suffered from a collapsed lung. After he recovered, he and I moved to Cleveland, Ohio, where Dad got a job as a salesman with the parent chemical company for whom he had worked in Niagara Falls. At the same time, I graduated from high school, got a job as a mail boy with Standard Oil Company, and was later promoted to the Payroll Department. The rest of the family followed us to Cleveland six months later and Mom and Dad scraped enough money together to make a down payment on a house right next to the railroad tracks. But it was home for Mom, Dad, and all seven kids!

During that time, I played shortstop in Class "A" softball in East Cleveland. A scout for the Cleveland Indians saw me play and asked me to try out for their professional team. Six hundred hopefuls showed up the first day! I got a hit in a game, stole second, at the coach's urging, and made it to the third day along with 90 others hoping to make it to the "Big Leagues." I missed the cut and went back to my job at Standard Oil content that I had tried and satisfied with the outcome. But my life was about to change again!

In October of 1950, I was drafted into the U.S. Army. The Korean War was going full bore. I took my basic training at Camp Atterbury, Indiana, with the Pennsylvania 28th National Guard. On one occasion, we marched in review for General Mark Clark. He was SHARP! He was also very interested in our training, as he knew that we would soon be shipping out for Korea.

Basic training was over and I soon found myself on a troop train heading to Fort Laughton, Washington. I was dead broke and dependent upon the U.S. Army. As we lumbered across the country, I one day asked the conductor, "Where's the next stop?" His answer,

War in the Land of the Morning Calm

"Helena, Montana, arriving in about twenty minutes." I went down the aisle hollering, "Give me money, I'm going for beer."

In minutes, I gathered a fistful of bills. I was off that train even before it stopped and headed for a bar not far from the station. I slapped the money on the counter and said to the bar keep, "Give me all the beer this will buy!" We must not have been the first troop train to stop there because they were ready with huge bags of beer. I grabbed my change and beer and took off at a run - toot, toot - the train was about to pull out.

The train was in motion, my arms were breaking from the weight of the beer, and I was about to stumble and fall. But next thing I know, two guys reach down and grab me by my shirt collar and hoist me aboard - beer and all. I kept a couple of cans for myself, $15.00 in change and received a round of applause as I passed the beer down the aisles. With money in my pocket I no longer had to worry about my paycheck ($18.50 a month or thereabouts) that would eventually catch up with me.

We processed through Fort Laughton very quickly and were on our way to Korea aboard the Liberty ship, H.B. Freeman. We landed in Pusan on the southeast coast and were soon on our way by troop train toward Seoul, the capital. I was put on guard duty standing on the platform between the cars. It was near midnight and I had my M-1 rifle but no ammunition. If there had been an enemy out there, I wouldn't have known what he looked like and couldn't have shot at him anyway!

John Meyers far right.

Episode Twenty-nine - Medal of Honor

I finally arrived at company headquarters (I Company, 7th Infantry Regiment, Third Infantry Division) somewhere north of Seoul. My first night I was on guard duty from 2:00 AM to 4:00 AM. I could hear ripples on the nearby river and in my mind, I feared the enemy was swimming across and I was the target. I know I was hallucinating as I could see North Koreans behind every rock. Finally time passed, nothing moved and I relaxed a bit. I had been scared as all Hell and thanked God that no one attacked me, as I STILL had no ammo for my M-1!

A few days later, I saw my first dead Chink. The top of his head had been blown off in an artillery barrage. There must have been a million flies swarming over and around him. Someone finally buried him but not soon enough. I'll never forget that scene. I served on the line for several weeks with two other replacements, Marina and Marino. We were the three M's as we came to the company in alphabetical order. Marina was killed in action not long after our arrival.

One of our company officers saw that I had some clerical experience and I was soon made Company Clerk. My duties included making the Morning Report, which contained statistics on KIAs, MIAs and WIAs and other pertinent information. Those numbers showed that in the eleven months that I was there, 149 GI's were wounded, and 49 killed in our company. So I figured, statistically, if you got hit the odds were 3 to 1 that you would not be killed. Comforting? Not much. Particularly since I had to take these reports daily to our Company Commander who was on the MLR. Frequently, I got caught in artillery and mortar fire as well as small arms skirmishes between our guys and the enemy.

I was with the Company Commander one morning when a platoon sergeant came in off a night patrol and reported to him. He told the Captain that the only enemy his patrol had seen was a wounded North Korean. The Captain responded, "He was wounded? Did you kill him?" The sergeant replied, "No, Sir, we didn't." The Captain was irritated and said, "Why not? You know if the son of a

143

bitch heals, he'll come back and try to kill us!" The sergeant felt that he would have been committing murder so he just left the wounded enemy soldier there to die. There were times when we were called upon to make those kinds of moral judgments. What would you have done?

On another occasion, Sasek our company jeep driver was returning from the front lines with two injured South Korean soldiers. Bouncing along on the rough road, one of them began yelling, "Etai, etai!" which translates into, "It hurts, it hurts!" We thought for sure he had been shot in the butt. When they got to the aid station, one of our doctors examined the man and found that he had a bad case of hemorrhoids.

The other man did not fare as well. He had been hit in the elbow by enemy rifle or machine gun fire. Our medic on the line had placed the man's arm in a sling and taped it to his chest. When the doctor removed the bloody sling, he found the only thing holding the arm together were two small strips of skin. He snipped them with his scissors and the forearm fell to the ground. The doctor asked Sasek to take the arm and bury it - which he did, just before he vomited.

Sometime later, we had pulled off the line and were in reserve. There was a Corporal in our outfit by name of Hogan. He was a good man but a heavy drinker. One night he decided to "attack" our company officers tent. He entered their tent, Thompson sub-machine gun in hand, got them out of their sacks and made them line up as if to be shot. Of course, he didn't but scared the Hell out of our officers. Needless to say, he was busted back to private for that episode and probably would have been court-martialed except he was invaluable in a fight.

On another occasion while we were still in reserve, he came into the tent where I was sprawled out on a cot reading. He had a grenade in his hand and said to one of our buddies, Homer Howard, "Homer, I'm gonna pull the pin on this baby!" Homer was a bit gullible and Hogan figured to terrify him. I looked at the grenade and could see that the pin was already gone. I hollered, "Hogan, you dumb son-of-a bitch, you already pulled the pin!" Hogan had done so without realizing it, panicked and screamed, "Holy Shit!" and headed for the great outdoors. Of course, the grenade would not explode until the handle came free by throwing the grenade - which Hogan did - straight toward the crapper, which was a hole in the ground with an ammo box for the seat.

A few seconds later, there was a fine explosion with shrapnel and shit flying everywhere. Some came whizzing through the tent. The ammo box stool was nothing but splinters. Callie, another buddy, had gone out to take a crap and was nowhere to be found. Luckily, he saw what was happening, dove into a foxhole, and crawled out screaming and cursing like a maniac after the dust settled. Our Captain came bursting out of his tent on the double, somewhat apoplectic, and screaming, "What the Hell is going on?!" As soon as he saw Hogan, he knew. The Captain hauled Hogan into his tent and gave him an Article 15 (the lowest grade of a court-martial). I doubt it made much of an impression on Hogan but the Captain was temporarily satisfied.

I received some awards while in Korea: the Combat Infantry Badge, the Bronze Star Meritorious, Presidential Unit Citations, etc., but nothing compared to the exploits and awards of a young man by the name of Charles L. Gilliland from Yellville, Arkansas. Private First Class Gilliland was a member of our company and had stopped an assault on our company perimeter. As a result, he was missing in action. When our company commander learned of Gilliland's heroic action, he felt that Gilliland deserved the Medal of Honor and asked me to investigate the matter and submit the award for approval. I interviewed men in his squad who were with him at the time, wrote the award, and submitted it to our Company Commander for his approval and submission to higher headquarters. It was not until 50 years later that I found out that the MOH had indeed been awarded posthumously to this incredibly outstanding youngster. It gave me a great sense of satisfaction to have participated in having our nation's highest award for bravery in combat bestowed upon the youngest man to receive the Medal of Honor during the Korean War. He was only seventeen.

Following is the account of his heroism as published in the Congressional Record and noted on the internet under Medal of Honor Recipients:

KOREAN WAR MEDAL OF HONOR RECIPIENT
CHARLES L. GILLILAND

Charles L. Gilliland

Corporal, then (Pfc.), U.S. Army, Company I, 7th Infantry Regiment, 3rd Infantry Division. Place and date: Near Tongmang-ni, Korea, 25th of April 1951. Entered service at: Yellville (Marion County), Ark. Born: 24th of May 1933, Mountain Home, Ark. G.O. No.: 2, 11 January 1955. Citation: Cpl. Gilliland, a member of Company I, distinguished himself by conspicuous gallantry and outstanding courage above and beyond the call of duty in action against the enemy. A numerically superior hostile force launched a coordinated assault against his company perimeter, the brunt of which was directed up a defile covered by his automatic rifle. His assistant was killed by enemy fire but Cpl. Gilliland, facing the full force of the assault, poured a steady fire into the foe, which stemmed the onslaught. When two enemy soldiers escaped his raking fire and infiltrated the sector, he leaped from his foxhole, overtook, and killed them both with his pistol. Sustaining a serious head wound in this daring exploit, he refused medical attention and returned to his emplacement to continue his defense of the vital defile. His unit was ordered back to new defensive positions but Cpl. Gilliland volunteered to remain to cover the withdrawal and hold the enemy at bay. His heroic actions and indomitable devotion to duty prevented the enemy from completely overrunning his company positions. Cpl.

Episode Twenty-nine - Medal of Honor

Gilliland's incredible valor and supreme sacrifice reflect lasting glory upon him and are in keeping with the honored traditions of the military service.

    Such are the men and women of our armed forces. For my part, I was honorably discharged from the Army with the rank of Sergeant in July of 1952. I was 24 years old. I graduated from John Carroll University in Cleveland, Ohio, thanks to the GI Bill. I went back to work for Standard Oil and five years later married the girl of my dreams and started our family. Now with my wife of 53 years, an MBA from Santa Clara University in California and five children, seven grandchildren and one great grandson, I can honestly say that I have had a very good life. If fact, one of the children said, "Dad, you should write a story about your life." And so I did, mostly for my own ego and entertainment, I guess. But should you care to read it, the book is in print and entitled: THE MEYERS CHRONICLES.

- JOHN B. MEYERS

DEATH ON THE IMJIN
Dale Geise

We came down out of the mountains from the Chinese side of the Imjin River thankful that another patrol was over. We slumped down on the wet ground to wait our turn to cross the river. It was very dark, but we could hear the river rushing by somewhere out in front of us. "Nervous" turned to me and said, "I don't like the sound of that!" My senses came alert since "Nervous" always took the worst things with a Midwestern calm that usually offered only low-key warnings. He had just made a very strong statement.

A high running river, when you can see it and measure it in the daylight, is one thing; to hear that low roar of water and think about approaching and crossing it in darkness is another. It made us quickly agree with "Nervous" - but that's part of what basic training taught us: get in line, wait your turn, and do what is ordered. So we sat there in the mist - there was always mist along the rivers - and waited.

We would be the last ones to cross. Men in our platoon who were ahead of us got into boats and began to pull themselves across the river with a rope that stretched from shore to shore. We couldn't see them but we knew how it worked. We didn't know, however, how high the water had risen since our original crossing.

It was very quiet. The heavy wet air deadened any sounds. No one felt like saying a word. The leaden tiredness of exhaustion had settled on us when a whispered message came back from someone at the river's edge: "Stay put, there's been an accident." The boat ahead of us had tipped over. We didn't know the names of those lost until later; Sgt. Dicerno, Melvin Kuehl, and two others had drowned.

For years, I have thought of that scene - the men in that boat, the dark and black rolling water. They were wearing heavy boots and damp fatigue clothes, heavy ammo belts, grenades and flak jackets. They probably dropped their weapons and helmets when the boat went over but they didn't have a chance. It is no wonder there was not a sound. They would have gone under very quickly without a chance to help themselves or to cry out for aid. I think about them out on that river with the water rushing by in the blackness of the night, knowing when the boat tilted, that there was no hope - they were going to drown.

My squad was left behind that night. We stayed on the enemy side of the river for almost a week on a little hill called "The Bubble." We took turns standing guard outside a hole, like a small cave, while others slept. We walked, with little enthusiasm around the hill picking up scraps of C-rations left by patrols before us.

The days dragged on while we got hungrier and watched the river that still ran dangerously high and fast. Our company knew where we were and on the third day, a helicopter approached with a heavily wrapped bundle hanging under its door. Food for sure! They dropped the package directly in the center of a minefield that circled the hill. We would sit in the dirt and study all that food lying out there but no one was inclined to go get it.

I have often wondered why the Chinese didn't come for us. During daylight, they would be in danger of our artillery and mortars as they crossed a level open area surrounding the hill. But at night, they could have sent a force to easily dispose of our small group. Did the minefield make them as uncertain as it did us? Or they could have shelled us to shreds at any time. Why not? Perhaps they thought our little group wasn't worth the bother.

How does one measure the balances of luck and loss? We could have been chosen to go in the boats earlier. Then there would have been a search for OUR bodies somewhere down river.

During our last two days on "The Bubble," the river dropped dramatically and we were able finally to cross to safety and food. We didn't talk much about the whole experience. There was too much "wonder why" and "what ifs" in it.

- DALE GEISE

THE ENGINEERS
George Collett

I first set foot in Korea on May 1st in 1952. We were trucked from the dock in Pusan to a "repel depel," (Replacement Depot) somewhere on the outskirts of Pusan. That was the most stinking place I've ever been in; raw sewage ran in open ditches along the sides of the roads.

We were assigned to 12-man squad tents and I was given guard duty the first night. When our guard detail was assembled, one of the truck drivers called for me to ride with him. My job was to ride "shotgun" for his "taxi." His duties were to take Korean civilian workers back to the shack areas where they lived.

Once we cleared the gate, he handed me two 30-round clips taped together end to end to replace the one 15 round clip I had been issued. I was armed with an M-2 automatic .30 caliber carbine. My driver said it was May Day, a big Communist celebration, which might cause us some trouble. He wanted me to be prepared to shoot if need be. My welcome to the war.

We headed back to camp after a couple of hours. Once there he took the two clips of ammo he had given me, and removed the .45 caliber pistol that he wore on his belt. He then hid them under the dash of the truck. It seems that only officers were allowed to carry side arms (pistols). It all seemed a little strange to me. At any rate, he said we were done for the night and it was time for a beer. We had a couple, and a few minutes later, I discovered that the urinals were pipes stuck in the ground. You would just walk up to one, take aim, and do your thing. Seemed to work.

The next morning we got on a "Mickey Mouse" train (very small) and headed for Seoul. There were several hundred of us and it was quite crowded. The seats were wooden and very uncomfortable as they were designed for the smaller Korean population. As best I can remember we rode all day and all night, arriving in Seoul the second day. Pretty much beat.

We were formed up into several groups and put on busses or deuce and a halves (trucks) pulling trailers loaded with our gear. We crossed a river to Yong Dong Po and there joined D Company, 84th Engineer Battalion. After spending the night we loaded on to the mail and supply truck and headed for the Headquarters and Supply Company of the Battalion. It was quite a ride north.

After supper that evening, the Chaplain came to meet us and give us his blessings. He took us outside our tent, pointed to some hills and mountains, and told us that was where the Chinese forces were located - some 6 or 7 miles to the north.

The following day, a truck from B Company (our final destination) picked us up and we headed further north. On that trip, we passed a sign stating that we were now crossing the 38th parallel. Not long after we arrived at Baker Company, our new home.

Baker Company was building a bridge called the White Front. If memory serves me right, we had 240 men plus or minus working on it. We arrived at the site very early each morning. The riverbanks were quite high and the road and the bridge were about fifty feet above normal water level. The piers that supported the deck consisted of five "bents." There were large frameworks that were put together on the banks and then lifted up and placed on steel pilings that had been pounded into the riverbed.

The bents were made of timbers that were 12 inches by 12 inches and about 40 feet in length. They were notched and bolted together with one-inch diameter bolts. The bents were lifted by crane and then bolted together with 4 x 12's which meant we swung around on ropes to get into position to do all of this somewhat intricate drilling, bolting, pounding, etc.; that was our job and we got it done, hell or high water as the old saying goes. We worked under both conditions.

Episode Thirty-one - The Engineers

After the completion of the bridge, icebreakers were built on the upstream side to keep ice from forming dams against the piers during the spring thaws. The breakers were formed by pile driving steel beams into the riverbed in a triangular pattern and then lacing the uprights together with smaller steel beams. We had all the Army welders that could be found as well as Korean civilian welders. To this day, I have no idea as to where all that steel was procured. I doubt South Korea had the capacity to provide it so it probably was manufactured in Japan to the required specs and shipped over by freighters.

It was somewhere about the time that we were close to finishing the job when I was approached by our company clerk, a stateside buddy and good personal friend. He asked me if I'd like the job of being our Company Commanders jeep driver. I jumped at the opportunity and was transferred to the motor pool as the CO's new driver.

When I was not driving, I spent my time in the shop tinkering with "our" jeep. It had removable top, sides, back panels and doors made of canvas. They fit loosely allowing much cold air to enter. I secured the panels to the top using thin wire. Around the bottom, I fastened the panels to the metal floor using sheet metal screws and washers. When done, it was pretty darned tight. I then got some white paint and applied it to the tire rims in a ½ wide stripe - looked jazzy.

I found a flat piece of round metal from a wire reel about the same diameter as the spare tire mounted on the rear end and had one of the Korean workers paint the Engineer logo in the center. On the outer edge of the circle was painted, "Company Commander B-84 Engineer Const. Bn." It was mounted on the spare. I then made floor mats out of straw and covered them with rubber cut from destroyed truck inner tubes. Next, I mixed a little motor oil with diesel fuel and with a towel "polished" the exterior of the jeep. That gave it a pretty good shine - as much as olive drab green could shine.

153

When cold weather arrived, I installed a heater. It sat above the wheel well on the passenger side and kept us toasty warm. Next came my Zenith "Trans-Oceanic" battery powered radio. One of the Korean carpenters made a wooden case, lined it with sponge rubber out of an artillery ammo can, and mounted it over the rear wheel well on the driver side. There the radio resided, safe and with good sound!

I picked up my Commanding Officer one morning after all of this work was completed. We headed for the bridge three or four miles away. I reached back and turned the radio on - set on an Armed Forces radio station in Japan that played mostly country music. The Captain never looked up, as he was busy studying paperwork piled on his knee.

After a few minutes, he said, "George, I don't know what I'm going to do with you seeing as how you and this jeep keep me in trouble with our Battalion Commander. He doesn't like our pretty jeep. I think he's envious." Then he told me he was going to miss me as he was instructed to get another driver.

I was crushed, really disappointed, speechless. I'd been driving him for several weeks with no complaints. Finally, I was able to ask him why I was being "fired." He responded that our company motor pool dispatcher was heading stateside and I would replace him. I was to be the new dispatcher and had to learn fast to keep our large fleet of vehicles moving - when and where needed.

My new job earned me another stripe and a lot of responsibility! I was now in charge of all our rolling equipment and the assignments of all drivers and equipment operators. The Sergeant in charge of the Maintenance Shop was a nice guy; he stopped by my tent one day (my sleeping arrangements didn't improve with the promotion) and made me an offer I couldn't refuse. He was a friend of an Australian Supply Sergeant who could get whiskey and would sell it to us. I bought a couple of bottles and from then on had some kind of booze in my footlocker. Only officers were allowed to have alcohol (and

Episode Thirty-one - The Engineers

side arms) on hand. I had both. My trusty nickel-plated .45 caliber semi-automatic pistol was always close by.

One night, I was given permission to visit a stateside pal that was dispatcher for a trucking company about 20 miles to our south. I called him to make certain he would be there and the phone was answered as follows: "You call, we haul. We're the double-clutching M-----F------from the Six Double Deuces, CQ (Charge of Quarters), speaking, SIR!" Another buddy was with me and we were on our way.

When leaving the company area, we were required to be armed. I had my trusty nickel-plated .45 and by friend had his .38 revolver. While we were gone, our Commanding Officer was ordered by battalion to have a surprise inspection to see if any of the enlisted men or non-commissioned officers had any side arms. I never understood this policy.

The Commanding Officer inspected the Dispatcher's tent (mine), saw my footlocker that I had stored there and opened it. My guys knew I had my pistol with me so they weren't concerned. However, there in front of my Captain was a fifth of Canadian Club. As he left the tent, he turned to my pals and discreetly told them that there would probably be a whiskey inspection the following night. And in fact, there was - but oddly enough, no whiskey to be found. Our Captain was a good guy!

One evening, reviewing our vehicle activity for that day, I came across a trip ticket with no miles logged showing distance, etc. traveled. Every vehicle had to have a ticket or they would not be allowed out the gate. The mileage had to be recorded and made part of our records. Don't ask me why.

I was not happy. I called the driver in to my hooch and asked why didn't he record the beginning and ending odometer miles, subtract, and enter the total miles driven for that day. His reply, "Sarge, I don't know how to do that." He could not do simple

155

War in the Land of the Morning Calm

arithmetic. In fact, he could neither read nor write! I calmed down and asked him if he would just get someone at each stop to write the numbers down for him, turn the info in to me at the end of the day and I'd do the calculations. He might have been illiterate but he could drive the pure Hell out of a deuce and a half.

On one occasion, I sent him on an important run in the dead of winter. Colder than you know what! He was to pick up 4000 pounds of dynamite from a base several miles to our south and to return ASAP. About six that evening, he was back. He pulled into the yard and parked a few feet from our "office." Everyone knew what he was hauling.

He came up to my desk - I was buried in paperwork. He stood there a moment and announced that he had a flat tire. I didn't look up but said, "OK, Kim will take care of it in the morning." Then he informed me that he had a second flat tire. Again, I told him that Kim would fix both in the morning. His next reply was to the effect that both tires were on the same axle, side by side. With that, I lost my cool and said, "Bill, I don't give a good F-----F--- if they're on the damned steering wheel. Kim will take care of it in the morning! He gave me a kind of forlorn look and replied, "But Sarge, they're on fire."

About ten of us were in the tent that we cleared in about one-thousandth of a second. Bill was absolutely right - the tires were burning smartly with 4000 pounds of somewhat volatile dynamite directly above. The ground was frozen solid so we couldn't shovel dirt to smother the flames. We grabbed every five-gallon can of water, every glass of water, anything wet--one of the guys might have tried pissing on the flames - I don't remember. It was a madhouse but we finally got the fire extinguished. I think we might have broken out the Canadian Club shortly thereafter.

Jim asked me if our unit set up pontoon bridges. We didn't - that was a job generally performed by one of our Combat Engineer outfits. On one occasion, the Chinks blew one of our ammo dumps to

Episode Thirty-one - The Engineers

Hell and back. It was on the north side of some river. There were many casualties. That pontoon bridge was covered with vehicular traffic rushing our wounded to the rear. Had it not been for that bridge there would probably have been much loss of life and suffering. The Combat Engineer guys were usually working very close to the front.

There was an unfortunate incident though, involving one of our men. We were working on a bridge somewhere several miles behind the MLR. He was laying communication wire for our EE-8 phones (Double E8's as we called them). This was his last day and was to rotate home within 24 hours. Unfortunately, he stepped on an old Chinese anti-personnel mine and was severely wounded. Taken to a MASH unit and then to a hospital in Japan he finally recovered. In fact, a couple of months later he returned to duty looking like death warmed over. Somebody screwed up - he should have been on his way home. Eventually he made it.

On some dark nights, we might get a visit from "Bed-Check Charlie." He would probably be some ill-trained young North Korean flying an old matchbox, two winged, fabric covered, single engine aircraft, an antique from WWII. The Chinese would not waste one of their better-trained pilots on such a mission. Charlie would look for lights on the ground and then proceed to drop mortar shells, grenades, or whatever kind of small explosives he could cram into his open cockpit. Needless to say, if he was in the vicinity all lights were turned off. If he had made the mistake of trying to attack a front line unit, they'd have blown him out of the air in a heartbeat. And they had no lights so we rear area guys were the target. We generally had some kind of lighting - probably from a generator.

In our tent, we had rigged up the headlight from a destroyed truck. It hung from one of the tent poles and was connected to a vehicle battery. Worked like a champ. We were having a "dinner party" one night consisting of a lot of cans of C-rations. We placed them on our pot-bellied stove for heating. Sure enough, here comes Charlie. We disconnected our light - and suddenly things started

157

exploding. I was near one of the tent exits barefooted but with a warm blanket wrapped around both feet and stuffed in a wooden box for warmth. I could hardly move all bundled up like that so I was trampled pretty badly by my brave buddies making for the exit.

After things calmed down a bit, we reentered the tent to find it filled with smoke, the stovepipe knocked off the stove, and the stove and that area of the tent covered in mush. We had not punctured the C-ration cans to allow the heat and steam to escape and they had all exploded. There was corn beef hash, spaghetti, pork and beans, etc., everywhere - the tent floor, the ceiling, the sides. What a mess. Took a while to clean it up. I suppose, had Bed Check Charlie known the damage he had wrought he'd have considered that a good mission! Probably get a medal.

As best as I can remember, during the early spring of 1953, our company was moved south near the Imjin River. We were to participate in the construction of a new bridge, The Freedom Gate Bridge, later named the General Libby Bridge. I had two draglines working on the north side of the river taking out stone from the riverbed. The stone was then trucked to a rock crusher where it was broken up into gravel-sized pieces ready to go in the concrete when needed. It was stacked into huge piles about a hundred feet long and fifteen feet in height.

Our mid-day meal was brought to the site. One day, we were all standing in the chow line waiting for our food when suddenly the rock pile began to explode - gravel flying in every direction. Chinese mortar and artillery was zeroed in and was raising hell. I dove behind a pile of formed steel and hoped for the best. The barrage lasted several minutes. When it ended, the sky was black from the explosions and flying dust. The gravel pile was destroyed, gone, disappeared, none left. I doubt we could have gathered a truckload.

We never could understand what the Hell that was all about but we guessed that the Chinese were sending us a message - "Build your bridge and we'll blow it to pieces."

Episode Thirty-one - The Engineers

Finally, my tour of Korea came to an end and I was on my way home. That boat trip back across the Pacific seemed to take forever. But then one very foggy morning, we peered into the distance and, lo and behold, two towers became slowly visible. As we inched forward (or so it seemed) the sun broke through and there was a most beautiful sight - the Golden Gate Bridge! We were back in the good old U.S. of A.

I was soon honorably discharged and returned home. A couple of weeks later I had a date with a local girl. We went to a movie. In those days, Pathé News or some other such organization came on first with a five minute or so update of world events. The very first episode showed a headline about a bridge opening in South Korea. I remarked to my date that I might see some of my old pals. The camera panned in on some General cutting a ribbon on the General Libby Bridge! And HELL, there was my former entire outfit on camera! I could probably have named a hundred of my old buddies. I kind of silently saluted them, the movie ended, I took my date home, kissed her goodnight, and said to myself, "Welcome home, Pal."

- GEORGE COLLETT

WATER, WATER, EVERYWHERE
DALE GEISE

Korea, 1952. We were out on another patrol today. The sun was scorching us and for whatever reason, I didn't take my canteen. Chinese mortars, hidden behind a hill to our front, began searching for us in force. Their fire was so intense we had to drop off the paddy dikes where we had been zigzagging and take cover down in the watery muck.

I had been thirsty long before the mortar fire began and down in that scorching paddy, my brain must have been baked because I did a very stupid thing. We were there in the mud and hour or two. I wish we had taken our chances and run for home but we didn't. The heat was fierce and the little pools of water here and there in the paddy began to look cool, clear, and good. I scooped up some in my hands and drank it.

How often would I have to see the "honey buckets" used to fertilize the paddies to know never to drink any of that water? "Honey buckets" were containers in the Korean homes that were filled with human waste and then used to fertilize those fields of rice.

My first year home, I had a very high fever that lasted two to three days. Mom and Aunt Bess put cold wet towels on me and gave me quinine tablets that finally stopped the problem. Was that malaria from the rice paddy (delayed reaction) or something else? I'll never know but I was most happy that it was only temporary.

Author's Note: A day or so after the war ended, we had an incident somewhat similar to what Dale experienced. We had pulled off the line and headed for a reserve area. Tents with wooden floors and cots had been set up for us. We arrived late in the evening, threw our gear, packs, etc. on the floor, and slept the sleep of the dead. The next morning we awakened to find most of our belongings gone - stolen during the night by a couple of "slickey boys," as we called them. Cameras, pictures of loved ones, packs, etc. - all gone.

Three of us took off and were able to track the rascals for quite a distance as it had rained a bit during the night. We left in such a hurry we took nothing with us - just out the door! We were furious. Four or five hours later, we were desperate for water - and you guessed it - we drank from an old rice paddy. Fortunately, it had been long out of use and we suffered no ill effects - but we worried for a couple of days. We never did catch the scoundrels.

The only thing I lost of value was a 35mm color slide I had taken of a night attack on OP Harry. We were less than a mile away from the OP on a very high piece of terrain. I placed my camera on a rock and held the lens open for about 30 seconds. The result was a picture worthy of *Life magazine* - tracer streaks, flares, artillery and mortar bursts, smoke, and dust shrouding the base of the hill. The picture captured everything but the sound and horror of the battle. If I had that picture today, I'd give every OP Harry survivor a copy. Those guys were real heroes.

- DALE GEISE

LABOR SAVING DEVICE
Dale Geise

Thompson got tired of digging one day and DECIDED - a strong word for the mental process that produced the following action - to build a bunker the easy way. He had been pick and shoveling a hole in the side of the mountain without the aid of energy or enthusiasm. He would later explain his actions to an admiring group of buddies by saying, "Why not use plastic explosives, a proven labor saver?"

"Why not indeed?" replied his friends who were reluctant to criticize and barely capable of applying critical judgment to the project. We had easy access to plastic explosives and training in its use but commanders would likely frown on frivolous application of it. Blowing a hole in the mountain, rather than digging, would in their opinion, be frivolous. Manpower was cheap; explosives were not.

Nevertheless, Thompson was busy on his construction project molding his plastic bunker charge. Preston A. Sneed from Tennessee, a singularly nice guy and as lanky as it's possible to get, wandered by. He squatted on the uphill side of Thompson and studied the molding process.

"What are you gonna do with that?" he innocently asked. "I'm tired of digging and I'm going to blow a hole in this freakin' mountain," Thompson cheerfully replied.

Sneed leaned back on his elbows against the side of the mountain and looked up at the sky. "Blowin' things up over here might draw fire from our Chinese friends over there which might irritate folks around our neighborhood," he said slowly as he waved at the haze of hills across the valley.

"So what", replied Thompson, realizing that Sneed might have some suggestions that would help in his project. He stopped patting the high energy explosive and listened. "And another thing," added

Sneed, "You're gonna' blow rocks and dirt all to Hell and gone and halfway to the command bunker. The CO might not be happy."

"Could be," said Thompson, unwilling to accept that his plan might not be popular amongst the brass. Sneed went on: "Our company officers are going to ask who gave orders for this project, who issued you the explosives, do you know what you are doing, where are you going to get the other needed supplies, etc., etc. Are you ready for all that drill?"

"Dammit," said Thompson, "You're ruining my fun. What are they going to do, send me to Alcatraz? I don't think so. Besides, it couldn't be any worse than this!"

Sneed wandered away and Thompson sat pondering his mission, which he was slowly realizing, had no good ending. If he succeeded in blowing a sizeable hole in the mountain, the officers who came to investigate might appreciate his initiative and assign him to multiple bunker building projects - which, even with the high explosives, would still require a lot of pick and shovel work.

With a sigh, Thompson realized what might have been fun seemed only to promise trouble. He reluctantly put away the explosive and wandered off looking for a less laborious way to entertain himself.

Much later - in about 2002 - while visiting my dear friend "Nervous" Nissen at Grand Island, Nebraska, we laughed in fond memory of Thompson's bunker construction plan. Virgil was then battling prostate cancer and it was good hearing him laugh as we enjoyed reliving Thompson's "plan" that we had observed those many long years ago.

- DALE GEISE

BEWARE THE CAN IN THE BUSH
Dale Geise

Some lessons are learned almost too late to benefit the student. Our squad was swinging along a trail among the rice paddies and on top of the low dikes that enclosed fields of shallow water. No one was there to tend them so the paddies lay idle without crop.

Maintaining our five-yard interval with blue sky overhead, it was a good day to be out for a stroll. One of our missions on that daylight patrol, however, was to draw enemy fire. That can cloud the sky and the spirits a bit.

We had gone out through our "wire" - the barbed wire entanglements that protected our MLR from surprise attacks. We carefully unhooked the booby traps that were set to alert us to enemy movements to our front. These snares were simply fine wires stretched across the path and tied to various grenades fastened to a tree or bush nearby. We were with friends out for an afternoon walk. What could go wrong?

We passed through our traps but a few yards down the slope, I saw something shining in a shrub by the path and stopped to take a look. It was a tin can just dangling there. I bent to look at it closely and then lifted it for a closer look. It seemed out of place but no warning bells were ringing. Perhaps by bending over instead of lifting the can straight up saved me. My touch was not usually so gentle.

An almost invisible wire ran from the can to a GI grenade tied to a strong bush. How did the Chinese get an American grenade? Probably the same way we picked up some of their equipment. Then, too, it may have been placed there by some G.I. hoping to entertain a careless young Chinese soldier who, like me, was curious.

The grenade safety pin had been pulled to a half-inch of its length assuring that very little pressure would be required to detonate it. I carefully clasped the handle of the grenade and fully reinserted the pin. I took the grenade with me and tore away the can and its deadly wire.

So sometimes, we pass through life surviving moments when there is a beckoning from beyond. Or perhaps that great register where we are all entered simply stated that it was not our time. Lady Luck smiled on us that day and we were given a pass to look up at that blue sky once again.

Later, as we were about to turn for home, mortar bursts started walking up the valley coming closer to us fifty yards at a time. We had been spotted.

My good friend and comrade, Virgil "Nervous" Nissen, turned to me from five yards ahead and made his well-known statement that always washed away part of our fear: "That," he said pointing to the spouts of earth being thrown up by the impacting mortars, "makes me nervous." It was an understatement that always produced a chuckle in the worst of times. Our pace accelerated to a dogtrot as we turned at right angles here and there to confuse the Chinese gunners.

The path up our "hill" looked good that day as we rewired our own booby traps and then trudged to our various holes in the mountain that we called home. I should have berated myself for being so stupid with the can in the bush - but it was too good to be alive.

- DALE GEISE

CBR WARFARE
Walter Adams

I was born in Athens, Georgia and like many of my fellow Korean War veterans; I arrived during the Great Depression. I was born on October 23, 1929, very close to Black Monday.

After the end of WWII, my family moved to Atlanta where I attended Tech High School and where I joined the Naval ROTC program and later, the Naval Reserve. I really enjoyed my weekend duties with the reserve unit, as I was a gunner on a Navy PBY, a twin-engine amphibious patrol plane. This was before the Korean War.

Soon, however, I became enamored of Miriam who proved to be my future wife. Miriam was not too keen about my going off every weekend to fly around playing with my .50 caliber machine gun. I loved my job but she, of course, was more important. So I sort of dropped out of the Navy reserve program and soon we were married.

Shortly thereafter, I received a letter from President Harry Truman telling me that if I did not renew my status in the Naval Reserve, I would be classified as 1-A in the draft. I tore the letter to pieces knowing that as a married man, I was safe. However, one day after the law changed to permit the drafting of married men, I received my notice to report to Fort Jackson, South Carolina.

It so happened that I was temporarily assigned to my brother-in-law's company at Fort Jackson and he asked if I had any preferences as to where to take basic training. Since I had relatives in Virginia, I asked to be assigned there.

A few days later, I began Basic Infantry training at Fort Lee, Petersburg, Virginia. On one occasion, we were working with the Garand M-1 rifle and the Sergeant asked if anyone knew how to strip the weapon. So, I piped up and said, "Sergeant, with my eyes open or closed?" His quick response was something like, "You trying to be smart, boy?" Then he blindfolded me and said to proceed. While reassembling the weapon, I said to the Sgt., "Sarge, some SOB took the rocker arm pin." Of course, he had hidden it but laughed and said, "You'll do, son." I didn't tell him that I had an M-1 at home.

My ROTC and Naval Reserve training had paid off and soon I was the company commander of our training company. I also fired the highest score on the rifle range (with the M-l) in our battalion. I was proud of that accomplishment!

As we were approaching the end of our basic training, our Captain informed me that I had been selected to attend Officers Candidate School at Fort Benning, Georgia. Though I considered it an honor, I turned it down. I was now a married man, had an excellent job to return to after the war, and was not interested in the Army as a career.

There were eleven other men in my company who had also been selected for OCS but they too turned it down. The twelve of us were then ordered to report to Seattle, Washington, with 21 days travel time. This gave us adequate time to return home and get our affairs in order. Being recently married it was a bittersweet time for Miriam and me.

We shipped out for Japan and soon found ourselves in a replacement depot somewhere near Tokyo. I suppose there were three or four thousand from our shipment and each morning we assembled for further orders. Two or three hundred would head for Korea, others to some base in Japan for further training and so on. But the twelve of us seemed to be going nowhere.

At last one morning we were pulled out of formation and were told, "You twelve are going to be in a movie - an American-Japanese production." We were stunned, needless to say. The name of the movie was, "Ever My Love" or something like that. Later, I told my son of this and he hooted - I told him to bring it up on the Internet

Episode Thirty-five - CBR Warfare

and there it was. Our part in the movie was strictly as extras but it was a welcome break from the monotony of waiting.

Around this time, I received in the mail my honorable discharge from the Navy Reserves. Of course, I waved it around and told everyone within earshot that I was on my way home - I was now a civilian. I did add that when we shipped out for Korea that I would go along just for the boat ride. Needless to say, my story didn't fly but anything for a laugh.

We returned to the Replacement Depot. Suddenly, one morning we were taken out of the dwindling formation and told that we could not speak to anyone from that moment on. We were put under guard and even escorted to the chow hall - one guard in front, one in back. If we went to a movie there at the base two guards escorted and sat with us, one at each end of our group. We kept asking, "What is all this about." Why the secrecy - but no answers. It was really getting a bit scary.

Then one night (in the middle of the night), we were awakened, told to pack up, and in a matter of an hour or so found ourselves on a train headed south. We didn't know where we were going; we didn't know anything and no one in charge would tell us.

Finally, we arrived at the very tip end of Japan and the secret unfolded - we were taken to a Chemical, Biological, and Radiological Warfare School. Top Secret. We started classes immediately and I remember taking notes in class and then being told to burn them. This was serious stuff and we took it seriously.

But the living conditions were excellent. The food was good, attendants would come in, clean our rooms, make our beds, do our laundry, etc. Who could complain? It certainly beat living in a foxhole on some Godforsaken mountain in Korea! Little did I know.

Finally, after several weeks we graduated. Something called Operation Mushroom was apparently in some stage of planning - a nuclear attack on North Korea. I think there were about 50 in our

169

graduating class and we were soon on our way to South Korea. We were to be farmed out so that all of our major units in Korea would have a trained expert CBR man attached.

We landed at Pusan and headed north by train to Seoul. I remember that the engine was pushing a flat car that mounted a manned Quad-.50 machine gun. We were armed with our trusty M-1 rifles and some of us were assigned to stand in the sandbagged passenger car doorways to be able to fire on any would-be attackers. Welcome to the war.

We arrived in Seoul and headed North by truck. Things were pretty fluid so we didn't know what to expect. We traveled for two or three days with little food and virtually no sleep or rest. We finally arrived at our destination - we didn't know where we were but soon learned that it was called the Iron Triangle. It was late in the afternoon and tracer bullets started flying around.

We leaped from our truck and dove into a ditch. There was a South Korean soldier standing near-by and he broke into laughter. I guess one of us shouted, "What's so damn funny?" His reply: "Bullets this way, duck; bullets that way OK." I guess we were a little chagrined but appreciated his advice.

A Sergeant from the unit we were joining came over and told my buddy and me that we could occupy a hole that he pointed out. He said, somewhat ominously, that the former occupants would no longer need it. It was fast approaching total darkness so we pitched our shelter halves (pup tent) over the trench and prepared to get some much-needed sleep.

I placed my duffel bag at the rim of the foxhole - it held everything I owned, including pictures of my wife, and even my discharge papers from the Navy. The two of us got down in the cold ground but I decided I couldn't sleep with heavy trousers on so I stripped down to my long underwear. I removed my boots and used them for a pillow. My helmet was over my face.

Episode Thirty-five - CBR Warfare

The two of us were beyond exhaustion. Chinese artillery shells started pounding the area but we dozed off! Hard to believe but we slept the sleep of the innocent. When we awakened the next morning, the first thing I noticed was the bright blue sky - our makeshift roof was gone and so was my duffel bag!

As we crawled out of our hole a GI from the unit came over and said, "Where'd you guys come from?" We told him that we had just arrived last night and had slept soundly. He was astonished and said, "Last night? We lost this hill last night and just took it back this morning." Apparently, the Chinese, if they noticed our foxhole, thought we were dead. I'm glad neither of us snored or we probably would have been. But they took everything we owned. Fortunately for us, they were not interested in occupying the position and left when the counter-attack came.

8 inch Howitzer

So there we were, ready to report in to our new Commanding Officer with our only possessions - boots, helmets, underwear, and our new carbines. One of the Sergeants rounded up a few things for us and we reported in to our new home, the 424th Artillery Battalion (known as the Big 8) that was an 8-inch howitzer outfit. It was a National Guard unit out of Indianapolis, Indiana, and I guess we were the only outsiders but we were welcomed.

An 8-inch howitzer is a fearsome weapon. It can lob a 220-pound shell eighteen miles and it can also fire nuclear ordinance. At the time, it was the only artillery piece capable of doing so. In the case of this battalion, the firing positions were close up behind the MLR to give the weapons extended range. Normally, most artillery pieces are somewhat further back; I suppose that's to prevent being

171

overrun in case of an enemy breakthrough. I recall on one occasion, the battalion was firing a mission so rapidly that even Jeeps (which could haul only four of those 200-pound rounds) were called upon to bring up ammo. And as for accuracy, the 8-inch howitzer was unexcelled. Once the target was identified, the Fire Direction Center would give the guns their target coordinates. The first round was the registration round - the remaining rounds would be ON the target and it would be annihilated.

On one occasion, a Marine unit quite a distance from us was having a problem with some Chinese caves directly to their front. The Chinese would roll their 76mm cannon up to the front of the cave, blast away and then disappear behind a camouflage net. So the Marines called upon our battalion for assistance. Their lighter artillery pieces weren't doing the job. Our Battalion Commander sent one gun and crew and achieved the desired results. The eight-incher was set up in a direct fire position and commenced firing. In short order, the caves were signed, sealed, and obliterated.

At any rate, here I was with an artillery outfit and no one (except probably the upper chain of command) knew what I was there for or what I was doing. So I had a lot of latitude in how I spent my time. In the CBR School, we had been issued all of these little detectors, a film badge of sorts. The function of the badge was to tell me (if people started dropping dead around me) the cause of death. But what it didn't do was to tell me how to prevent myself from joining them. Obviously, if the badge changed color it was time to get out of Dodge, and bottom line, my job was to give the warning.

Another of the things that we were taught in CBR training was how to construct a bunker that would offer protection against a CBR attack. I had also been in the construction business in civilian life so I helped and directed the construction of some of our battalion bunkers. I don't believe the Chinese had any intention of using any kind of CBR attack against us but it was better to be somewhat prepared.

Episode Thirty-five - CBR Warfare

I also spent time just helping out in the usual chores - sometimes pulling outpost duty, checking the perimeter defenses, anything I could do to help. For example, on one beautiful sunny day I was with a buddy checking our perimeter. We had trip wires hooked up to grenades in any likely avenues of approach so we wanted to make sure they stayed in working condition.

As I approached one area that still had a fair amount of foliage, I saw a hand reach out in an apparent attempt to remove one of the wires. Unfortunately, I had left my carbine in the jeep and I had not strapped on my .45 caliber pistol. I had automatically reached for it but it wasn't there! The gorgeous day had lulled me into a sense of false security, I suppose, and I was about to regret my *carlessness...*

But I was carrying a small hunting knife that my wife had given me as a going away present. My reflexes kicked in when I saw the other hand in the bush holding some sort of automatic weapon. Somehow, I grabbed the enemy soldier by the hair, pulled his head out of the shrub, and had my knife against his jugular vein. My hand was shaking so that it's a wonder I didn't kill him by accident. It all happened so fast that it's difficult to remember.

My buddy came over and fortunately had had sense enough to bring his carbine so we quickly had the infiltrator under control. When we disarmed him, I took a close look at his sub-machine gun and it had markings indicating that it had once been in the use of Chiang Kai Shek's Chinese Nationalist Army, probably when they were fighting the Chinese communists prior to WWII. I wanted to bring that weapon home as a souvenir in the worst way but unfortunately, that was not allowed. Our Chinese friend was sent to the rear to become a POW. I wonder if he is still around - if so, I know he remembers that day!

On another occasion during darkness, a friend and I went down to the fuel dump to get some kerosene for our lanterns. That was our illumination in the bunkers. This time I remembered to grab my carbine but didn't realize that I had removed the ammo clip! At some point in the fuel dump, we separated. Suddenly I was confronting another infiltrator - this guy was intent on blowing the fuel dump, which would not have been good. I took quick aim, pulled the trigger - and nothing. I decided I was a slow learner as a would-be Infantryman. I reversed the carbine, tried to hit him in the head with the stock of my weapon, and missed again. Fortunately, my buddy heard the commotion and came to my rescue. He shot and killed the Chinese soldier and my day was saved once again.

One afternoon, one of my pals was on OP duty and was running low on ammo. He radioed me and asked that I bring him a couple of clips for his carbine. He also said that he had a prisoner that the South Koreans had brought in but added that the Chinese soldier was just a kid and said, "Bring along some candy bars." He was really feeling sorry for this young prisoner. So I picked up the ammo, grabbed some candy and this time, remembered to load and take my carbine.

As I approached the OP, the young prisoner took off up the hill. There were a few South Korean soldiers standing around laughing and shouting, "He sayonara, he gone, gone."

As the kid disappeared over the horizon, I asked my buddy, "Why didn't you shoot him?" He said he just couldn't do so since the young Chinese was a mere boy. Then he asked me, "Why didn't you shoot - you had a perfect opportunity." My reply: "Just cleaned my carbine - didn't want to have to do it again." He cracked up. And the young Chinese sixteen year old made good his escape.

On another memorable evening, we were sitting around in our bunker and our Sergeant informs us that someone has to go man one of the OP's - the guy on duty got pulled off for some reason. So we flipped coins to see who would go. I lost. I picked up my grease gun and headed out. The OP was well sandbagged and even had a small roof overhead. It held a .50 caliber machine gun and was well stocked with hand grenades.

Episode Thirty-five - CBR Warfare

I settled in (I don't remember why I was alone, this was usually a two man job) and as I relaxed I could hear my guys back down the hill laughing and chatting. It was a beautiful night and the moon came up bright and shiny over my hill. I was feeling lonely and very downhearted - and then I saw a little dot silhouetted against the moonlight - and another and another. And here I am, all by myself. I rubbed my eyes and knew company was coming. I jacked a round into the .50 caliber, placed my grease gun at my side, and pulled the box of grenades closer to me. I called back to my platoon CP on the EE8 phone to tell the Sergeant. He asked how many were coming and I told him I wasn't sure but probably 15 to 20. He then told me that he'd bring a squad to my rescue as soon as he heard any shooting!

He seemed to think that if he and the squad moved too early it would give away my position. So I'm sitting there for what seemed like three or four hours and am very nervous. I know my heart was pounding loudly enough to be heard by the approaching enemy. Suddenly, the EE8 phone rings - not very loudly but I immediately threw my helmet over it and then sat on it to muffle the sound. I rang back to the CP and the Sergeant asked, "Have you seen anymore of 'em?" I said, "No, but they damn sure know where I am now!"

Suddenly, the sky lit up off to my left and automatic fire was blazing away like crazy. Boom Boom Boom - mortars were firing. As it turns out, that Chinese patrol attacked a trench line manned by some South Korean infantrymen. The South Koreans wiped them out so once again good neighbors saved me! Needless to say, I was very grateful.

Not long after that episode, it was late at night and I was chatting with one of my pals. Suddenly, we noticed a North Korean trying to enter our perimeter. We zinged off a couple of shots to get his attention and he promptly surrendered. The noise startled the guys on outpost duty so they let loose at any imagined target - trees, bushes, shadows, etc. Tracers were flying, lot of shouting and confusion.

And out of his warm bunker, stumbles our "good old boy," a 30-year corporal clad only in his underwear and somewhat inebriated from his 190 proof alcohol and canned grapefruit juice. But he had the presence of mind to bring his M-2 carbine loaded with a 30-round clip. He sat in the snow and proceeded to empty all 30 rounds into the ground at his feet. He tried to reload but he was somewhat disoriented which was fortunate. As we marched the prisoner off, one of our officers came running out of the Command Post yelling at all within earshot that everything was under control. All in all, mass confusion. I often wonder what that North Korean soldier thought of us.

A few days later, we were watching as three or four of our F-86 Saber jets made an air strike on the Chinese positions directly to our front. One of the jets got damaged pretty badly by ground fire and turned to head south and to safety. As the plane approached us, part of a wing fell off and the pilot rapidly lost altitude. As he came across our positions, he ejected and his aircraft crashed into the side of a mountain. The pilot came down safely and we jumped in a jeep and went to pick him up. As we did so, his buddies came over us

Episode Thirty-five - CBR Warfare

very low and slow with flaps and landing gear down to check things out. Realizing he was in safe hands, they waved and took off for home. He was one happy man!

Speaking of the F-86 Saber jet reminds me of the time that one of my buddies from Hqs. Battery had to take something to one of our forward batteries. Somehow, he took a wrong turn and unknowingly was ten miles into enemy territory. He said that when he noticed a mule train crossing over a hill he knew was in big trouble - we didn't have any mule trains! Then he saw an old bi-plane close to the road and partially concealed under a straw roof - one of the "Bed Check Charlie" planes used by the North Koreans to harass targets of opportunity during hours of darkness.

My friend got out of there as quickly as possible and headed home after having located the forward battery. He gave them a pretty good indication of where he had seen the bi-plane and the coordinates were called back to battalion headquarters. Battalion gave the information to an F-86 squadron and soon one of our fighter jets was on the way. Shortly after, the pilot radioed the message; "Bed Check Charlie is Beddy-Bye - for good!"

Shortly after that incident, the Chinese forces mounted a major offensive and broke through one of the South Korean's best divisions. We were told not to run, panic, or pass out but to begin an orderly withdrawal. Which we did. The Chinese offensive must have driven us all the way back to the 38th parallel. We dug in and started pounding away at the unseen enemy. Other artillery units were adjacent to us on both sides, everyone firing like crazy. We were hub to hub and the din was unbelievable. Tons of artillery ammo was expended in a short period of time.

We kept firing. The second or third night we got the word that the cease-fire would go into effect at midnight. The war was finally over. Oddly enough, our unit moved back north on some kind of prisoner exchange deal and we found ourselves back in our old position near Papa-san Mountain in the northeast corner of the Iron

177

Triangle. And there were our former opponents, lounging around in emplacements and bunkers that I helped construct! I snapped a few pictures of them, which I still have. They, like us, were a bunch of young kids and I suppose they were as happy as we that the shooting and killing was over.

I returned home shortly thereafter grateful to be alive and felt that my life was starting over - I have been blessed.

- WALTER ADAMS

CBR, SEARS AND THE ENGINEERS
WALTER ADAMS

When I started to remember things about my tour in Korea, it opened up my mind and things that I had not thought of in years came tumbling back. As I said in my earlier account, being a CBR specialist in an artillery outfit left me with a lot of time on my hands. Obviously, I couldn't sit around and do nothing so I helped where I could.

In civilian life, I had a fair amount of experience in the building industry so I put my knowledge to good use in constructing and improving our bunkers. When we needed lumber and so forth, we would requisition the materials from the engineer depot, which was located far south of the MLR near Seoul.

On one occasion, I drove a five-ton ammo truck to the depot and presented our requisition for 1000 board feet of 2 x 12's for a bunker roof. The corporal in charge said, "What's a 1000 board feet?" I pointed to a stack of bridge timers, 3 x 12's, and told him that would about cover it.

He had his men load the lumber onto my truck until it could hold no more. He then asked, "How do you know when you have a 1000 board feet?" So I showed him an official looking tally that I had been notating as each piece was loaded and told him that we had one piece too many. I asked him to have one of his men to unload it, which he did. I thanked him kindly for his help and headed North with enough lumber to roof three or four of our bunkers! I was very pleased with myself.

I suppose I should have been ashamed of taking advantage of that young corporal but those guys were living in good housing, with good food, etc. and not in danger of being killed by our Chinese friends. I was taking this back up front where the action was - enough lumber to perhaps save some of my buddies from harm.

War in the Land of the Morning Calm

A month or so later, I was back at the depot for some small item we needed when I spotted a large electrical generator mounted on a trailer. I backed up to the generator and said in a firm voice to a couple of GI's standing around, "Hey, guys I've got orders to take this over to the Colonel's headquarters. Give me a hand and help me hook it up to my truck." Which they did. I thanked them profusely and headed north - again with a very slightly guilty conscience.

Shortly after my arrival with the generator in tow (I was given a hero's welcome), we had electric lights in all of our bunkers. I often wondered if those young engineers ever realized they'd been conned. The Lord helps those who help themselves and I figured I was simply adhering to those words of wisdom.

Not long after this episode I ordered a water pump, a couple of showerheads and several packages of zinnia seeds from Sears, Roebuck. We built a shower room over a nearby creek and pumped water up to two 55-gallon steel drums. One drum had a pan under it that we dripped diesel fuel through from an old truck carburetor. When the pan was ignited, the water eventually got good and hot so we had hot and cold running showers!

The only shower in about 300 square miles running all the time. I ordered the pump from Sears in Atlanta, GA.

Everyone who knew of this luxury came by and enjoyed our hospitality. Unfortunately, in the winter when the temperature dropped to 30 degrees below zero, the shower wasn't of much use. We melted snow in our helmets to sponge off.

By the way, when the Chinese drove us back to the 38th parallel, we backed a truck into the creek, loaded up the drums, etc. and

Episode Thirty-six - CBR, Sears and the Engineers

advanced to the south! We weren't about to let those bums enjoy our handiwork.

Before our retreat (advance to the rear), I continued to work on my bunker shared with two or three of my buddies. I had placed another 55 gallon drum on top of the bunker and kept it full of water - rigged it with a hose so we could have running water inside the bunker. We had a pot-bellied stove so with heat, electric lights, and running water we had all the comforts of home!

My Bunker - Lawn chair from 105 artillery boxes. This is about 6 months before the communists ram us back to the 38th.

I had planted the zinnia seeds outside the bunker and they came up promptly and looked pretty good. One day the IG (Inspector General) came to our battery to check things out. His job was to look for problems, solutions, condition of the men, morale, criminal activities, etc. That last one should have gotten my attention considering my "borrowing" the generator. But he took one look at our bunker and said to our commanding officer, "What the hell kind of bunker is that?"

Before the CO could answer, the IG walked over to where I was standing. I snapped off a salute and invited him to enter. I had just finished building an easy chair of scrap lumber, woven parachute lines for the seat, which was padded with a GI blanket. It was a FINE chair, very comfortable. The General looked around, spotted it, and asked, "Mind if I sit?" I said, "Of course, Sir, please do."

He noted my Southern accent and asked the location of my hometown. When I told him Atlanta, Ga., turns out he was from there also. In fact, we discovered that out homes were only 5 blocks apart and that we shared many of the same friends. We had a nice visit and then he was on his way.

About two months later, I got a call from my CO to get back to my bunker pronto. The IG was back and wanted to see me. When I got there, our colonel, a couple of captains, and two or three lieutenants were standing around in front. I saluted all and my CO told me to go in. There sat the IG in my easy chair - again.

He was just passing through and stopped by to chat. He said, "You have the nicest bunker north of the 38th parallel." We continued to talk about home and our mutual friends, etc., and then he was gone. As soon as he left, all of our officers wanted to know what he wanted with me. I told them that our conversation was Top Secret and related to my primary job as CBR specialist. I said no more, we all went back about our business, and I'm sure my officers were left wondering!

So life on the line was not always horrible - sometimes monotonous, often scary, occasionally humorous, even boring - but compared to what many of our compatriots had to confront on a daily basis, we were indeed fortunate.

- WALTER ADAMS

THE MOSQUITO PILOT
JOE HOLDEN

I spent several days at Camp Stoneman, California, before shipping out for Korea. We went by barge across San Francisco Bay to board the troop ship, General W.A. Mann, of WWII vintage. As a point of interest, this ship in August of 1950 carried Republic of Korea government cargo including a million and a half dollars-worth of gold and silver bullion to San Francisco for safekeeping.

The accommodations aboard ship were very comfortable. As officers, two of us shared a very decent cabin with spacious bunks, toilet, etc. We were on the promenade deck so I had no complaints. Officers were assigned as compartment commanders to oversee conditions in the troop areas below deck. The troop accommodations were not quite as luxurious as ours - canvas cots five deep, very crowded conditions, etc.

We hit a severe storm a few days out. The ship was rolling and pitching - one of the crew told me that the bow was rising and falling by over fifty feet as we ploughed into the huge waves. In fact, the screws (propellers) would come out of the water as the stern was lifted causing the ship to shudder from end to end. We gave out copious amounts of Dramamine during that event.

The food aboard ship was very good; we even had entertainment such as Bingo. Oddly, we had dependents on board, wives and children of men stationed in Japan. I believe this was the first group to be allowed to join their husbands since the outbreak of the Korean War.

Some of the wives got pretty wild and disgusting particularly since they were given a lot of attention by the young, single officers. One lady in particular, an Army Captains' wife, was so obnoxious that the Captain of the ship would not allow her to disembark when we docked. He brought her husband aboard, explained that this lady was not a good representative of our country, and would bring only discredit to our military serving in Japan. I think she was sent back to the states.

The trip across the Pacific took about three weeks. I checked in at an Air Force base outside of Tokyo. There was still much devastation from WWII. We were billeted in what had been Japanese barracks. I'm not tall but I remember often smacking my head on the low doorways. Soon I was on a train headed for one of our air bases at the southern tip of Japan. There, I boarded a C-47 (transport plane) piloted by a Greek crew. We had to land two or three times before reaching our destination at K-6, our airfield 30 miles south of Seoul. I thought the Greek pilots were OK but somehow they managed to make each landing an adventure. I've been in crash landings that were mild compared to what they considered a normal landing.

At K-6, we were greeted with knee-deep snow and total darkness. A jeep eventually showed up and gave me a lift to the transient officers' quarters. I stopped off at the mess hall (which was open 24 hours a day) to get a bowl of soup. They were also serving scrambled eggs that looked pretty hideous and were barely edible. These eggs had been in cold storage forever and were fairly green in color. I took a pass on them.

My initial assignment at the air base was to be the maintenance officer. However, there was a shortage of pilots so I was told I'd be flying combat missions. That suited me since after 100 missions I'd rotate home - which would be quicker that waiting out a year plus tour of duty. I would be flying the LT-6 Texan monoplane, a two-seater; two sets of eyes being better than one. We were known as mosquito pilots - probably because we were a real damned nuisance to our enemy.

I believe there were six corps areas across the Korean front each covering about 20 miles. My squadron was assigned to fly the three eastern sections - each had a name, Palomino, Snowflake and Marlin. The MLR was marked by brightly colored panels at different intervals making it easy for us to determine the front lines from the

184

Episode Thirty-seven - The Mosquito Pilot

air. I was quickly given a couple of orientation flights riding the back seat position with Captain Horowitz, the pilot. His nickname was Captain Horrible. But he was a good pilot and helpful.

Our first flight was very enlightening. We were flying around in the Punchbowl area where major ground action had taken place and it was still hot. As we approached our sector, we saw one of our Navy ground attack planes coming down trailing smoke. A parachute popped open and the pilot hit the ground safely but confused. He had no idea whether he was in enemy territory or friendly. We saw some of our guys on the ground heading for his way so we buzzed him to let him know help was on the way.

Our next flight was a low recon behind enemy lines checking out the locations of their bunkers and trenches. We could see them taking shots at us but fortunately, we took no serious hits and returned safely to base.

My next mission was with another Captain instructor whose name I've forgotten. We were flying near the east coast with nothing much going on. We headed in for a landing at K-18, a Marine Corsair base. They flew ground support missions. Our flight had been dull but the landing was not. I think the runway was near the beach and mostly sand. We came in and next thing I know, we were standing on our nose. Then the plane fell back on to its main landing gear.

We were thrown forward pretty violently, and suffered some beat up and scraped knees. An ambulance took us to the Flight Surgeon who patched us up and said we would both qualify for the Purple Heart if we wanted it. My Dad had lost two fingers in WWII for which he received that award. I just didn't think my slight injuries were on the same par so I refused the honor. If I had it to do over, I'd have said, "Hell, yes, lemme have it!"

We did receive a couple of shots of what was called "Mission Whisky," I guess to settle our nerves. That was the nastiest tasting booze I'd ever put in my mouth but it did help perk us up a bit.

Having flown my checkout flights, my next and future missions would be in the pilot's seat. My back-seater was to be a Lt. Pierre (can't remember his last name), a French Canadian. He was a huge guy and looked every bit the part of a Canadian lumberjack.

He spoke with a heavy French accent. And Pierre always carried a Thompson sub-machine gun along for company. He flew a couple of missions with me that I can only describe as unforgettable. On the first occasion, we were flying low on a normal routine track along the MLR looking for the bad guys.

Suddenly, I felt a rush of air and as best I could, turned and looked over my shoulder. There was Pierre half standing, parachute and safety harness removed, pissing over the side. When we returned to base, I explained to him the proper way to handle such a situation was to use the funnel located at his feet that would then expel his urine into the wind stream - and perhaps on the enemy. He was impressed and promised never to do that again!

A week or so later Pierre and his Thompson were riding shotgun with me again. We were flying low over enemy territory looking for targets for our Corsairs. Suddenly, back goes the rear canopy followed by the bark of Pierre's Thompson. This time he was shooting, not pissing - which I suppose could be considered an improvement. Of course, this annoyed the bad guys so they were returning fire. I got us out of there pronto and vowed Pierre would no longer be my back-seater. No more peeing or shooting from MY airplane. He really was a great guy and rotated home shortly after our last flight. But truly, I can't say that I really regretted seeing him go.

I flew a few missions on the southwest side of Korea below Inchon and Seoul. When General McArthur made the famous end run with an amphibious landing at Inchon, a considerable part of the

Episode Thirty-seven - The Mosquito Pilot

North Korean Army was cut off. Some of them were holed up in a very mountainous area south of Seoul and Inchon. They had shot down a couple of AF planes. They were, therefore, on our list of things to do.

The mountains were very rugged and covered in deep snow. How to fly in this kind of situation without getting killed was a challenge. The terrain created severe updrafts, which could be a real danger. Also, flying up a valley running parallel and close to the mountains was a little dicey. If confronted with a very high peak to your front, you might have to do a quick 180° turn rather than try to rapidly gain altitude. Also, there had to be room to execute that 180. All of this while looking for targets as well as being a target!

But it was easy to spot enemy activity. It was pretty certain that no civilians would be in that rugged terrain so any trails or footprints in the snow had to be the bad guys. My plane was armed with 2.5mm white phosphorous rockets that were fairly accurate. They were great for marking targets for our ground attack planes. Exploding on impact, they burned fiercely giving off great amounts of white smoke.

On this particular flight, a joker silhouetted on a ridgeline was taking pot shots at me. He was highly visible against the snow and made a good target. Just to be ornery, I fired one of my rockets at him striking a rock practically next to that poor soul. I really had not expected to come close. And it was not a pretty sight - one I would not care to see again. He was pretty much engulfed in flame.

By now, I had flown 20 or more missions so I was reassigned to a TAC (Tactical Air Control Party). My job was Forward Air Controller on the ground with the ability to call in air strikes as needed. I had a jeep with a trailer and a driver, and a second jeep full of radio equipment with a driver, a radio operator, and a radio mechanic.

187

I was assigned to the 57th Field Artillery Battalion, 31st Infantry Regiment, 7th Infantry Division. The 57th was in reserve at the time so I had time on my hands. The Army guys treated me like royalty. I shared a large tent with about ten other officers. The battalion commander's tent was very close by.

One afternoon, there was a loud explosion only a few yards away. I landed on the floor of the tent flat on my face with one of my fellow officers on top of me. We rushed outside - an incoming Chinese mortar or artillery round had exploded directly on top of the ridgepole of the CO's tent wounding him severely. His Executive Officer was in the tent also but suffered only a shredded air mattress. The Battalion Commander was air evacuated to a MASH unit.

Not long after that episode, I was visiting one of the Artillery Forward Observer bunkers in our area. Those bunkers faced the enemy positions and were extremely well built and protected. As I approached there was a loud pop, a small explosion, and I found myself flat on my face again. I had hit a trip wire that created the loud but harmless explosion, an early warning system to the occupants of the bunker. I was beginning to think I was safer in the air.

It didn't take long for me to find out why the Army guys were so good to me - the tent mate even throwing his body on me during the aforementioned incoming artillery round.

It was difficult if not impossible for them to make trips to Seoul. But I had a jeep, a trailer, a driver, and time on my hands. So their request was that on my next trip, they wanted me to load up with booze. I told them no problem and took their orders for bourbon, scotch, and beer, or whatever.

On the way to Seoul, we were stopped by a pair of MP's. I was not wearing my helmet!

I explained that I was Air Force and didn't own one. "No excuse, Lt. Sir." They gave me a DR (Deficiency Report) and warned

Episode Thirty-seven - The Mosquito Pilot

me that one more would get me sent to the front! I couldn't help but wonder where I'd been?

Needless to say, when I returned to the battalion I was greeted as a hero. Drinks all around. The only problem was the beer - Budweiser. It had frozen at one time or another, and when a bottle was popped open, it more or less exploded, thereby losing half the contents. But no one complained. Plenty more where that came from.

After some two months with the 57th FA Bn., I was reassigned to my former job flying combat missions. I was stationed at K-6, an airfield several miles south of Seoul. All of our missions were to the north as the southern half of the peninsula no longer held any enemy units.

I flew missions for the Navy AD Skyraiders and Marine Corsairs. Both saw a great deal of action in WWII. In Korea they were used for close ground support and were extremely effective. The Corsairs carried four 20mm cannons, rockets, and frag bombs. The Douglas Skyraider was unsurpassed as a ground attack plane. It could carry 8000 pounds of bombs and armed with rockets and 20mm cannon, it was a formidable aircraft. When either of these planes made a strafing and/or bombing run, someone on the ground suffered. We were in a "hot" area, and my job was to locate and mark potential targets for the ground attack planes.

On this particular mission, I had put my smoke rockets on the target and the Corsair guys made their runs. But I had been hit. The fighter jocks wanted to make a second run. I told them to go ahead and I'd follow right behind them to see if there was anything left to hit. I was confident my aircraft would get me home. But as we dove, my plane started shuddering violently from end to end and I was scared out of my wits. I knew I was going down. But as I checked my instruments things seemed to be OK.

We made it back to the base and I told the ground crew I had taken some serious damage. They could find nothing, no holes, no rips or tears, so I was beginning to feel a little foolish. The T-6, however, has a reinforced area on the bottom of the fuselage called a jack point. There is a nipple on the fuselage in which the jack is inserted. The plane can then be lifted up for maintenance, etc. One of the crewmen found that the nipple had been cleanly shot off - thus causing the severe shaking I felt. Since the hit was in the reinforced area, that made the shuddering more pronounced. That made me feel much better as I'm sure the ground crew thought I might be losing it!

Later, we flew a long mission over on the west coast of Korea. Had to stop at a Navy base for refueling as we were going to be on station for over two hours. Pat (I've forgotten his last name) was my back-seater. He was from Boston and intended to return home and become a politician. Probably not much safer than his current job.

At any rate, we were flying an area between the mountains and the ocean where enemy activity had been spotted. Sure enough, we spotted a large convoy of vehicles partially concealed aside the road. We made a low pass and saw a couple of Russian built T-34 tanks as well as other vehicles. There was a C-47 control ship on hand so we gave them the coordinates.

Very quickly, a flight of F-84's arrived. I dropped down and marked the target for them. They informed me that I was being fired upon – I wasn't aware of that and didn't believe that I had taken any hits. They made their runs and did a helluva job. The convoy was destroyed and this was later confirmed by after action review. Whatever damage I had received was minimal as we made it back to our base with no problem.

We were debriefed at K-6 by the squadron CO. The date happened to be May 1, big communist day of celebration. Some PR guy got hold of the story and it made some stateside newspapers or so I was told. I was quoted as saying, "It might have been May Day for the Reds, but it was the 4th of July for us." Gimme a break - I'd never have said anything that corny. By the way, we received the

Episode Thirty-seven - The Mosquito Pilot

Distinguished Flying Cross for that action. That's an award that every pilot covets and I was most proud to receive it.

Sometime after this action, I was back flying on the east coast. The Navy had several ships off shore including destroyers. They carried 5-inch guns and were quite accurate with them. I had become fairly proficient at directing artillery fire and calling in the 5-inchers was no different. We fired some good missions. One of which was an enemy truck park. One of our pilots had spotted truck tracks going into an area and disappearing. He made a couple of low passes and discovered what appeared to be a vehicle park disguised as a village, thatched roofs and all. But he never saw any activity. He was about to rotate home but he gave me the coordinates so I could monitor the area.

I had no trouble locating the place and I flew over it frequently but never saw any evidence of vehicles. It was in the eastern corps area and about half way between the mountains and the ocean and a few miles north of the MLR. The buildings appeared to be hollow, just roofs, and no sides. I flew the area several times with no results and no positive sightings. But I kept checking. Time passed, the snow melted and winter turned to spring. But I knew it was a potential target.

Finally, on one of my many recon flights over the area I went in low and saw vehicles everywhere. I made a couple more runs to be certain and then called my control ship, Peter Shirley, a C-47, giving them the coordinates and asking for an immediate air strike. Unfortunately they responded with, "No assets in the area." A moment or so later an unidentified voice came in on my radio: "Hey, Li'l Buddy, maybe we can help?" At first, I had no idea who he was but he was certainly laid back and casual about the whole thing.

I described the target and asked if they would be interested. "Yup, give us the coordinates." I looked out toward the ocean and saw a boat, a really big boat - in fact, one of our battleships. It was the USS Iowa. That was my "Big Buddy!" They fired a round that

191

was a little long and I gave them the necessary corrections. Next came a salvo from one of their sixteen-inch 3-gun turrets.

A 16-inch projectile weighs anywhere from 1,900 to 2,500 pounds of high explosives depending on the target. A moment later when those three rounds hit, the area just disappeared. I am not exaggerating when I use the word obliterated. I radioed the Iowa with a "well done" and a "thank you kindly."

On the way back to my base, I noticed a puff of smoke coming from my cowling. I seemed to be OK. One of my buddies flew alongside and he didn't see anything alarming. The Iowa heard our radio conversation and informed me that they had rescue assets aboard if I needed to ditch at sea. I thanked them profusely and kept on going. I felt I had enough altitude to make it back to base and make a crash landing if necessary. Or I could always jump. But I just wanted to get "home."

Finally, I made it to K-18 and set her down. As I taxied in, I noticed one of the ground crew appeared to be quite animated. When I popped the canopy he said, "Where have you BEEN." I climbed out to see 30 or more holes in my plane. The engine had taken several hits. One cylinder was punctured and the oil was gone. I guess I was so full of adrenaline during the engagement that I didn't know I was getting hit - and often. How my sturdy bird kept in the air under those circumstances I'll never know. Grateful would be an understatement.

I later moved to another base, K-47, which was further north. I had been spoiled at K-18 as there we lived in Quonset huts, and we were a safe distance behind the lines. Here, we were close to the MLR and living in tents. The runway was made of some kind of composition stuff that tended to be slick in wet weather. And our traffic pattern took us very close to a large peak that came to be known as "BustYourAss Mountain." Nothing much was going on except that I was very close to flying my last mission. On mission #96 I found myself flying a bit higher; on #97 I was up there; on 98,

99 and 100 I probably needed oxygen. To say I was being very cautious would be an accurate statement.

Finally, I was on my way home. Fortunately, I was on a C-54, one of the big four engine military transports. Beats a slow boat for sure. We stopped at Wake Island, which is a very small dot in the ocean with a very small landing strip. Next to the runway and half submerged was an old rusty Japanese landing craft from WWII. The red meatball insignia was still visible. Its war was over, as was that of our men who died there in the early stages of the war in Pacific.

We made it home in about three days. People were not too interested in the Korean War.

I suppose that hurt a bit from my standpoint but I was just thankful and glad to be home. The 6147th Tactical Air Control Group flew something like 40,350 sorties during the Korean War. As a result, I believe we were responsible for an inestimable amount of damage wrought on our enemy. I am proud to have served.

- JOE HOLDEN

TWO HUNDRED CHINESE
JIM CAMPBELL

I was a brand new 2nd Lt. rifle platoon leader and had been on the MLR but a few days. Late one night a call came in from my LP to inform me that a couple of hundred Chinese troops were milling about in the valley two hundred yards or so in front of our position. Our company occupied a very high piece of terrain with steep approaches so I didn't feel that we were about to be attacked.

However, I immediately informed my company commander by radio of the situation and he instructed me to take my platoon sergeant (who was to rotate home the following week) with me and take a closer look. Sgt. Gonzales and his replacement, Sgt. Etheridge, were in the platoon CP at the time. (Our command bunker was a very small, stuffy hole carved into the reverse slope of our ridge.)

The temperature seemed to drop from 90 degrees to about 60 in those few seconds. I commented to the two of them how cold it had suddenly become. They broke into laughter and said, "Lt., didn't you ever hear the expression cold fear?" Naturally, that cracked me up and the three of us stood there laughing like idiots.

Then Sgt. Etheridge requested that he go in place of Sgt. Gonzales in that Gonzales was about to head back home to Puerto Rico. I readily agreed – we grabbed our weapons and took off down our mountain headed for the valley below. The descent was steep to the point that we were more or less running which was not very smart. Had the Chinese been coming up from the valley, we'd have met them head on and would have found ourselves in deep trouble. Two hundred versus two were not good odds.

We reached a point where we had a clear view of the valley and, fortunately for us, the Chinese had moved on. It was not until sometime later that it occurred to me that they were heading for OP Harry (which was close by) to participate in that battle. I doubt that many people know of that fight.

OP Harry was a pretty sizeable hill that was situated in a rather strategic spot in the Chorwon valley, a few hundred yards in front of our MLR. The Chorwon was a natural invasion route into South Korea and its capitol, Seoul. The OP was defended by a reinforced rifle company - slightly over 200 men and was attacked nightly by anywhere from three or four hundred to three thousand plus Chinese troops. I believe the onslaught lasted for 7 or 8 consecutive nights and the casualties of those defending were so high that a fresh company was sent in on a daily basis to take over the battle. Every man who defended that hill was a true hero.

From our position, we could only watch - too far even to give supporting fire. The attacks began at night. The hill was shrouded in dust and smoke in short order. Artillery flares lit the sky and tracers were streaking in toward the attackers making crisscross patterns of every angle. Our artillery was zeroed in, and was firing continuous defensive barrages into the Chinese troops. I read later that the artillery units expended something like 300,000 rounds of ammunition in defense of the outpost. Our men were often engaged in hand-to-hand combat - it was a truly vicious fight.

The Chinese were taking tremendous casualties and finally quit the battle. Had they persisted, I'm certain that our company would have had its turn in defending the OP. I feel I owe a debt of gratitude to our men (and those of our allies) that fought there. I often wonder if our turn had come, would I have performed as well. And I often think of Sgt. Etheridge and Sgt. Gonzales. He returned home to Puerto Rico safely and Sgt. Etheridge was my right arm for the duration of the conflict. I never thought to tell him that I admired his selfless act of putting himself in harms' way so that a friend could return to his family. Perhaps a small thing in the minds of some - but not in mine.

- JIM CAMPBELL

BROTHERS
Perry Rubart

We were on a troop ship out of Sasebo, Japan, on our way to Inchon, Korea, through very choppy seas. We arrived without incident, and due to the great rise and fall of the tide in that area, our ship anchored a few miles short of the harbor.

We debarked by going over the side and down web nets into waiting landing craft. At the same time, men who were heading home were climbing up nets on the opposite side of the ship so there was quite a shuttle ship to shore and vice versa.

When our landing craft hit the beach, we were walking on slatted wood matting similar to snow fencing to keep us from miring in the mud. The tide was out and the mud was like glue. The guys who were heading home were coming at us in the opposite direction with about ten feet of mud separating our two lines.

They were a happy bunch, shouting and laughing, and giving us the business with jabs like, "Joe Chink is gonna get ya," and "Watch out for Bed Check Charlie," etc. I guess we didn't find much humor in their comments - they were going home, we were going into the unknown.

Suddenly, both lines stopped. All the laughing and joking stopped. Two men, one from each line, slogged into the mud toward each other. They hugged and burst into tears - two brothers thousands of miles from home meeting on that forsaken beach. Dead silence all around and then the Sergeants started shouting for the lines to move once again.

I've often wondered over the years of the meeting of those two, one coming, one going. Obviously, one survived. Did the other? In later years, were they able to sit around the kitchen table with their loved ones and talk about the day their paths crossed in that far-off, war torn land of Korea?

Sixty years have passed since I witnessed the love of two brothers standing ankle deep in the mud of a country we were there to defend and to give the people of South Korea their freedom. I served with the 39th Field Artillery Battalion of the Third Infantry Division and perhaps in some small way, I helped in that endeavor.

- PERRY RUBART

AMBUSH PATROL
Bill Mitchell

My orders for that particular night were to take an ambush patrol and set up on the Chinese side of the valley. I took one squad from my platoon and beefed it up with two extra BAR guys and swapped out M-1 rifles for M-2 carbines to upgrade a couple of my riflemen. Fifteen of us, and we were loaded for bear - extra ammo, grenades, etc.

One of my BAR men (it took me awhile to understand what he was up to) had apparently appointed himself as my bodyguard. Every time I took a patrol out, he insisted on going with me. He was 18 and I was 24. I guess he figured an old guy like me needed all the help I could get. He was probably right. I wish now that I had thought to tell him how much I appreciated his concern. The kids in my platoon were great guys and I knew I could depend of them.

We were to cross the LD at 2100 hours. It seems strange that our nerves would be strung out tighter than a violin string during the preparation and then the waiting - but once we crossed the LD we settled down and felt little or no fear - just get the job done.

Immediately prior to our departure, the company executive informed me that the Battalion S-2 had called to tell him that the Chinese patrols were using small penlights for nighttime signaling devices. I appreciated the warning but it seemed strange that they would risk giving away their location by using such a light during hours of darkness.

At any rate, we headed out and set up at the base of the Chinese held mountain. It took us about an hour to arrive at our destination. It was almost directly in front of our company position back on the MLR. I put us in an L shape ambush formation - I anticipated that if an enemy patrol were out they would be coming up the valley from our right heading for home.

199

We settled in and waited. Suddenly, a burst of quad .50 fire came in over our heads from behind us smacking the ground 50 yards up the Chinese slope. Tracers lit the sky for a few seconds then all was quiet. I immediately radioed my company commander and asked him, "What in the HELL is going on?" Not very respectful toward my CO but his response - "No problem Lt., the quad .50 guys just wanted you to know they have you covered in case you need their help." I told the Captain to thank them kindly!

Quietness descended and again we waited. About two hours later, a small blinking light appeared to my right just where I had expected a Chinese patrol to approach. It flashed off and on a few times and appeared to be quite close. I fired off a quick three round burst and a couple of my guys on the long side of the L fired a few quick shots immediately afterwards.

All was quiet, no return fire, and then a groan. One of my men had been hit by our fire! Fortunately he was wounded in the leg - not life threatening - but he had to be evacuated. Two of the patrol members volunteered to take him back to the company. The rest of us stayed in position until dawn with no further activity occurring.

Needless to say, I felt pretty horrible about that incident. I have no idea what the light was, but other members of the patrol saw it as well. Nor was I able to determine how the man who was hit happened to be in what I anticipated as the kill zone. He was already headed for the rear when we got in the next morning so I never had an opportunity to talk with him. I only hope that his wounds were not serious. And I have puzzled over that incident ever since.

A few nights later, a South Korean patrol ran into another of our ambush patrols and the results were tragic. Several of their men were killed in the encounter. There must have been some bad communication somewhere as they were way out of their assigned area. Such are the vagaries of war but too often with horrendous results.

- BILL MITCHELL

RAID ON HILL 412
Jack Greene

Hill 412 (elevation 412 feet) was a pretty small knob almost directly in front of my platoon position. It was just slightly on the Chinese side of the valley and completely barren of trees or foliage. We never saw movement on it but the Chinese had an outpost there that probably consisted of squad or so. I'm not a tactician, but I couldn't see value in that piece of ground for neither the Chinese nor us. Our portion of the MLR was on a very high mountain and ridgeline. We looked down on Hill 412 from about 1400 feet - naturally, we called our position the Eagle's Nest. But the Chinese mountains that we faced (in back of Hill 412) were even higher. Hill 412 seemed untenable from either standpoint.

But for some unknown reason (at least to us), higher authority decided to execute a small raid on 412. It took place in broad daylight by what appeared to be less than a platoon from one of our adjacent companies. The men advanced up the hill with no opposition and as far as I could tell, met no enemy fire even at the top. There might have been some small arms fire exchanged but very little. Our guys came back down and headed home.

The next day a similar daylight attack took place by what might have been a company-sized force. Again, they encountered what appeared to be light resistance but did take some incoming Chinese artillery fire. They had no cover and apparently started taking casualties and withdrew.

The next raid was again staged in daylight and when our attacking force (I think it might have been another company size) reached the top of the hill, they were hit with a TOT. A TOT is an artillery term meaning that assorted artillery pieces of different caliber and different distances from the target are fired so that the entire ordinance hits the target at the same moment. It is an awesome display and the consequence to those on the receiving end is brutal.

Our men were in the open, suffered a lot of casualties, and were forced to retreat.

I believe there were one or two more raids directed at 412, perhaps at night. One might have been supported by a tank or two. For some reason or another, I was not aware of those - didn't see or hear them. But they apparently met with the same fate as the others - casualties and withdrawal. Those night raids, we learned later, were diversionary attacks to draw some of the Chinese attackers away from OP Harry. I doubt that the Chinese fell for that little ruse. Hill 412 was a fairly good distance from OP Harry and as said before, the Chinese knew that it was an untenable position for them or us.

Shortly after these failed attempts, our company executive officer called each platoon leader to tell us that we were scheduled for the next raid - probably in a couple of days. He also informed us that our entire company would participate and that casualties were expected to be heavy. His final statement was for us to tell our men that if they had anything of value that they wanted their next of kin to receive, to turn them in to the company clerk with instructions, as he would be the only man to stay behind. I recall that our exec officer always carried a Nazi dagger on his belt that his father had removed from the body of a German officer during WWII. He wanted to make certain that the trophy dagger was returned to his dad. On that solemn note, we tried to get some rest.

The following morning, all platoon leaders were told to report to the company commander's CP at 1200 hours (noon). When the four of us entered the bunker, we were most surprised to find the Commanding General of the Division awaiting us along with our Company Commander, the Company Executive Officer and the General's aide. I was pretty amazed-- the Commanding General of the division sitting there with 5 lieutenants and our company commander ready perhaps to give us a pep talk.

I don't recall the entire conversation but the gist of the general's comments seemed to be apologetic for sending us on another raid of

Episode Forty-one - Raid on Hill 412

Hill 412. The others had proved disastrous, gained no ground, and proved that the position was of no real value regardless of who owned it. So I'm sure all my fellow company officers were thinking the same as I - why are we going to do this? And General, Sir, YOU can cancel the attack. Needless to say, none of us voiced an opinion or questioned the orders. We were dismissed and went back to our respective platoons to give our men preparatory orders. Not a happy occasion.

That evening, we were again called to the Company Commander's bunker. We were expecting to get the final orders for the attack, time of departure, etc. Instead, our CO informed us that the raid on Hill 412 had been called off, and to his knowledge, no more attempts would be made to attack or hold it. When we four platoon leaders expressed a sigh of relief in unison, I think we probably expelled all the oxygen from the Captain's bunker. We returned to our men to give them the new orders and to tell them they could tear up their final letters home.

- JACK GREENE

ROCKET ATTACK
Roger Ward

This is one of those little situations that arise in a combat zone. Not funny, not serious, just another day at the office. Lt. Wallace and I were good friends. He was a platoon leader from the Division tank battalion. As we were in a defensive situation, one of his tanks was dug in with us on the MLR. We also had a quad .50 mounted on a half-track. Both powerful weapons and we appreciated his company along with his toys.

One afternoon, the two of us had to go back to battalion headquarters on some kind of errand so off we went in his jeep. Pretty neat, him having a jeep. Anyway, on the return trip the Chinese started lobbing a few rounds in our direction. They were missing the road and hitting in an open field off to our right. But close enough that we vacated the jeep and hit a ditch for cover. I realized they were firing their heavy-duty rockets. We were familiar with artillery fire but having never seen their rockets at work, I kind of crawled up a bit from the ditch to get a better view. I never much believed in the curiosity and the cat thing and the explosions were 2 or 3 hundred yards off. No problem.

Lt. Wallace, my buddy, thought otherwise. I'm 5'6" and weighed about 120 lbs. He was 6'2" and weighed about 180. And he proceeded to throw himself on top of me. My first reaction was, "Hey, you're blocking my view!" Not to mention the fact that he about crushed me. The rocket fire stopped and it was all over quickly so we proceeded on our way back to the company with no further untoward incidents.

I don't believe I even thanked him for what he did. The next rocket might have been close enough to do serious damage but yet he protected me. The rest of the trip, as I remember, was just our normal conversation - neither of us gave the little diversion another thought. Our position on the line received Chinese artillery fire every night, all night, so I guess we just didn't consider it as a big deal. But, Bob, if you're still with us; let me take this opportunity to thank you. I wish we could meet so I could do so personally.

- ROGER WARD

SILVER STAR TARNISHED
Anonymous

NOTE: The contributor of this article chose to remain anonymous for obvious reasons.

He is a good friend, and like me, was a rifle platoon leader in our battalion. We were in close proximity when on the MLR but never saw one another during that period. Not much time for social visits under those circumstances.

After the war ended, we were in the same training area and saw each other fairly often. We were chatting one evening and he came forth with this story.

Toward the end of the conflict there was a Chinese artillery piece throwing random fire into our battalion headquarters area much to the annoyance of our battalion commander. The location of that artillery weapon was in an area fairly accessible to a ground attack as opposed to being atop or in a tunnel of one of the Chinese held mountains.

The Battalion Commander ordered my friends' company commander to send out a night raiding party and destroy the offending weapon. That seemed a little odd as the Chinese would simply replace it after the raid was over - but orders are orders. His company commander ordered Bill (I'll call him) to make the raid.

He took two reinforced squads, one as the assault group and the other as back up and to cover the withdrawal. They caught the Chinese off guard - the weapon and crew was destroyed. The raiding party returned safely though it was a truly dangerous assignment.

A day or so later, Bill was called to his company commanders CP and was instructed to write him, the company commander, up for the Silver Star for his gallant action in the raid! Of course, the Captain had not participated except to give the order. He never left his bunker that night. Bill wrote the recommendation, submitted it to

Battalion and the company commander was awarded the Silver Star, the Army's third highest award for bravery.

Bill was a decent person so I asked him why he wrote the recommendation and submitted it. His answer was simple - his commanding officer threatened him; told Bill his career in the Army was over if he didn't do as told. Bill, like me, was Regular Army (not a reservist) and hoped to make the military his career.

The services give out many awards, medals, commendations, etc. for numerous of reasons. Some are called "attaboys" and don't mean an awful lot. But the Medal of Honor, the Distinguished Service Cross, the Silver Star, and the Bronze Star (with a V for valor) are given only to those who performed exceptional acts of bravery. And I would guess that 99.5 percent of those awarded were legitimate and earned. The Captain's was not, and brought disgrace only to himself.

- ANONYMOUS

KUMHWA VALLEY PATROL
Bill Jorgenson

We had moved to another area on the MLR. I think we were facing the Kumhwa Valley, a very large flat expanse to our front, which at one time appeared to have been a fertile rice growing area. A Belgian company had held the position before our arrival and I remember being much amused by the large quantity of empty beer cans on the forward slope. In their defense, I don't think anyone could have approached the position without making quite a racket. The odor of stale beer would probably have had some kind of adverse effect on an attacking Chinese unit as well!

A couple of days after relieving the Belgians, my company commander called and told me to double time to his CP for orders. When I arrived, he informed me that I was to take a patrol across the valley that night and would I mind if a Korean line crosser, a scout dog and his handler accompanied me. Would I mind? Did I have a choice? But that's the kind of guy he was and I admired him greatly.

Of course, I replied that I would be delighted for the company but what was it all about? It seems that the South Korean line crosser was in enemy territory gathering information when he was spotted by a Chinese patrol. To escape capture he had to ditch his ANPRC 10 radio and conceal it as best he could. It was a fairly heavy piece of equipment. I don't know why the radio was so important but our task was to take him to the area and hope that he or the dog would find it.

We set out at dark that night and headed across the valley, which seemed to me to be a jaunt of four or five miles. To make time, we stayed on what had been the dikes of the rice paddies. About a mile out, we passed within a couple of hundred yards of a Chinese outpost. We were close enough that I could smell (pretty horrible odor) whatever it was they were cooking. I guess they heard us as they tossed a few flares in our direction. We dove into what had been verdant and green fields of rice. Fortunately, they were now dormant. The farmers fertilized the paddies with human excrement so we were spared that unpleasantness. We lay low until things calmed down and then proceeded, thankful that the Chinese had not interrupted our progress.

We finally reached our destination - just south of some river the line crosser had forded and where he had hastily concealed his radio. The dog searched, we all searched, the line crosser searched - to no avail. I was afraid that we would be caught in the middle of the valley during daylight if we didn't leave very soon. That would have been suicide alley for us as there was no cover. The man was quite distressed that we couldn't find the radio but he understood our predicament. We had to cross that flat terrain quickly so we headed for home empty handed. We arrived safely and the line crosser, the dog, and his handler headed back to their respective units. I wished them well and of course never saw them again.

But I've always wondered about the significance of that radio. I'm sure the Chinese had access to any number of our frequencies and probably could tune in on us at random. It obviously must have been important to risk the lives of 14 men and one beautiful German shepherd war dog. I regretted that we had failed in our mission but was pleased and relieved that we returned with no casualties.

- BILL JORGENSON

SNOOPER SCOPE
Roger Beatty

The snooper scope was my baby - at least for a short period of time. I think it was developed toward the end of WWII and probably saw limited use during that period. It was a night vision, infrared device mounted on an M-2 carbine.

This piece of equipment weighed about 30 pounds with the scope and battery pack. It was very cumbersome. There weren't many around as far as I know but our company got one and for whatever reason it was given to our platoon. And of course, I was assigned to carry the damned thing. I messed around with it for several nights preparing for a patrol that was sure to be coming. I wanted to get accustomed to this new-fangled equipment - it was high tech for those days. I wasn't impressed - everything looked a hazy green and it seemed to me to be difficult to pinpoint any particular object. When all else fails, read the owners' manual - which apparently got lost in the mail!

Not long after, sure enough our platoon caught a night patrol mission that was given to our squad. Normally our platoon leader would have led the patrol but he could hardly walk from a severe ankle sprain. Our platoon sergeant got the duty. By the way, I'd heard stories of patrols being led by a Lt. or a platoon sergeant and once out of sight, he'd drop out, hunker down, and tell the squad leader to go ahead with the mission. When the patrol came in, if it came in, the legitimate leader would then rejoin, and come home safe and sound never having put himself in danger. No one dared rat him out. I don't know how true those stories are - but the Army thrives on rumors.

Our guys weren't like that. My platoon leader and platoon sergeant would volunteer to lead a patrol and we grunts would want to be chosen to go. How crazy was that? So our turn came and you guessed it - obviously, my job was to carry that 30 plus pound night

211

scope - more like 37 pounds attached to the carbine. I think it was kind of a test run to see how it worked.

There were twelve of us and we crossed LD well after darkness had set in. It was very dark - ink black and overly warm, muggy and humid. We were covered in sweat as much from nerves as from the heat. This, in my limited knowledge, was the most dangerous type of patrol activity - a combat patrol. An ambush patrol was spooky enough and dangerous, a recon patrol could be pretty darned hazardous. But a combat patrol meant going into no-man's land or enemy territory, find them, and engage their unit in a firefight. In other words, we were looking for a battle.

We moved down our mountain trying as best we could to be quiet. As we approached the lower levels and then the small valley floor, silence was next to impossible because of thick undergrowth. Artillery hadn't stripped these areas as it had on the upper slopes. So we stumbled, slipped, fell, and silently cursed. I'm sure we sounded like stampeding horses. But we kept moving, heading into Chink held real estate.

We'd frequently stop so I could attempt to see what or who, if anyone was in the neighborhood. Our platoon sergeant was right next to me and he'd occasionally take a peep through the scope. He also thought the thing was fairly useless. But a few minutes later at another stop and scan pause; I did detect a movement quite a few yards to our front. It appeared to be the upper part of a human almost motionless so I wasn't certain. A lot of fuzziness and that darned green background. Sarge took a look and he wasn't sure either - but told me to go ahead and put a couple of short bursts on the target.

I did so which sure as Hell broke the silence of what had been a very quiet night. We were all hunkered down expecting immediate return fire. None came. We split into two fire teams and hopscotched toward whatever was in front of us. Still no return fire. All quiet. All of us nervous and fingers on the triggers. A moment later, we were there - to find the body of a very young, very dead Chinese soldier slumped forward from his well-camouflaged foxhole. Our scope had done its job.

He was in a well- concealed position dug somewhat into the base of a small hill. A couple bags of rice, water, and a sniper rifle of Russian WWII vintage made his mission pretty obvious. He must have made his platoon sergeant madder than Hell to have gotten that kind of assignment. During daylight hours and shooting only at targets five hundred yards distant or more, he'd probably have survived for a while. In fact, he might already have killed several of our fellow GI's before we nailed him.

As his weapon was a Russian model, it reminds me that I once read the true story of a WWII Russian sniper who knocked off a lot of Nazis, mostly officers, before himself being discovered. He had cleaned out the insides of a dead cow located several hundred yards from a road carrying a lot of German traffic to and from the Russian front. He would fire only on a German staff car thus insuring himself of an important target. Pretty clever but the Germans finally caught on and killed him.

I did feel some remorse and guilt about sending the young Chinese kid to his ancestors only because he was so young - 16 or 17 at the most. But we were youngsters as well and his job was to kill us. My remorse didn't last long. War is not a nice game.

As to the snooper scope, we sent it back to battalion. We were not impressed. Since it didn't come with a Sears, Roebuck guarantee of satisfaction we didn't want it. Nor did it come with an instruction manual - perhaps that would have helped. I suppose that in today's money it was a $50,000 piece of equipment. I have to think that it paid for itself that night, as it no doubt saved the lives of some of my buddies down the road.

- ROGER BEATTY

THE 38TH FIELD ARTILLERY BATTALION
Bob Mehler

I grew up in Newark, New Jersey. I attended High School there and after graduation joined my father in the family trade. He had started out working on horse and buggy bridles, wagon covers, and all sorts of things requiring canvas. It was a small but successful business and I was learning the craft.

WWII was winding down and I attempted to join when I came of age. However, my three brothers were already in the service so I was turned down. The war ended and our business and my training continued. As nuclear power plants came on line, we were providing asbestos coverings and other such products for those facilities. Then the Korean War broke out and I was drafted! Now I found myself in the Army.

I went to Fort Dix, NJ for 16 weeks of basic Infantry training which covered all that a neophyte infantryman needs to know. However, we didn't get much instruction in the heavier weapons like the .30 and .50 caliber machine guns. I mention this as it later came into play.

We shipped out from Fort Lewis, Washington, and I found myself in Korea with the 38th FA Battalion, 2nd Infantry Division. This was during the latter part of the war and a fairly major battle was taking place in an area known as Old Baldy - a sizeable mountain owned by the Chinese. My CO asked me if I knew how to drive a truck. Having never driven anything but a car I had to reply "no."

But he proceeded to teach me - he showed me how to clutch and double clutch and then pronounced me a trained deuce and a half driver. My assignment for the next two weeks was hauling 105mm howitzer ammunition to our gun emplacements that were busy shelling the Chinese positions.

I received a couple of promotions, Pfc. to corporal, etc., and soon I became a sergeant and a squad leader of a machine gun section. I don't quite know how that came about - from truck driver to machine gunner but that's the Army for you. My problem was that I had exactly one hour of instruction on the .30 and .50 caliber machine guns during basic training.

My new job was to set up a perimeter defense around our area. We emplaced the weapons on the high ground with good fields of fire and I ran communication lines to each position. I also had radio contact with each of my gunners. As luck would have it, we never had to fire a shot in our defense. The Chinese were engaged elsewhere, but our 105 howitzers stayed busy.

Occasionally, we'd get a little grief from one of the Infantry units because of one of our artillery rounds bursting over their positions. These were called "short rounds" meaning that for some failure of the fusing or other defect, the round didn't make it to its intended target but instead exploded over the head of one of our infantrymen in a trench somewhere on the MLR. Thankfully, those type misfires exploded high enough that usually no damage was done to our guys. But, unfortunately, in combat our own men are sometimes tragically killed by "friendly fire."

Even with those kinds of accidents occurring, any foot soldier will tell you that our artillery is the infantryman's best friend. In a defensive situation, artillery barrages and concentrations are pre-plotted to hit the most likely avenues of an enemy approach. And when the enemy attack comes, it is not only met by the men in the frontline trenches and foxholes but also by a wall of flying steel laid down by "the big guns!"

The war finally ended for which we were all grateful. My unit was fortunate. We did our job but did not suffer some of the really bad experiences that others faced. We returned to the states and my tour was over. I returned home, married my sweetheart, took over my father's business - in short, we've had a good life and I hope in some small way, I helped give the people of South Korea a better life as well.

THE STRAWBERRY GRENADE
John Girard

We had been relieved by another unit and pulled off the MLR for a few days of rest. We left our position about midnight - the swapping out of men and platoons took a while so it was almost dawn when we finally got back to the rear area. Everyone immediately sacked out for an hour of two of sleep. The sun came up way too fast; we were awake and soon small cooking fires were started and C-rations and coffee were heating up. It was a beautiful morning, hard to believe that there was a war going on in the neighborhood.

Suddenly, a sound like a rifle shot rang out. One of our young guys jumped upholding his face and screaming. What appeared to be a large amount of blood, seeped out between his fingers. Someone shouted, "Sniper," and we all found ourselves hugging Mother Earth. We were in an open field with no cover and no place to go.

It took a couple of seconds for it to sink in - the "blood" was strawberry jam from a C-ration tin that had fallen into one of the cooking fires. Must have been there for three or four minutes when the young trooper saw it, bent over to retrieve it only to have it explode right in his face.

There was a lot of relieved laughter followed by one of our platoon comedians suggesting that the injured man be awarded a Purple Strawberry. That seemed somewhat disrespectful of the Purple Heart so his buddies gave the victim a bunch of knuckle punches instead. He took it in good humor. We finished breakfast, such as it was and moved out.

It's quite amazing how fast the human brain and animal instinct can react in such a situation. My brain, in a second, told me that what I heard was not a rifle shot; didn't sound like one. But my instincts acted even faster, and I, like the rest of our little breakfast club, hit the dirt looking for cover. One thing for sure, there was a lot of spilled coffee that morning.

- JOHN GIRARD

LIFE OF AN ARTILLERYMAN
Paul Bonham

I graduated from Purdue June 16th, 1950. The Korean War broke out on June 25th, just nine days later. There was a lot of soul searching on my part about what to do. As I had just graduated and the summer work was starting up on the family farm, my twin brother Richard and I decided to wait and see if Uncle Sam was going to draft us.

His "greetings" came in September of 1950. We went for our physicals and our notice of induction followed shortly thereafter. We left with one of the largest groups ever to go into the Army from Huntington County, Indiana, at one time - 21 young men.

It was cold that January 29th in 1951, when we arrived at Camp Breckenridge, Kentucky, long after dark. There is nothing more depressing than to arrive at a strange Army base late at night - the transition from civilian to military life was stark. There were a few soldiers walking about. All the barracks looked the same and all had red lights above the doors. There was snow on the ground and the temperature was 29° below zero. We knew we had arrived in a frozen Hell.

We had each been issued an army overcoat and our bunks had one blanket. The soldiers who were supposed to fire the furnaces that night didn't show up so hardly anyone could sleep. It was freezing cold. The next morning we were able to get the furnace going but all the water pipes and toilets in the barracks had frozen and burst during the night.

Later that day, we saw soldiers cutting the dead grass with razor blades - where grass was visible through the snow. They had obviously aroused the ire of some tough drill sergeant who had a mean sense of humor. That got our attention as we were soon placed in an Infantry training company with the 502nd Infantry Battalion, 101st Airborne Infantry Division. That was the famous Screaming

219

Eagles Division that participated in the Battle of the Bulge in WWII. We knew we were in for some tough times - though we never saw a parachute.

The basic Infantry training lasted 16 grueling weeks in which we endured cold weather, rainy weather and even hot weather. During that time, we marched many miles, drilled incessantly, spent hours on the rifle ranges and took tests of all sorts. One of those was for OCS, Officers Candidate School, which Richard and I were both fortunate enough to pass.

Those who didn't make it to OCS were shipped out to Germany or Korea. The two of us stayed at Camp Breckenridge for Leadership School. After completion of that, we were both assigned as instructors there for another 12 weeks awaiting our next move to OCS. In November, 1951, we were sent to the Field Artillery Officer's Candidate School at Fort Sill, Oklahoma. We were both assigned to the same unit in OCS. Class #12, "L" Battery.

OCS is an experience that a person will never forget. From the very beginning we were under the gun - nothing was ever done fast enough, well enough, loud enough, or on time. If you spent too much time shaving, you were accused of growing a beard. If you thought your area was spotless, the DI would find a speck of dust somewhere. We double-timed everywhere, but stopped long enough to salute every officer within sight.

With all the harassment, there was a great deal of good associated with OCS. The classes were difficult, the training was harsh, and we had to learn fast. If we didn't, it was very possible that we would get a pink slip and find ourselves on the way to Korea. But we were motivated and wanted those 2nd Lieutenant bars.

Oklahoma was cold that winter. The wind never stopped blowing across the plains and over the Wichita Mountains. We spent many hours being taught everything we needed to know to become expert artillerymen. Days and nights were spent in learning to adjust artillery fire on enemy targets. Every artillery 2nd Lieutenant was a potential FO (forward observer) for an Infantry unit. Most important of all, we learned about the qualities of being a good leader.

After the 22 weeks of intense training was over, we were commissioned 2nd Lieutenants in the United States Army. Our parents drove all the way from Indiana to be there for the commissioning ceremony. It was a proud day for Richard and me, and for Mom and Dad. It was April 22nd, 1952 - a good time for farming - and as we had a two-week furlough, we drove back home with the folks. There we helped to get the spring plowing and field work done. The two weeks went by quickly and we returned to duty.

We were assigned to the 932nd Field Artillery Battalion of the 31st Infantry Division. The 31st was called the "Dixie Division." It had fought in WWII in the South Pacific. Its mission now was to train reservists and National Guard units. We were at Camp Atterbury, Indiana from May until October of 1952, and then sent to Camp McCoy, Wisconsin. While there, we trained a great number of companies and batteries of reservists.

An interesting thing happened during that time. Several of the men with whom we had taken basic training at Camp Breckenridge in the winter and spring of 1951, rotated back from Korea through Camp McCoy while we were there. They had already seen their share of the war and were on the way home.

The summer went fast as we were busy doing things that were new and challenging. The battery to which we were assigned came from Tupelo, Mississippi, hometown of Elvis Presley.

We spent quite a bit of time on the firing ranges which was a real learning experience as we were able to fire and train with many different weapons. Also, we had the opportunity to explore a lot of Wisconsin that summer. While there, I received my orders for Korea, leaving in October. Richard was to leave a month later.

After arriving back at Camp Atterbury we found an army regulation that allowed twins to be stationed in the same post, camp, station, or unit. We wrote Washington, D.C. and then waited to see if the army "Brass" would honor our request to set back Richard's departure date to coincide with mine. Finally, we got the word - we would both ship out for Korea from Fort Lewis, Washington, on November 2nd, 1952.

We left Seattle by air. I was on a Northwest Airlines flight and Richard was on a Canadian Air Force Plane. My plane arrived in Tokyo in about 36 hours. Richard made it about nine days later. His plane had engine problems and their navigator got ill so they sat in Alaska. I stayed at Camp Drake near Tokyo until Richard got there. During that nine-day period, I had the privilege of touring several Japanese factories where the army was reconditioning WWII vehicles brought in from the South Pacific. The Japanese workers would put them back in prime condition and the tanks, trucks, etc., were then sent back to duty in Korea.

We attended a two-week school in Gifu, Japan, at the site of a former Japanese air base. The training was in Chemical, Biological, and Radiological training. Very interesting. On the weekend of December 7th, anniversary of the Day of Infamy, we went to Nagoya, Japan, by train and visited that city. The people were friendly but obviously, communicating was difficult. It was quite an experience as rebuilding was underway to repair the damages of WWII.

After graduating from CBR training, we took another train trip down the middle of the Japanese islands to the port of Sasebo. We went through Hiroshima but it was night so we were unable to see the city. From Sasebo, it was an overnight trip on the troop ship Sgt. Brewster, to Pusan, Korea, on the southeastern tip of Korea. This was where the Chinese and North Korean armies almost pushed our forces into the sea in the early stages of the war. By the way, the waters of the Pusan harbor were the bluest I've ever seen.

Episode Forty-eight - Life of an Artilleryman

We were in Pusan a short time and then loaded on to a Korean train - built to accommodate the average small Korean adult. It was a bit cramped. The day and night ride to Seoul through the South Korean hills and country was a most interesting experience. We were traveling the area where American troops fought and died during the first two years of the war. We were told there were still guerillas in the hills and each car had armed guards. It seemed every man on that train had his own sidearm - like something out of the "Wild West."

We arrived in Seoul and there was still destruction everywhere. After much confusion, we managed to get to the Army Replacement Center to receive our assignments, which was to the Third Infantry Division, United States Army. Another train ride took us north to the town of Chang Yang Ni and to the Third Divisions Replacement Depot. There we were issued our winter gear: parka, field pants, "Mickey Mouse" boots, (rubber lowers and somewhat insulated and waterproof) and a trusty .30 caliber carbine. This was much better winter clothing that the troops had during the first winter or so.

At the Replacement Depot, we were assigned to the 9th Field Artillery Battalion, 3rd Infantry Division. We would be in the Chorwon Valley (9th Corps) sector. All of this happened very quickly, I hardly remember eating or sleeping - and I soon found myself with B (Baker) Battery of the 9th FA Battalion. This was my unit from January 1st, 1953 to September of 1953. The 9th was a towed 155mm howitzer unit, it could fire a 96 pound projectile a distance of 12 miles plus. Most of the time we were about five miles behind the MLR.

155mm Howiter

223

Most of the firing done by the guns of the 9th Field Artillery during January of 1953 was on targets far north of the MLR and on known enemy bunkers. Our howitzers were kept in camouflaged bunkers constructed of sandbags, timber, and rails taken from the Chorwon railroad. Many days were used for practice in moving to other areas and putting our guns in firing positions. It was a stable time on the line.

We fired direct support for the men of the 15th Infantry Regiment who were holding defensive positions on the MLR. Many times, we fired on targets of opportunity called in by our FO's such as Chinese troops in a chow line or other large groups. On one occasion, we fired at "enemy on horseback." Don't know what that was about but hope we didn't injure the horse. These targets were generally six or seven miles distant but we could be very accurate.

I spent Christmas Day, 1952, as a new officer in Baker Company of the 9th FA Bn. Richard was assigned to Able Battery adjacent to me. We were living pretty good and ate well as we had some excellent cooks.

I began my new assignment as Motor Officer and Rodent Control Officer! The motor pool pretty much took care of itself if it had a good non-commissioned officer in charge. But with temperatures reaching 20° below zero our M-10 tractors, the prime movers for our guns, had to be ready to go at a moments' notice. Drivers and mechanics had to just about live with their vehicles.

Each motor pool was like its own garage and each motor pool sergeant had his own methods to keep everything running, even if it meant using tin cans and baling wire. The drivers were all great scavengers. Railroad rails made good tracks to store fuel barrels on. The Battery CO was Captain Smith from Minot, North Dakota. My motor sergeant was Sgt. Dawes of South Dakota. Cold weather didn't faze either of them one bit.

Episode Forty-eight - Life of an Artilleryman

Baker Battery Chorwon Valley

In our positions, we supported the left flank of the Third Infantry Division in the Ninth Corp Sector. We could also support the 25th Infantry Division in the Whitehorse area, a high hill northwest of Chorwon in the Chorwon Valley. When it was necessary to move, we moved at night since we had to cross much open ground under enemy observation. On the reverse sides of the hills, many fires could be seen warming the ROK troops. Probably a somewhat dangerous practice since the Chinese artillery was ever-present.

In March of 1953, the Third Division moved to the right into positions in the Kumhwa sector. Large emplacements were built for our artillery pieces. Timbers from the states and many thousands of sand bags were used in the construction of these bunkers. Our crews lived in dug in bunkers - practically everyone was underground to some extent with the exception of the mess (cooking areas) and the FDC (Fire Direction Center). Rats were unpleasant and unwanted guests.

The Korean Service Corp built the officers of Baker Battery a first-class bunker that we dubbed "The Chalet." It was large enough to accommodate four men and had all the comforts of home - beds and basins, a bar and cooler which was made from a VT fuse container. Buried in the floor it kept everything at the right temperature.

One thing we had in Korea besides the many hills and mountains was plenty of snow and cold weather. It was often cold enough to make diesel fuel congeal so the men in charge of keeping the stoves going were always busy. They were easy to spot as the diesel fuel and soot turned them very dark. Could have passed for Indians.

Later, during the spring and early summer campaigns of 1953 our battalion fired thousands of artillery rounds in support of OP Harry and other areas along the MLR. The Chinese were determined to take OP Harry as it was in a strategic location of the Chorwon Valley. The Chinese attacked the OP every night for seven or eight nights with anywhere from two-hundred to two or three thousand troops. Our artillery support was vital and we were given the green light to fire as much ammunition as needed. The Chinese took tremendous losses and finally gave up their attempt.

We were also engaged in a bunker busting campaign and fired daily on enemy targets, seen and unseen. Our battalion had Forward Observers on OP Peter and others in front of Papa-San Mountain and Green Knob, Chinese territory. Richard spent 39 straight days on OP Peter as a forward observer for our Third Infantry Division Artillery Battalion. I managed to get a couple of days in that area to relieve some of the FOs who needed a break. It was an interesting experience but the Chinese lines were only a few hundred yards away so I was glad to get back to my guns as Executive Officer.

We had another Observation Post that was occasionally used as a VIP bunker from which visiting dignitaries could get their view of the war. A Lieutenant, a Sergeant and three or four men manned these OPs around the clock. I met Colonel John Eisenhower there in the spring of 1953. I asked if there was anything I could explain to him concerning the front. His reply was "No." As he was the Division G-2 (in charge of intelligence and planning). I don't guess there was much I could have told him.

These OPs were accessible only by jeep, which due to the snow made such trips sometimes difficult to accomplish. Our VIP OP did have a helicopter pad but was rarely used. In fact, the artillery didn't use many choppers during the Korean War. Occasionally, a high-ranking officer would come in by helicopter and we'd have to cease firing for fear of shooting him down!

Many nights as we fired interdictory rounds on enemy held hills, we would be awed by our Air Force flare ships dropping their cargo on enemy targets. They would illuminate an area so bright we could read our "Stars and Stripes."

All the hills had names – OPs Tom, Dick, and Harry, Heartbreak Ridge, Porkchop Hill, Papa San, Jane Russell, Jackson Heights, Triangle Hill, Old Baldy, T-Bone, and many others. The Chinese were entrenched on many of them; the American forces and our Allies held others. They frequently changed hands. The Chinese forces would normally attack at night, sometimes with mass attacks, sometimes with feints and infiltration.

During the battle for OP Harry, which was in our divisions' sector, our 9th FA Bn., we would fire steady defensive fires all night long. Our barrages and concentrations were pre-registered by our Forward Observer so the Chinese suffered huge casualties as a result. Some of our guys would be so exhausted that when it came time for them to get a short break they could sleep right through a thousand round barrage without waking – fifty feet from our howitzers!

On days when there would be a lull in the action, the men played softball, pitched horseshoes, or just rested. And, of course, there was always care and cleaning of equipment which was ongoing. Our trucks were continuously bringing up ammo, fuel, and supplies to be unloaded and stored. The ammo dump would be full and then just as quickly depleted. The roads were always busy and it took a top-notch motor pool sergeant to keep all the vehicles maintained and ready to roll at a moments' notice.

Our bunkers were constantly being up-graded and weekly inspection assured that they were kept ship-shape. At night, if there were no firing missions, we had movies on a hillside in the Headquarters Battery. Occasionally, the movie would get an extra boost when "B" Battery got a firing mission. The little area also served as the church for the Battalion on Sunday mornings.

The rain and mud (and snow in the winter) made movement slow, and the practice "RSOP's" (Reconnaissance, Selection and Occupation of Position) were sometimes a lesson in futility. However, when things were quiet the practice missions kept everyone trained and ready for any kind of action. Also firing at enemy positions during the day and interdictory missions at night became a routine we endured, but kept us sharp. And the gun crews kept their howitzers in prime condition.

Episode Forty-eight - Life of an Artilleryman

Kumhwa Valley 1953 - observation obscured by smoke screen

I was promoted to 1st Lieutenant on June 17th and named the Battery Executive Officer. I was now in charge of 6 howitzers, their respective crews, and the FDC (Fire Direction Center).

In late June and the first days of July 1953, we got the word that something big was happening. The Third Division (our Division) was preparing to move and move fast... Our Battalion was to go into action near Chorwon. But then, the big Chinese offensive hit the Kumsong sector to our right and we had gone into high gear. The division was on the move in early July, to be replaced by the Second Infantry Division in the Kumhwa area.

Thousands of Chinese troops crashed through a couple of ROK Divisions and were over running everything in their path – including the 555th Field Artillery Battalion (the Triple Nickel). I believe the 555th was supporting one of those divisions and when the ROKs collapsed under the Chinese onslaught, the Battalion was overwhelmed. Apparently, there was mass confusion as the retreating South Koreans, followed by the Chinese and North Koreans,

229

descended upon the men of the 555th. I heard they lost about 45 KIAs and as many captured. Tanks of the Third Division went to the rescue. We fired VT (variable timed) shells to cover the tanks so that the beleaguered artillerymen could ride out – those who were left.

While the 3rd Infantry Division moved into a blocking position, division and corp. artillery was moved into a six-mile long valley firing constantly, everything from the 105's to the 8-inch howitzers. There might even have been a battery (2 guns) of the even bigger 240mm weapons. The guns were hub to hub and the gunners were firing, reloading, firing, reloading – tons of firepower went raining down on the Chinese.

Kumwah valley 1953 - Baker Battery gun pitts.

Our Forward Observers up on the line with the Infantry units would report Chinese troops attacking by the hundreds. The FO's would call the Fire Direction Centers giving the coordinates of the target and would call for a TOT (Time on Target). That meant that in a matter of seconds all of the artillery weapons would fire so that all the rounds would hit the area at the same instant regardless of the varying distance of those guns to the target. The next comment from the FO would be something like, "They're all gone" or "Target destroyed – good shooting."

There was no let-up in the artillery barrages or the infantry fighting, right up until 2300 hours (11:00 PM) on 27th of July 1953. The cease-fire went into effect and an eerie silence extended over the entire front. There was no celebration, just a time to be wary and try to relax. After the formalities of the armistice were handled, the guns of the 9th FA Battalion were silenced and covered for the first time in nearly three long years of continuous fighting. Excluding the ROK and other UN units, there were somewhere in the vicinity of a thousand plus artillery pieces employed during the war by our army. I believe any Infantryman will tell you that our artillery is his best friend.

During July and August much time was spent in training and keeping a wary eye to the north in case the North Koreans and Chinese wanted to start something again. Our equipment was kept clean and ready. During that period, Richard and I helped train a Korean Artillery Battalion for a few weeks. That was a unique experience to say the least. To watch the discipline given out by the Korean officers was astonishing.

Finally, our orders to rotate home came in late September. We boarded the General Grant and managed to cross the blue Pacific without getting seasick. We came in under the Golden Gate Bridge and then on to Camp Stoneman. All the houses looked funny with TV antennas sticking out from them. TV's were somewhat of a novelty when we left in the fall of '52.

I went on to Camp Carson, Colorado, for separation on October 7th, 1953. My mustering out pay was $300.00 with an advance of $100.00. Wow! In a matter of days I was back on the farm helping my Dad pick corn. And it was sure good to be home for Mother's home cooking. Richard arrived shortly thereafter. He was held over in California for a court-martial hearing, involving one of the troops under his charge as a compartment commander on board ship. He also spent a little time in the hospital at Camp Carson but was finally separated with a clean bill of health. Needless to say, for the family to be together once again was a wonderful feeling.

As a postscript to all of this, our commanding officer had recommended both Richard and me be awarded the Bronze Star Meritorious for service against an armed enemy of the United States while serving with the Third Division Artillery in Korea. It was very gratifying to receive the award and I am proud to have served.

- PAUL BONHAM

CHINESE BREAKTHROUGH
Roger Blakeney

We had just come off the MLR and going into reserve - or so we thought. We were exhausted having had little or no sleep in the nights preceding our move. Instead of rest and relaxation we were told that the Chinese had just broken through the Capitol ROK Division, the South Korean Army's very best. Our Triple Nickel (the 555th Field Artillery Battalion that was in support of the South Koreans) was also overrun. The battalion suffered 22 killed, 19 wounded, and 46 captured. The war was winding down, the armistice about to be signed, so obviously the Chinese were trying to grab as much terrain as possible to improve their bargaining position.

Our division, the Third Infantry Division, was ordered to move into a blocking position to stop the Chinese offensive. I was sent back to division headquarters to receive our orders and our destination - our assigned assembly area. We were warned that the situation was fluid to the point that we should be prepared to get off of our trucks fighting.

I was assigned a driver, jeep, and guide and we took off in the middle of the night to locate what was to be our assembly area. It would be my task the next morning to lead our battalion there assuming we didn't encounter the Chinese offensive en route. I don't recall the distance that we traveled but my guess would be about 15 miles. The night was blacker than coal and I vividly remember our artillery lined up hub to hub along that road. It seemed to me that every artillery piece in Korea was firing at the Chinese onslaught. (I read an article recently, which stated that 2.7 million artillery rounds were expended by U.S. forces in June and July alone, 1953.)

The crews were bare to the waist, covered in sweat and firing, loading and firing without pause. The noise and the flashing explosions in the darkness were incessant. I was pretty much mesmerized by all this but I still had to try and remember the turns and landmarks. In total darkness that was next to impossible. We made the round trip without incident; I returned to my unit and alerted my company commander that we would be moving out at daylight.

We had assembled at division headquarters and moved out about 0600 hours heading for our assembly area. I was in the lead jeep with my CO followed by our company, the battalion, and in my imagination, the entire division. Probably, only our company was in this column. But to say that this lieutenant was nervous would be a gross understatement.

But much to my relief and surprise, there were MP's stationed at the first three or four turns so I relaxed a bit thinking that we would have guides at various intervals and cross roads until we reached our assigned area. As luck would have it, one of the MPs directed us to a left turn, which I remembered as a right - but I figured the MPs had to have had the route correctly plotted so my nerves settled down to a slight roar. And we took the turn to the left. Big mistake.

Unfortunately, we had gone only a three or four miles when I realized there were no more guides and we were lost, pure and simple - with a whole lot of folks following along behind us. I told the company commander and we stopped. With that he pulls out a map - I didn't know a map of the area even existed. I'd never seen one. Why didn't the division briefer have one? Sure would have made my task easier.

While standing there studying the situation, we hear small arms fire a few hundred yards off the road. My CO says, "Let's go up there – maybe we can get oriented." Turns out a company of Marines was engaged in a firefight with a Chinese unit. We're standing around watching when the Marine CO nonchalantly strolls over and asks if he can be of assistance! We explain our dilemma and he says, "Well, if you're looking for the Chinese, they're right out there." Which was pretty obvious. His men were about 50 yards to our front banging away at the Chinese. And they, in turn, were returning fire with gusto. We chat for a few more minutes as if it were a Sunday

Episode Forty-nine - Chinese Breakthrough

picnic-- during which time he was able to show us our current position. All of this while the firefight was still ongoing.

We thanked him most kindly, wished him and his men well, and we were on our way again. Fortunately, this didn't take long and as it turned out we were only a mile or so off course. I was much relieved as this move rested heavily on my shoulders.

An hour or so later as we approached the assembly area, the Chinese started interdicting the road with artillery fire. One round had disabled a deuce and a half carrying a squad of riflemen directly in front of us. Our progress was blocked as we were on a narrow dirt road, ditches on both sides. My CO got out of the jeep and I followed. We were standing there trying to figure out our next move when a few more incoming rounds landed nearby.

I looked back at our column. Without any command or hesitation, three or four of our trucks (some pulling supply trailers) were turning around in the middle of the road and heading the opposite direction. How the men detached the trailers, manhandled them aside while the drivers turned the vehicles around (which seemed impossible considering those ditches) is something I will never understand. This happened in a matter of minutes. The human body can do amazing things under such conditions. The artillery fire stopped, we got everyone turned back in the right direction, the disabled truck to our front had been shoved off the road, and we proceeded to our assigned area without further delay.

Lady Luck smiled on us that day. The Chinese offensive was stopped. We saw no action and a few days later the war was over. I was one more relieved young 2nd Lt., as I was totally embarrassed over my part in getting us lost. The Chinese offensive bothered me - getting lost bothered me more. Fortunately, to this day no one knew except my company commander of our little problem and me. Being the leader that he was, he never mentioned it. He rotated home not long afterward and I lost track of him. I have tried unsuccessfully over the years to find my former friend and CO, Captain Joseph H. Poole. Joe, I hope you are alive and well.

- ROGER BLAKENEY

THE FOG OF WAR ON HILL 620
Robert D. Heslep

Robert Heslep imitating Patton.

I arrived in Korea in the middle of April 1953, and became a voice radio operator in Headquarters Battery, 9th Field Artillery Battalion, 3rd Infantry Division, which was located in the vicinity of Kumhwa. My job was to relay target instructions to our battalion's firing batteries as given by our forward observers and our aircraft spotters and then report the results of those missions. Most of the ground action was a matter of probes by each side to find the others weak spots.

Because the 3rd ID had taken a lot of hits during the first half of the year, it was scheduled to swap positions with the 40th ID in the middle of July. The 40th was in the Chorwon Valley, west of Kumhwa. The South Korean Whitehorse and Capital Division were to the east of the 3rd ID in the Kumsong area. Advance units of the 3rd ID, including elements of the 9th FA, began to switch with similar units of the 40th ID around July 12th. Enemy loudspeakers on the front lines screamed that they were aware of our troop movements and would be waiting.

On Sunday evening, July 14th, at 10:00 pm, our battalion CO received a phone call monitored in the Headquarters Battery Fire Direction Center stating that the Chinese and North Korean troops had routed the Whitehorse and Capital ROK divisions. Further, they had advanced six miles in the Kumsong area in a pouring rain. The 555th Artillery Battalion (the Triple Nickel) and the 5th Regimental Combat Team were both pretty much destroyed. The 9th FA immediately retrieved it's advanced parties at Chorwon and moved the next morning with the rest of the 3rd ID to Kumsong for the counter attack.

The 64th Tank Battalion, attached to the 3rd ID, sent tank patrols into Kumsong's no-mans' land to probe enemy positions. However, those patrols suffered rocket and mortar attacks and occasional swarms of enemy infantry. It was then decided at division level for the 9th FA to provide direct fire support of such probes if radio communication could be maintained between our battalion and the tanks. The first and last attempt at such coordination was undertaken around July 20th.

Pfc. Gabriel Broussard, a jeep driver and I (also a Pfc.) volunteered to set up a radio relay station between a tank patrol and our Fire Direction Center. We proceeded up Goat Trail about five miles to Hill 620. We approached the area around 8:45AM. It appeared to be beyond the 3rd ID's Main Line of Resistance. I contacted the 9th for a routine radio check and then, for security reasons, shut down temporarily.

Meanwhile, Broussard had left the jeep and gone into a rice paddy to retrieve a flare parachute for a souvenir. He hastily returned shouting, "Gooks out there!" I saw about eight of them setting up an ambush but could not re-establish radio contact with Battalion Headquarters.

Just in front of Hill 620 was a road running to our left. We took it hoping to find friendly forces. On our right were destroyed and smoldering artillery bunkers. After driving another mile or so we turned around and headed back to where we had been. As we approached the intersection at Hill 620, we saw another squad of enemy personnel preparing an ambush.

Episode Fifty - The Fog of War on Hill 620

Stopping the jeep, we crouched behind it and began firing at them. Broussard was at the right rear of the vehicle armed with a grease gun and two clips of ammo. I was at the jeeps' left rear with an M-1 rifle and eight clips of ammo - 64 rounds. Almost immediately I noticed bullets hitting about a foot from my leg. I spotted a guy shooting from a rise in the middle of a rice paddy about 200 yards from me. I fired several rounds but couldn't tell if I'd hit him. He promptly stopped shooting so I was pleased with that! Meanwhile, Broussard had killed one of the enemies on our right front and I got another one on our left.

Running low on ammo, we decided to abandon the jeep, which was shot all to Hell and useless. Broussard had only one round left and I had only two or three clips. We found a draw in the hill opposite Hill 620. It rose toward the 3rd ID line so on our elbows and stomachs, cradling our weapons in our arms, we proceeded to crawl up the draw through brush and stunted trees.

From the top of the hill, we looked down and watched the enemy troops set fire to our jeep. We thought about killing some more of them but decided we'd better keep what was left of our ammo in case of another possible encounter on our way back to our lines. I also discovered that I had lost my spare clips while crawling on my stomach.

We decided to go back to the road where we had made the radio check and then work our way back to the MLR. Somehow, we became separated. Broussard ended up in a rice paddy where he found a couple of grenades and began walking upstream. I reached the road and crawled in a ditch toward our lines. There being no imminent threat I got up and started walking. Enemy mortar rounds started landing nearby so I picked up the pace. It was also comforting to see two of our air force jets bombing enemy positions across the valley.

Soon, I met up with Lt. Bacci who, along with Lt. Taylor, had come to search for us. Broussard had been located and returned to

Headquarters with Lt. Taylor. Lt. Bacci and I returned to our Battalion in his jeep. Upon arrival, our Battalion Commander (who had been in Korea only a very short time) demanded to know why we had not defended the jeep and returned with it! He did not readily accept our explanation that we were low on ammunition and that the jeep was in no condition to drive in as much as it had been shot up and set afire. As I was a lowly Pfc. I did not feel comfortable arguing with a Lt. Colonel so I kept my mouth shut. What I thought of the man, however, would not make for polite conversation. Nevertheless, and probably in spite of the Colonel, Broussard and I received the Bronze Star for Meritorious service.

The sergeant in charge of our intelligence section for the 9th FA in July of 1953 was one Sgt. Simms. He confidentially acknowledged to me that the Chinese had captured the hill the night before Broussard and I had attempted to establish the relay station. He went on to say that he did not receive that information until after we had set out on our journey and could not establish radio contact with us to warn of our impending problem! The 64th Tank Battalion must have known that Hill 620 was in enemy hands for it sent out no patrols the morning we drove up Goat Trail and into trouble.

All in all, I guess Broussard and I were pretty lucky. We didn't accomplish our mission but it wasn't for lack of trying. The war ended a week after these events and for that, we were all very grateful.

- ROBERT D. HESLEP

THE MiG AND ME
RON HILL

SFC Ron Hill at Outpost Harry April 1953.

My name is Ron Hill, currently living in Sautee-Nacoochee, Georgia, in the northern portion of the state. It's a beautiful area and quite mountainous. Reminds me a bit of Korea except most of the mountains there were pretty barren with very little foliage or trees left. Fighting back and forth over those areas had damaged the landscape to the point that those scarred mountains looked more like moonscapes. Thousands of rounds of artillery fire from both our guns and those of the Chinese had left craters and damage that will take a lifetime to heal.

I arrived in Korea toward the end of the war and was assigned to the 9th Field Artillery Battalion, Third Infantry Division. Our weapon was the Cannon, M1A1, 155mm caliber, which could lay down devastating fire. I handled much of the paperwork for the battalion, which included command reports that were sent up the chain of command. One such report indicated that our battalion had expended 47,000 rounds of ammo in one month. Sadly, one of those rounds was a short round - a premature explosion. It hit our motor pool area killing one and wounding four - one of the many tragedies of war.

Compared to what happened shortly before the war ended, that expenditure of ammo was small potatoes. The Chinese mounted a huge offensive and attacked and broke through the Capitol ROK Division, one of South Koreas best units. Unfortunately, one of our sister battalions, the 555th Field Artillery (known as the Triple Nickel), was attached to and giving supporting fire to the ROK

Division. It was overrun. The battalion suffered 22 killed, 19 wounded, and 46 captured. I believe all their guns were captured or destroyed.

To stop the Chinese, our Third Infantry Division moved into a blocking position. Meanwhile our battalion along with other artillery units of the division, units of Corps artillery, and an 8-inch howitzer battery from 8th Army lined up hub to hub and rained down what could only be described as tons of artillery fire on the Chinese troops. That was a real expenditure of ammo! But the Chinese offensive was stopped. Not many days later, the war ended.

Our unit moved back somewhere south of the Chorwon Valley area and peace prevailed. We were living pretty comfortably in tents and with our own mess hall. There was not a lot going on but we maintained some semblance of security with regular guard details around the area. We also had a couple of .50 caliber machine guns set up on a hill not too far from Kimpo Air Base.

I believe I was Sergeant of the Guard that morning, September 21, 1953, some two months after the war had ended. It was a beautiful morning and I was making my rounds when someone started yelling that a MiG was fast approaching our position. The MiG was the top of the line jet fighter flown by both North Korean and Russian pilots. I made a mad dash to the top of the hill to man the 50-caliber gun. As I swiveled the weapon to take aim, someone shouted, "Hold your fire, hold your fire." The plane was so close that I recall feeling almost eye-to-eye contact with the pilot. The view of that jet and its pilot is still a delightful memory. It seems that someone got the word that the pilot was defecting and fortunately passed it down the line in time for him to make a safe landing at Kimpo. I learned later that our intelligence people debriefed him, his jet was tested and retested (for comparison against our F-86 Saber jet), and the young North Korean pilot was eventually given sanctuary in our country and later became a citizen. His name is No Kum-Suk and his book, "A MiG FLIGHT TO FREEDOM," is well worth reading.

Any number of odd things occur during a war and its aftermath, but I truly believe my brief (almost) encounter with a MiG jet fighter has to rank very high on the scale of strange and unusual occurrences. I know I will never forget that moment!

- RON HILL

R AND R
Bill Jamison

Seoul City Air Base waiting for planes for R & R to Japan April 1953.

The war was over and several of us were going on our first R and R to Japan. We were flown to Pusan and from there were to go by ship to Fukuoka. Unfortunately, when we arrived in Pusan there was a typhoon raging in the Sea of Japan and the Korean Straits. So there we sat waiting for the storm to abate, totally disgusted.

Finally, after a couple of days of boredom, we boarded a very small ship. I think it had been a Japanese destroyer escort of WWII vintage but much smaller. More like a small yacht of about 100 to 150 feet in length. There were about ten of us and a Japanese crew. The distance across the strait should have been a matter of a few hours.

However, half way to our destination, we encountered the typhoon head on. It had either turned around or stayed in the area but the bottom line was that we were in big trouble. In those days, storm tracking and predictions were definitely not as scientific or as accurate as now.

I think everyone on that small ship except the captain, the first mate, and I became violently ill. Probably some of it caused by sheer terror. The boat was being tossed about like a leaf. I always thought that I could swim before I could walk but under those circumstances it would not have mattered. Had we capsized, no one would have survived.

The little vessel rolled and pitched with the bow disappearing under huge waves. But the captain and his mate did a masterful job of handling her - I know it was exhausting for the two of them. If we had lost power, it would have been game over.

We finally made it to port, battered but relieved and glad to be alive. Our ordeal was over. Then we received shock number two. We reported to the Army post as required only to be told that we would be restricted to base for the next two or three days. The following day was May Day, which was a big turnout and celebration by the Japanese Communist Party. Our superiors were afraid that the presence of American military personnel in the midst of all that might spark a riot. We were not happy.

I've never been a big drinker, but that night we hit the Officers' Club and proceeded to get roaring drunk. We made real jackasses of ourselves and if my memory is correct we were invited to leave. I don't think we sobered up for a day or so and we were finally permitted to resume our R and R. Fukuoka wasn't much of a town in those days so our leave was pretty pathetic. We headed back to the Land of Morning Calm shortly after, and to our relief the seas were calm.

- BILL JAMISON

THE MEDIC CAPTAIN
Roger Jenkins

The war had been over a couple of months and for some unknown reason our company was moving again. We were taking over an area occupied by another battalion from our regiment. There seemed to be no hurry or timetable so we made several trips back and forth coordinating the coming move.

During that time, I became friends with a Captain who was, I believe, their battalion medical officer. He was an exceptionally nice person and played a really mean game of ping-pong. Special Services had kicked in and their unit was well supplied with recreational equipment. I was pretty fair at the game so every time we visited his unit the two of us got into some wild competition. He usually won.

They moved out, we moved in and I never saw him again. To my regret, I learned later that he was killed shortly after his outfit relocated. Seems that their area encompassed an old Chinese minefield that no one knew was there. The men had set up a baseball diamond, which unfortunately bordered on that field. Some of the mines were inert from age and weather. But not all.

At any rate, two men while shagging balls ran unknowingly into the danger zone and set off one of the mines. Both were severely injured and lay there helpless. The doctor was close at hand, saw what happened and without hesitation grabbed his medical kit, and ran toward the injured men. Unfortunately, he didn't make it - he triggered a mine that instantly killed him. The two men were brought out as quickly as possible and survived.

It is difficult to forget things like that. He was a bit older than the rest of us so I often wonder if he left a wife and perhaps, children. If so, I hope that they know he died a true hero. How ironic - he survived the war, treated many wounded or dying men, never shirked his duty, and died on a baseball field trying to save the lives of others. May he rest in peace...

THE SEAPLANE PILOT
Anonymous

NOTE: I have no idea why the writer of this very interesting article prefers to remain anonymous; I think he is simply way too modest. Here is his story:

The Seaplane Pilot's plane.

In the spring of 1945, I joined the Marine Corps and reported to Parris Island. I completed boot Camp and along with a large number of marines boarded a train bound for the west coast. I ended up at Camp Pendleton Marine Base for more combat training. We were told that after six weeks we would be headed for the Pacific Theater. However, our departure was delayed for unknown reasons. The war ended in August, 1945, and I was sent to Cherry Point Marine Air Station for airborne electronics training. In July, 1946, I was released to the Reserves for six years (inactive duty) as I had been accepted for college.

I had just completed my third year at UNC, Chapel Hill in June 1950. In early July of 1950, I received notice that I was to report to Cherry Point Marine Base. The Korean War broke out that month with the invasion of South Korea by the North Korean Army, which was backed by the Russians and later, the Chinese.

When I reported for duty a Marine aviator interviewed me. He asked me if I would like to go to flight school and I said YES! I took all the tests and medical exams and three days later reported to Pensacola, Florida, for flight training. It was there, in the last few weeks of Basic, that I had my first experience of seeing the death of a friend. Unfortunately, there were more to follow. Myron had reported to Pensacola with me, a fellow Marine.

He was one plane ahead of me in Field Carrier Landing Qualification. Turning downwind Myron stalled and the plane flipped over. He was still alive but could not get out of the cockpit as it was compressed from the crash. All of us heard him begging for help, as there were five other planes in the pattern and all on the same radio frequency. The aircraft burst into flames and I, along with the other pilots, listened to him die. He wanted to be a Marine Aviator more than anything. It was tough to handle, something one can never forget.

I qualified on the USS Cabot, a WWII carrier and asked to fly seaplanes. My request was granted and I was commissioned and received my wings, a proud moment. I was ordered to Naval Air Station Coronado and reported to my squadron. Six months later we completed pre-deployment training in the PBM-5A seaplane and were sent to Sangley Point, Philippine Islands, in August, 1952. Our PBM seaplanes were sisters to the famous PBYs of WWII but technically a far more advanced aircraft.

I had considered being a fighter pilot but there was a need for seaplane pilots and there was something about those beautiful planes that appealed to me. The first aircraft that the U.S. Navy purchased was a Curtis A-1 and it was a "flying-boat." That was May 8, 1911, so

Episode Fifty-four - The Seaplane Pilot

there was a history to this type aircraft. By mid-1918, the number of seaplanes outnumbered land aircraft. In fact, the first 2500 Naval Aviators received their Wings of Gold as flying boat aviators.

From the early 1930's until the 1940's, the Consolidated Aircraft Company designed, developed, and produced the PBY "Catalina" seaplane. The "Y" was the designation for Consolidated. Later the Glen L. Martin Company became the major supplier and developed the PBM (Martin).

The PBY Catalina first flew in 1934. It saw a great deal of service during the Second World War flying missions such as anti-submarine warfare, convoy escort, bombing runs, search and rescue missions, cargo transport, mine laying, etc. It was a very versatile aircraft. In fact, it was a PBY crew that first spotted the Japanese Naval Armada and gave warning to our fleet for the upcoming Battle of Midway. Their warning was surely instrumental in giving our fleet a great victory over the Japanese. Also in the Pacific Theater several squadrons of PBY's were outfitted with the latest magnetic anomaly detection gear, painted flat black and with a torpedo slung under each wing, proceeded to raise havoc with Japanese convoys during hours of darkness. Those squadrons were, of course, known as the "The Black Cats".

Sangley Point was our first tour and there we lost two aircraft. One in a failed ditching attempt and one in an attack by North Korean MiGs. We lost fourteen crewmen - two of four pilots and twelve airmen. The four pilots had been in my advanced training class and we were all close friends.

We returned to Coronado in January of 1953. In June the squadron arrived again at Sangley Point to begin our second tour. Four of the First Pilots (who qualified) were designated Plane Commanders in February and I was one of the four. We flew various missions, some quite different from in the past. In fact, several months after the Korean conflict ended, several of our planes flew Under-Water Demolition Teams and dropped them off the coast of

251

Viet Nam. They went ashore in large inflated rafts and they were very heavily armed. We had no idea of their missions and of course never saw them again.

P5M-1

Our squadron on this deployment was flying the P5M-1 seaplane. It entered the service in January 1953, to replace to the PBM-5A. The PBM first entered service in 1939 and had a very high rating with pilots and crews who flew these planes during WWII and Korea. The P5M was equipped with the latest ECM (electronic counter measures) and advanced radar. It also had the updated LORAN (Long Range) navigational system. The aircraft weighed 72,000 pounds with full fuel tanks. At this weight JATO (jet assisted take off) was required during lift off, especially in a sea condition of light winds and "slick" water. JATO was also used in rough seas to shorten the length of the lift-off run. Cruising speed was 175 knots, serviceable ceiling of 12,000 feet, and a range of 3,000 miles.

The missions flown were normally of 12 hours duration and were tracked by Chinese and Russian radar. It was not possible to

Episode Fifty-four - The Seaplane Pilot

evade their radar on night patrols; the enemy was always close by in their MiGs. They would cut in and out of the tracks our seaplanes flew and they operated with full ordinance aboard. We had little defense should an attack occur. Their speed on a pass would be 550 to 700 knots. Our only defense was to push the yoke full ahead and dive for the water hoping their rockets would overshoot the target.

P-5 M-1 - Waiting for a lift.

The P5M-1 was designed to support Navy vessels and to gather information concerning enemy submarine locations, radar location and to detect all shipping that might be supporting enemy facilities. It could handle open sea landings to facilitate the pickup of downed pilots and crews. Three of the twelve aircraft assigned to the squadron were rotated every seven days to operate with a seaplane tender out of Buckner Bay, Okinawa. The USS Pine Island was on station. The ship was capable of hoisting a P5M on deck, if necessary, for repairs. Aircraft on the water were tethered to buoys and it required that one pilot and two crewmen to remain on the plane for security and for emergency assignments.

On July 27, 1953, the Korean Armistice was signed. One of the stipulations in the agreement was that no UN aircraft would fly closer than 30 miles off the coast of North Korea. If this was violated, the aircraft would be shot down. That was more than just a

253

mere threat as the North Korean Air Force flew the MiG-19, a new version of the MiG. In September and October of 1953, MiG's attacked and destroyed several Navy PBM aircraft resulting in a number of our air crewmen being killed. The question was whether or not these aircraft were inside or outside that 30-mile zone. A moot point to those who died.

The following is an interview with the Plane Commander of a P5M-1 as he told of an incident that shares such a combat encounter between a MiG and a P5M-1. This particular aircraft was on its second tour. The crew had completed fourteen previous patrols. The Plane Commander had 810 hours Plane Commander Time and 900 hours in the PBM-5A.

"On a November day, we were buoyed off Pine Island, a crew consisting of myself as Plane Commander, a First Pilot, navigator (all Naval Aviators must spend time as a navigator), a radio operator, and five crewmen. At the pre-flight briefing the assigned track was "Red Fox." That track was direct to a location 30 miles east of Shanghai, then direct to a point 30 miles off Pyongyang and finally to Buckner Bay. The weather was clear at lift off then a cold front over the Yellow Sea. Expect head winds to Pyongyang then tail winds to Buckner Bay, Okinawa. Yellow Sea water temperatures varied at around 25°. Total flight time was estimated at nine and a half hours. Lift-off was at 0400 hours (4:00 AM). All patrol flights required that the crews wear survival suits referred to as "Poopy Suits." Somewhat cumbersome but necessary.

"As we lifted off, that 30-mile restricted area was on our minds. We were cleared by ComAirPac control to a cruising altitude of 4000 feet. The weather was a mix of clouds with some ice and sleet. The outside air temperature was in the low 10° F. Everything was normal. We cycled our deicers and sent our position report to ComAirPac. We were approaching our 30-mile position off Pyongyang when the two crewmen in the after station shouted over the intercom, "Two bogies on our tail." Just as that alert came over, a rocket passed our plane about 50 yards to our starboard. I pushed the yoke full forward

Episode Fifty-four - The Seaplane Pilot

and at that same instant the First Pilot rammed the throttles full ahead. The aircraft had dropped about 2,500 feet when another rocket slashed through the overhead of the flight deck right over the navigation table and exploded about 50 yards off the starboard wing tip. Had it exploded on impact, I would not be here to speak of this action.

"The altimeter indicated that we were less than 400 feet above the water when we pulled the aircraft's nose up and leveled off at 40 feet. The plane was "red lined" meaning the engines were in danger of total failure, our air speed being about 260 knots. As we pulled up, the crewmen reported some pieces of metal hitting the fuselage as the MiG's passed to starboard climbing steeply. At the same time, our radio operator sent a "help wanted" to Air Force Control. They responded with two F-86's vectored to our position. We were ordered to find a cove or a place to set the plane down. We were about 6 to 8 miles off the coast of South Korea at an altitude of 200 feet. The water surface was extremely rough with winds out of the north at 40 knots and swells moving northeast. Visibility was limited due to heavy snow.

"The impact of the rocket that hit the overhead ripped a gash about 3 feet long and a foot wide. It took out five of the antennas connected to the radios and LORAN. The emergency channel was operative. The freezing ice and cold air quickly entered the aircraft along with insulation, packing, wiring, and other debris. The two F-86's passed by and reported that the starboard engine was leaking what appeared to be oil. The after-station crewmen agreed that it was definitely oil. Not a good sign. One of the F-86's cut back on power, lowered his flaps and pulled up to starboard and reported that there were a number of holes and surface tears on the starboard side of the hull and on the surface of the starboard wing.

"I decided to set the plane down about 200 yards off shore. The aircraft landed safely in a full stall cross wind on a swell. We set down in about four feet of water and the plane was beached. The crew climbed out and moved to shore. All crewmen were then pleased with the "poopy" suits. There were no injuries except for slight facial scratches to the navigator's face. An hour later two choppers arrived. The pilots informed us that one of them would take 5 or 6 of the crew to a K strip. These were airstrips scattered about South Korea and used for emergency purposes and also as bases for our AD attack planes and Corsair attack aircraft. One or two crewmembers and we pilots would stay with the aircraft and wait for the recovery boat to arrive. We taxied the aircraft to the beach and made it secure. It was later moved by barge to Seoul for repairs. This was just one of 43 encounters with MIG's flown by Russian and Chinese pilots. They were well trained and flew an outstanding fighter aircraft."

Plane being towed to safety after being hit by a Chinese Missile.

Episode Fifty-four - The Seaplane Pilot

Two weeks after this mission, one of our planes blew up just after lift off from Sangley Point. The crew was headed for Hong Kong for three days of R&R and to take documents to the U.S. Navy affairs Office. This was a normal flight that took place every three weeks. Once again, I lost two of the 20 Ensigns that joined the squadron fresh out of training. Two officers and three air crewmen survived. Five air crewmen were lost. Many of us had served together for quite a long time and their deaths were deeply felt.

P-5 M-1 Ground Crew

Three seaplane squadrons carried the bulk of the aerial recon work during the war. Thirty-seven pilots and crewmen gave their lives in combat. Six aircraft were lost and twenty-three others were damaged and retired from service. In the beginning of the Korean War, the Navy's seaplanes in use were built in the late 30's and mid 40's. The equipment was outdated but all missions assigned were

257

completed. We flew in all types of weather, sea, and combat conditions. During WWII, the PBYs and various models of the PBMs played a major role in the air war in both the Pacific and Atlantic Theaters. The era of the seaplanes, the flying boats, ended after Viet Nam and are no longer a part of the U.S. Navy.

I left active duty and returned to college. I later joined a Naval Air Training Unit and flew the S2F aircraft. Shortly after, I was called back to active duty and reported to the Naval Air Station in Jacksonville, Florida. My squadron flew six S2F's to Guantanamo Bay, Cuba, where we flew search missions for Russian ships bound for Cuba. They were suspected of carrying nuclear missiles capable of hitting the United States. After three weeks, the Cuban missile crisis ended and we returned home.

After having served almost eighteen years, I resigned my commission and left the US Navy. There were, or course, some regrets. Had I stayed on I could have retired with benefits but I felt that I had stretched my luck to the breaking point. I was not a hero; I simply did my job to the best of my ability and I had been well trained. Those who died were the true heroes and they will never be forgotten.

- ANONYMOUS

STEVEDORES
Bill Mason

The war was over and we pulled back from the MLR a few hundred yards and set up shop on some fairly decent and flat terrain. It was a nice change after living in holes or bunkers or whatever protection we could find on the top of some gawd-forsaken mountain or ridgeline.

Twelve man squad tents went up and the engineers even erected a Quonset hut mess hall in what seemed a matter of days. Fifty-five gallon oil drums were converted to showers and the weather was pleasant. Life was good - except that within a week we were ordered to start a training cycle. No one was in the mood for that but it was necessary - morale sinks if there is nothing to do but gripe. And so we half-heartedly started.

One class that I was assigned to teach was removal of anti-personnel mines. The night prior to the class (which was for our company) my Platoon Sergeant and I went to the assigned area and buried a half-dozen flatted C-ration cans, which we would then use as mock mines.

The next morning, the company was assembled and I proceeded to give the pitch on land-mine removal and then my Sergeant and I got down on our knees and began probing in the prescribed manner with our bayonets. But we had a problem - the matchstick markers we had placed to identify the location of each mine had been trampled into the dirt. We couldn't find the damned things! We cracked up, as did the rest of the company. Our laugh for the day - we just couldn't get serious about training.

Then an amazing thing occurred. We were ordered to immediately depart for the port of Pusan, our mission there to help unload cargo and supplies. Everyone was delighted with this change of events so we struck camp, loaded the trucks, and headed south. No training for us!

259

We arrived at the port and were shown around. We would be operating forklifts, cranes, front-end loaders, etc., whatever it took to get the backlog of materiel into the warehouses. We were like a bunch of kids with a whole set of new toys. After having been thoroughly oriented, we were shown our quarters. To us, they were luxurious - actual buildings with running water, heat, beds, and good food - all the amenities. We slept like lambs that night looking forward to a pleasant sojourn in something akin to civilization.

We turned out bright and early to receive our instructions on how to operate the equipment we'd be working with - our new playthings. What a hoot. But before we even got started our dreams were cut short. We were ordered to pack up and head back north! It seems that when our Commanding General learned of our assignment, he was not happy. His comments were along the line of, "I don't want my blank-blank combat troops doing the work of blank-blank stevedores. Get "em back up on line!

And so we reluctantly followed orders, gazing wistfully at what would have been our surroundings as we headed out. I suppose the ships were eventually unloaded, we went back to our training regimen, and our general was once again happy. Life went on. But we were a sullen lot as we headed back to our former "home."

- BILL MASON

TRAGEDY
BRAD WILLIAMS

The war had ended. The last Chinese offensive had been stopped. The armistice had been signed. We pulled off the MLR. No more incoming artillery fire, no more night patrols, no more defending or taking a hill, no more sleeping in holes or bunkers, no more C-rations, no more weeks without a bath. We began to live almost like humans.

But being an Infantry unit, it was not long before the inevitable training cycle began. Who could know what our former adversaries were thinking or what they might attempt? I doubt a piece of paper meant much to them so no doubt our training was an essential part of our life.

We started off with platoon and company size exercises. The usual infantry stuff - attack an enemy hill, set up a defensive position with final protective fires plotted, run an ambush patrol or a reconnaissance patrol or a combat patrol, map reading exercises, and of course practice with our various weapons.

It was all pretty dull and annoying but we had to stay busy or we'd all have gone bonkers. I got lucky during one period and was sent to Japan to attend air-ground coordination training. It only lasted a week but it was pretty interesting and would perhaps come in handy at some future date.

One day as I left the class, I ran into an old high school friend. His family was very wealthy. He had a pilot's license and his own Piper Cub by the time we were seniors in high school. Harrop was in Air Force blues with pilot's wings on his chest. He looked the epitome of a fighter pilot. We shook hands warmly and I said, "Harrop, buddy, you look great - I guess you're delighted to be an Air Force jock flying those hot jets? That's what you always wanted!" "Naw," he replied, "Bored to death - all I've done is fly photo recon missions. Fly over, take pictures, and fly back - worse than driving a Greyhound bus." I guess the old saying, "Be careful what you wish for, you might get it," is sometimes true.

I returned "home" to Korea a few days later to be informed that our Regiment was going to run a large training exercise. The Battalion Commanders and their S-3 Operations Staff had already been briefed by the Regimental Staff and our company commanders were to get their orders within the next few hours. Shortly, we platoon leaders met with our CO to receive our assignments.

The exercise was going to be an "attack" on a large enemy held hill, two battalions in the attack, one in reserve. There would be a platoon of tanks from our tank battalion in the attack and the usual artillery preparation prior to the jump-off. There was even to be a couple of air strikes as we advanced. And as the Infantry moved out, there would be live machine-gun fire overhead directed at the "enemy" positions. These weapons had been zeroed in and staked down prior to the event to prevent any accident and manned by experienced crews. That fire, of course, would be lifted when the troops got to a pre-designated point in their advance. It was all pretty basic.

We moved to the assembly area around 0400 with the attack to begin at daylight. No one got much sleep that night and I think we all were thinking the same thing - get this over with. My company commander had assigned me to be his liaison officer with battalion headquarters so I really didn't have much to do - and I didn't complain. My platoon sergeant would handle my platoon, as he was fully capable.

The artillery barrage began promptly at daylight lasting several minutes. In real life, it might have lasted several hours but no point in wasting ammo. The air strikes came in, the tanks and the infantrymen advanced with tracers from the machine guns streaming overhead. A few moments later, even before the attack had reached the base of the hill, a red parachute flare burst overhead which was the prearranged signal to immediately stop the exercise.

Then three or four ambulances came screaming up from the rear. We didn't know what had happened at that moment but in a matter of minutes the word was out. Two of the advancing infantrymen were hit and killed by errant machinegun fire. One of the weapons had jumped its tie down in the midst of a burst of fire from the gunner - in an instant, two young men died. To call it a tragedy would be a supreme understatement. Those two boys had probably survived some tough combat situations only to die in a peacetime accident. And the man behind the trigger probably suffered the rest of his life knowing what had happened.

For whatever reason, I was selected to write the letters of condolence to the parents of these two young men. What was I to say? "I regret to inform you that your young son (probably all of 19 years of age) was today killed in an unfortunate and tragic training accident, etc., etc." Like all of us, their lives had been at risk during actual combat. To die in this fashion was beyond tragic.

I have no idea what I wrote in those letters. I don't remember if they went up the chain of command for comments from my superiors or whether the letters were mailed directly to the parents. Either way, there were four heart-broken parents on the receiving end of that mail delivery. I think about them to this day. Things of that sort are never forgotten, nor should they be.

- BRAD WILLIAMS

AIDE-DE-CAMP
Justin Milnor

There is one thing certain about the military, change can come quickly and without warning. It happened to me even though the war had been over for a couple of months.

I was going about my business as a platoon leader and with the additional assignment as company executive officer. Things were very dull and we were going through the motions of a training cycle. A 25-mile forced march with full combat gear, a mock attack on a sizeable hill defended by a sister company, small unit tactics, etc., the usual business of an infantry unit. We were bored.

One morning, I was ordered to report to Regimental Headquarters where I was told that I had been promoted to the job of Assistant S-3. The S-3 is responsible for plans and operations, which is a very responsible and important job. I have no idea why I received such a promotion, as it was quite a leap from platoon leader to Assistant S-3. It was not a promotion in rank (or pay) but I guess you could say, in status. I considered myself to be just an ordinary officer, not particularly outstanding. So I was quite amazed but liked the challenge. Our S-3 was a major and a WWII veteran - and a real warhorse. His name was Morrison, Major Morrison, and I liked and admired him. I truly believe that war was his game, what he lived for.

But he was as bored as everyone else was. There would be only three of us running the S-3 operations - Master Sergeant Williams, the Major, and myself. We did little or nothing. Sent down a few training directives to the line companies and that was about it. I quickly discovered that I didn't like the assignment and would have preferred to stay with my platoon. But as long as I was there, I hoped that the Major would teach me something about being in S-3. Writing up orders for different combat situations or running mock exercises on paper, anything to fill the hours. But that didn't happen. I'd go back to my tent in the middle of the day and sack out - no one cared.

War in the Land of the Morning Calm

This is kind of funny but true - in desperation I ordered a course in animal husbandry through the Army's Education Program or whatever it was called. I dreamt of leaving the Army, going back to Winter Park, Florida; where I had lived as a teenager, buying some land around Kissimmee, (which in those days was a real cow town) settling down and becoming a rancher. Had I pursued that dream, I might be wealthy today since my 'ranch' would have been right in the middle of what is now Disney World. Oh, well.

I guess it was about this period when our boredom was broken by a potent rumor. As I've said before, the Armed Forces live on and love a good rumor. Ours was a dilly. Our division was shipping out for French Indo-China to help the French forces there. The huge French base at Dien Bien Phu (in the northeast corner of what is now Viet Nam) was under assault by the Viet Minh (the communist movement sworn to throw the French out). The base was encircled and in deep trouble so the rumor seemed logical.

Major Morrison came alive, a gleam back in his eyes. There seemed to be excitement in the air, palpable, inexplicable, crazy, hard to believe, but I'm sure the majority of the division (including this poor, dumb lieutenant) was thrilled at the prospect of another fight. As it turned out, the rumor (if it was a rumor) failed to come to pass and we went back to our day-to-day tasks. The French lost the battle of Dien Bien Phu and were kicked out of French Indo China. As you know, less than ten years later our forces were fighting the communist Viet Cong in Viet Nam. Sadly, we know how that ended, in my opinion, due to poor leadership from the White House. Second place doesn't count in a war.

After the excitement of the rumor, we settled back into our lethargic state and I started receiving my lessons on animal husbandry. The lessons were about as dull as my work.

Shortly thereafter, Major Morrison told me to report to Colonel Howard, our Regimental Commander. Since his tent (combination office and living quarters) was right next to our S-3 tent I had seen

Episode Fifty-seven - Aide-de-Camp

the Colonel on several occasions, just in passing and with a respectful salute. He was a kindly gentleman and impressed me as being somewhat the fatherly type.

I entered his tent very nervously as I had no idea what to expect: "Sir, Lt. Milnor reporting as ordered." With a smart salute, of course. The Colonel told me to stand at ease and proceeded to tell me that our Division Commanding General was in need of a new aide as the current one was departing for the states. The Colonel went on to say, "Lt., each regiment will send a representative for the General's interview and it will be a great honor for that regiment whose officer is selected. Lt., you will represent our regiment and I will be pleased and honored if you are selected."

Being young, dumb and bullheaded I responded with, "Sir, with all due respect I don't want the job. I prefer not to be an aide to the General." The Colonel was not happy with my reply and informed me in no uncertain terms that I would report to Division Headquarters the next morning at 0900 and that I would present myself as an eager and qualified officer for the assignment. I said, "yes, sir," gave the colonel a salute, did an about face and got out of Dodge. In my mind, a general's aide was no more than a lackey and that did not appeal to me.

But as ordered, I was at Division Headquarters promptly at 0900 and was shown to some Colonel's office who would conduct the interview. He welcomed me warmly and said something about how pleased I must be to have been selected to represent my Regiment. He went on to ask me why I wanted the job as aide to the general and my response was the same that I had given my Regimental Commander - I did not want the assignment.

He was somewhat taken aback and asked me why then was I there for the interview. I explained to him that I was ordered to seek the job though I had told my Colonel I didn't want it. The interviewing colonel then asked what I wished to do and I replied that I would like to return to my company and resume my duties as platoon leader-executive officer. He dismissed me and I returned to Regimental Headquarters.

I suppose that had Colonel Howard explained to me that the job would only be for seven or eight months and that if I performed it in an exemplary manner, I could pretty much write my own ticket for my next assignment. I didn't give that scenario a thought - I just wanted to be a platoon leader. And I felt I could advance on my own merit without a boost from being a gofer for a general. With 20-20 hindsight, I suppose I should have willingly fought for that plum, as it would have certainly been an impressive part of my military record. Bottom line - I just didn't want the job. Had I been a little more mature, I would have at least thanked Colonel Howard for his interest in me - but I didn't. I packed my duffel bag and 24 hours later I was back with my platoon.

My guys welcomed me back and I felt at home once again and with no regrets. But there is a moral to this story for you young folks, if you have read this far. At some point in your current career, whatever it might be, someone up the chain of command might see potential in you and become your mentor. I didn't even know the meaning of the word. He or she might make themselves known. If so, accept their guidance with graciousness and appreciation. Ask for more responsibility, be of assistance to your mentor, set your goals high, and attain your objective through hard work. But one word of warning - don't be a brown nose. You will lose the respect of your co-workers and if your mentor is any kind of leader, you will lose his respect as well. There is a big difference between that kind of activity and hard work. Good luck.

- JUSTIN MILNOR

THE SWAGGER STICK
JIM CAMPBELL

There are times in the military when one is called upon to perform above and beyond the call of duty. I had such an occasion though the shooting had stopped two months prior.

Our Regimental Commander's tour was up so he rotated home. He was a gentleman and well liked and we were sorry to see him go. His replacement was a WWII veteran and we were not impressed. He seemed a bit pompous but since I was a lowly lieutenant I would have very little contact with the Colonel so I gave him little thought.

A few days after his arrival, to his credit he started making the rounds of all the units of the regiment. He dropped by our company for lunch (such as it was) and to meet our officers and men. During the course of our conversation, he announced that every officer in the Regiment would be required to carry a swagger stick. The cost would be $20.00 per and someone would be dispatched to Japan to arrange for the manufacture and purchase of said article!

By way of explanation, a swagger stick is the modern version of the old riding crop when the horse cavalry was an integral part of the Army. It had a legitimate purpose such as encouraging the horse to go a bit faster. I have the one that belonged to my father. It was also a pretty potent weapon.

But the swagger stick on the other hand, was strictly for show in as much as neat things like tanks, trucks, jeeps, and vehicles of all sorts eventually replaced the horse. Nor was the swagger stick a legitimate part of the uniform. However, I think many of the old line officers continued to carry them - General Patton, for example. In those days, a general officer could pretty much do as he pleased when it came to the uniform.

To get on with my story, being part Scot I was much annoyed at being ordered to spend $20.00 of my hard earned money on such a useless and pretentious object. A lieutenants' pay was about $150.00 a month and combat pay had of course ceased. So like any good soldier I fumed, griped, ranted, and cursed the Colonel, as did most of my fellow officers.

A day or so after the Colonel's visit my company commander called me to his tent and said, "Lieutenant, the Regimental Commander has selected you to go to Japan and see to the manufacture and delivery of the swagger sticks. You leave in 24 hours." I was thunder struck - I have no idea why I was selected for that task - but I was certainly going to rise to the occasion! As we say in the South, "My momma didn' raise no dumb chillun." To get out of "town" for a few days and escape the boredom was like manna from Heaven. I suddenly felt our Colonel was an exemplary leader and a king among kings. A gentleman of impeccable taste!

I hopped a military transport plane out of Kimpo airfield near Seoul and was on my way. At least my flight did not cost the taxpayer a dime as flights were going back and forth daily. The aircraft had no heat in the passenger compartment and I was certain that I would freeze to death before landing. However, we did fly over Mount Fuji and that was a beautiful and unforgettable sight.

When I arrived in Tokyo, I made some half-hearted attempts to find a source for the Colonel's brainchild. I did manage to find a black pearl for my future wife as she had indicated that she would love to have one. I also bought a cultured pearl necklace for her and she wore it with her wedding dress several months later. She married me!

I returned to Korea and reported to the Colonel that though I had sought out every source, no one was interested in making said swagger sticks. Actually, had I tried I could have found some enterprising Japanese who would have willingly and quickly filled our order. By then WWII had been over for some 8 years and the Japanese had embraced capitalism and democracy with open arms. Department stores were full of merchandise and the populace was eager to do business with anyone with a dollar - and I never sensed any feeling of animosity toward us. The assignment was truly a simple one. But I headed for "home" purposely empty-handed.

The Colonel didn't seem to be too upset about my failure and thanked me for my efforts. I imagine that through the grapevine he had gotten word that his idea was not too popular with his officer corps. I shudder to think what my men would have done had they seen me strolling around with a fancy swagger stick under arm. But as I said at the outset, sometimes one has to rise above and beyond the call of duty regardless of the sacrifice - and so I did.

- JIM CAMPBELL

THE OFFICERS' CLUB
Robert Ludlam

The war had been over several months. We had pulled off the line and set up in a training area complete with tents, cots, a Quonset mess hall for the men, showers made from oil drums, and fairly good food. At least it wasn't C-Rations. I don't remember where we were but not too far north of Seoul, the capitol of South Korea.

Sometime near Christmas, our Battalion Commander decided he wanted an Officers' Club. I thought that was a little strange. The war hadn't been over that long. I also felt like the enlisted guys and the NCOs should have a club before us hotshot officers. Your men always come first in my book. But no one asked for my opinion.

Then for some strange reason, I am appointed as the Club Officer (in addition to my other duties). The Army has someone in charge of everything - latrine orderlies, Troop Information and Education Officer, Sgt. of the Guard, Officer of the Day, Chief Chaplain, etc. By the way, in my 14-month vacation in Korea I never saw a Chaplain. I didn't think about it at the time and I'm sure there were many sincere men in the Chaplain Corp. They were, perhaps, short-handed. At any rate I was in charge of the club and who was I to argue with my superiors?

My first assignment, of course, was to stock the club with goodies including as much liquor as I could find. I checked out a two and a half ton truck and I took one of my guys as driver. I was on my own without a clue as to where all of this was to be obtained. But my young driver was a natural-born scrounger and con artist. There's one in every company.

We headed for Seoul, which I think by then was where Corp Headquarters was located. That meant abundant stuff of one sort or another. We found a Quartermaster Depot, pulled in, and explained our mission to the Sergeant-in-charge. We explained that we needed booze and snacks. Jake, my driver, pulled a captured Chinese bayonet and cap from under the driver seat and allowed as how the sergeant might like to take them home as war souvenirs. Naturally, the sergeant hadn't been anywhere near the war so he was impressed. I think I had a few dollars in script (issued to us in lieu of real money) with which I greased the Sergeant's palm. He was grateful. Very cooperative.

In short order, we had a truckload of beer and whiskey of all sorts, canned meats, cheese, soft drinks, stateside snacks, tables, chairs, glasses, etc. We headed back to base with quite a haul. To reimburse Jake for his diligence, I dropped off a couple of cases of booze for him and his pals. Always take care of your men.

With the help of a couple of volunteers I set the place up with a bar, chairs and tables, all the amenities. Some Korean workers had even built a working fireplace of large stones at one end of the building, which gave it some real character. Opening night was a roaring success. Christmas was just around the corner and we were ready to party.

We even had a professional entertainer drop in - Dick Contino and a couple of his back-up musicians were scheduled to put on a show for us. I doubt many people remember him.

Back stateside he was billed as the "Worlds' Greatest Accordionist" and had performed many times on the Ed Murrow TV Show and with some of the Big Bands. However, he also tried to dodge the draft but didn't succeed. The Army cut him some slack, I suppose, and put him in Special Services as an entertainer. Special Services was established several years before as a way of increasing morale by providing recreational facilities, entertainment, etc., for the military. So that's how he came to be in Korea and played for us at our grand opening. He was very talented. By the way, if there was ever a USO show in the neighborhood, we weren't invited.

As Dick played his accordion, we got drunker and drunker. One of my very inebriated pals decided to take the Battalion

Commander's Jeep for a spin. He managed to drive off with wheels spinning but within a hundred yards or so ran it up an incline and into a large tree. He escaped with minor cuts and bruises but the Jeep was in serious disrepair. He limped back to the party, somewhat chagrined. As I recall, the Battalion Commander was feeling no pain saying, "To Hell with it - Jeeps can be replaced, good Lieutenants are hard to find," and bought my buddy another drink. Camaraderie at it's very best.

As for me, sometime during the celebration I wandered off to get some much-needed fresh air and passed out cold, flat on my face on the main dirt road in the battalion area. It was freezing cold and snow was several inches deep. Fortunately, not much truck traffic that late at night so I didn't get squashed into the snow. Otherwise, I might not have been discovered until spring. But eventually, my buddies found me and hauled me back to our tent were I awakened the next morning with a huge hangover. I'm certain all the other battalion officers were suffering as well. I'm glad the Chinese didn't decide to restart the war just then. We'd have had to ask them for a 24-hour sobering up truce - or perhaps have them over for a drink or two. Unfortunately, I don't believe they had much of a sense of humor.

It occurs to me that none of us thanked Dick and his group for their entertainment (none of us were sober enough to think of that) so I'll do so now - belated thanks, Pvt. Contino for a nice evening!

(On the serious side, let me state that during combat I never saw any alcoholic beverage of any kind anywhere near us. And drugs were unheard of.)

- ROBERT LUDLAM

KIM Q BONG
AL TAYLOR

I consider myself to be very blessed. God has been so good to me. I had loving, caring parents, wonderful siblings, a loving wife and two great children. I also had a career in which I looked forward to going to work every day. I have good neighbors and many good and true friends. I lost my first wife, whom I loved, to an illness. And now I'm fortunate to have a second wife who also loves me. It doesn't get much better than that.

There is one thing, however, that I would change if given a second chance, a "do-over." His name was Kim Q Bong, a seven-year-old child and an orphan of the Korean War. He had been passed on to me by the platoon sergeant I was replacing. I was given no choice in the matter. How could I tell this small child that I didn't need him? - or so I thought, soon Kim became my constant companion. Wherever I happened to be and whatever I was doing, he wanted to be a part of it. In a matter of days, I knew he was someone very special.

Kim Q Bong on my right and Johnny.

He spoke English fluently and could write in our language as well. He was the smartest child I've ever known. My young brother back in the states and Kim wrote one another frequently. They became pen pals and friends, two different cultures and worlds apart.

I remember many a night returning to my bunker after long and exhausting fire missions, filthy dirty, dead tired and hungry. In a matter of minutes Kim would serve me with steaming powdered eggs with cheese and Spam cooked on a gasoline-fueled stove. And, of course, a canteen cup of hot coffee. I didn't ask how he came by the food but I knew. Like any good GI, he was an outstanding scrounger and often visited the cooks. They would give him odds and ends, which he turned into a great meal for me. No one could refuse him.

If my uniform was covered in grime and filth, which was the norm, Kim would have my extra set of clothing washed and awaiting me. He would then scrub, scrape and clean my boots until they were almost parade ground ready.

He was an extraordinary child and I know now that I loved him like a son. Time went on and soon it was my time to rotate home. All of my thoughts were consumed by that magic word. I passed Kim off to another platoon sergeant that promised to take care of him and who would assure his well-being. And I was gone.

I can't help but wonder what became of Kim. He could be many things-- a husband and father, a corporate executive, or perhaps a responsible leader serving his government and nation. I am to this day, 60 years later, troubled by the fact that I was so selfish and interested in my own well-being and thoughts of home that I didn't do more to insure the safety and a good future for that small child who was so dedicated to those of us he served.

I wish that somehow I had stayed in touch with him. Even better I wish that I could meet him face- to-face. What a reunion that would be - that would be my "do-over."

- AL TAYLOR

THE PROVOST MARSHAL
Al Taylor

Finally, I was heading home along with a lifelong friend. We had joined at the same time so now we were shipping out together after thirteen months of combat. We arrived in Yokahama from Korea and disembarked. The depot was one huge building or warehouse, and I suppose there must have been two or three thousand men awaiting orders. Bobby, my buddy and I got separated but some hours later he ended up in line right in back of me. Then we loaded up aboard ship and headed out.

After a couple of days at sea, a Captain approaches us and said, "M/Sgt., you and your friend come with me." He took us topside and direct to the Officers' Quarters. Then he said, "You two can share this cabin." Needless to say, I was somewhat mystified but then he went on to add, "Sgt., I have been appointed Provost Marshal of this ship a job I did not ask for and do not want. In fact, I just want to kick back and have a pleasant trip home. Therefore, I am appointing you as Assistant Provost Marshal. So, unless the ship is sinking, do not call me. Deal with it!"

The very next night, I get a call from one of the cooks in the ships galley saying there was a problem. I took Bobby and a couple of other guys not knowing what to expect. We entered the kitchen area to find a very young, drunk GI with both hands full of hot dogs. He had somehow broken into one of the food lockers and was draped with about five pounds of cold wieners.

I dismissed my group telling them I would handle the miscreant! I put him at attention and proceeded to raise the Devil: "You little jerk; you just spent a year in Hell. We're almost home and you pull a stunt like this that could put you in the brig for six months. Why ruin your life for a few hot dogs?" By now he was in tears and sobering up fast. I released him with a few final words: "If you step out of line by one inch or even cross my path, I will personally throw your worthless ass overboard." He hurriedly departed. Needless to say, I didn't see him again and I truly hope he returned to civilian life a better man.

The remainder of the trip was uneventful and pleasant and now all of my thoughts were on but one thing - home. My war was over.

- AL TAYLOR

HOMEWARD BOUND
JIM CAMPBELL

My orders had come through and I was heading home. I do not remember much about the goodbyes but I do remember getting on that little train that had carried us toward the war so many months ago. Now it was carrying me back to Inchon and the first leg of my journey back to the States.

We were at the Replacement Depot for a couple of days. I went to the PX and bought a Rolex watch for $90.00. It just felt good to spend a little money on something, anything. After all, we had received an extra $50.00 a month for combat pay so why not blow some of it? There was also an outdoor movie set up and I saw Leslie Caron in "An American in Paris." That always stuck in my mind and in later years, if her name was mentioned I thought of that night passing the time, waiting to ship out. Strange memories.

Our day finally came and we boarded a small US Navy ship. We were just in time for lunch - there were about twelve of us - and we were invited by the ship's officers to their mess hall (or whatever the eating facility is called in the Navy). I was stunned to see a white tablecloth, nice silverware, napkins, and stewards in white jackets serving us, etc., and half a fresh honeydew melon was placed in front of me! I don't remember the rest of the meal but I remember that melon. I was thinking, "Why hadn't I joined the Navy?"

We were transported to a troop ship - I don't recall where the exchange took place. The harbor at Inchon was inadequate at that time to handle large vessels. My memory is a bit fuzzy but at some point we were on our way to Seattle. I was a little disappointed that we weren't going back to San Francisco as I dreamed of seeing the Golden Gate Bridge on the way in, not the way out!

But I was not complaining. We were headed home and that was all that mattered. What did matter was that a few days out, we hit a ferocious storm I was pretty much spellbound by the fury of nature and managed to find a small deck just under the bridge of the ship.

No one knew I was there and it would have probably been off limits to anyone but the crew. But no one else was anywhere to be seen so I had the view all to myself. And what a view! The wind was howling, the waves were tremendous and the ship was plowing straight into them. A troop ship is pretty large and I'd guess the bow was probably fifty feet from the water line to the deck - and it would disappear under every oncoming monstrous roller. I'd watch the bow disappear and wonder if it was going to resurface. Water was boiling across and over the deck almost back to the bridge.

I stayed there, fascinated, for an hour or so. I was pretty much worn out from just hanging on as well as being wet and cold. The storm eventually abated and the remainder of the trip was calm and uneventful. Had I been washed overboard, no one would have known until we checked off the ship in Seattle. I guess I'd have been declared as a MASS - Missing at Sea, Stupid. But it was an experience I'll never forget and seemed to be a fitting end to my Korean tour of duty.

Episode Sixty-two - Homeward Bound

We pulled in to Puget Sound after darkness had settled in. Our progress was very slow but the sight of the shoreline was a welcome one as well as very beautiful. Lights were on here and there in the many small towns lining the coast, blinking like so many diamonds and jewels. The stars, in a cloudless sky, seemed to be welcoming us home. All in all, it was a magical night.

We docked at the port of Seattle. An Army band was on hand along with a few families awaiting their loved ones. All of the insignias of the divisions, corps, etc. that fought in Korea were on display on the sides of the building where we debarked. It wasn't much of a celebration but we all shared one thought - we were about to step foot back into the United States of America!

We were bussed to Fort Lewis, not far from Seattle, to complete the necessary paperwork on which the military thrives - pay records, leave time, medical checks, next assignment, etc., and then we were on our way HOME.

I hopped the first commercial flight out of Seattle to Atlanta. One of my friends was with me. Somehow, he was still celebrating our return home and was falling down, out of his mind, drunk as we boarded the aircraft. I had to practically carry him aboard. It was a very embarrassing moment but I suppose the other passengers understood. Upon arrival in Atlanta, my first stop was at the Henry Grady Hotel in downtown Atlanta. For some reason, I wanted to have dinner there, as it had been a place where a former girlfriend and I had frequently eaten. Old memories.

The next morning I headed for a store to purchase civvies as I had only my uniform. I recall walking down Peachtree Street, in uniform, wearing a six-inch handlebar mustache. Passers-by looked at me as though I were from Mars - dogs barked, children cried, women fainted and strong men turned their backs. World War II had ended eight years earlier. I suppose the thrill of that victory was over and I don't believe the public knew the significance of the Korean War. There was no "Welcome home, Lt." There was no "Thank you for your service." Thankfully, today such comments are welcome and common practice as our military is so involved worldwide in the war against Islamic Terrorism. But in 1953 we were already members of the Forgotten War. Welcome home, soldier.

- JIM CAMPBELL

MY GUARDIAN ANGEL
Jim Campbell

This is not a war story and perhaps should not be included here. However, it has stuck in my mind for many, many years so those of you who believe in the paranormal might appreciate it.

I had received my orders for Korea along with 30 days leave time. My parents and little sister were visiting my older sister and her family who were then living in northern California.

Having nothing better to do, I decided to drive cross-country through the western states and then up the length of California to Marysville. I had purchased a .45 caliber revolver to take along to Korea. I was a poor shot with the Government Issue Model 1911 Colt .45 semi-automatic so I thought the revolver might be a better bet. And it was brutal in appearance, very intimidating. Strapped to my thigh, I looked the part of a western gunslinger. Or so I thought. (A month later when I met my platoon in Korea - with the six-shooter hanging off my hip, I know my forty young soldiers said, "Who *is* this guy!?")

Before leaving my training company, I told my supply sergeant of my need to practice so he handed me a couple of hundred rounds of ammo for my use when I got to the desert areas out west. I fully intended to improve my ability with a handgun. As I drove through Texas, New Mexico, Arizona, I frightened many a jackrabbit with that cannon.

Traffic was sparse in those days - I rolled down the window and shot on the run - or stopped and blasted away at a few innocent cactus plants.

I had a pleasant visit with my folks in Marysville but then it was time to report to Camp Stoneman (near San Francisco) for my departure toward war and the unknown. My folks, accompanied by my little sister, decided to drive me there and then take my car back across the states to our home in Georgia.

Looking back, I know that was a terribly sad moment particularly for my mother. They dropped me off at the front gate. I picked up my B-4 bag (I think that's what it was called) holding all of my uniforms, etc., that would be needed for the trip and Korea. We said our goodbyes' of which I remember little. My mind was detached. No time for tears. Would I ever see them again? I turned my back and knew that my world was about to change. A day or two later I was on a troop ship sailing off to war.

Fast-forward forty years. For some reason the subject of Korea came up in a conversation with my little sister (11 years younger). She told me that after they dropped me off at Camp Stoneman and had been on the road two or three days (she was eleven or twelve at the time), the following conversation took place between her and our mother. Melissa, snoozing on the back seat, said Mom turned to her and said, "What did you say, Melissa?" She replied that she had said nothing. A few moments later my mother repeated the question and Melissa asked her what she had heard.

Mom answered, "No, it wasn't you, it was Bessemary." Bessemary was her younger sister and the two of them shared a love that was unbreakable. Unfortunately, she died of breast cancer around 45 years of age and was staying with us at the time. That was in 1948. In fact, I had been home only a short time from my first tour in Korea. Aunt Bessemary's death was a sad event and I know my mother must have been heart-broken.

To get back to the conversation, my sister asked our mother what she had heard. Mom replied that Aunt Bessemary had said to her, "Beanie, (her nickname for her sister) don't worry about James. I will watch over him." Melissa said that my mother was never worried for my safety after those words from her dead sister. And I did come home from Korea, sound in mind (more or less) and body. I always thought our Battalion was the most fortunate in Korea; a huge battle might be just a half-mile from us but we weren't needed. I took patrols into enemy territory and found no one. Others died in that endeavor. We were hit nightly by Chinese artillery. We escaped injury. Friends in other units were killed or wounded. The Chinese mounted a huge offensive. We were sent to stop them. They retreated before we got there. Perhaps I was just lucky - or was it something else?

Logic tells me that my mother dreamt that conversation. She was probably dozing in the car. After all, thousands of men died in Korea. Surely, they had loved ones up above - why were they not protected? Why was I? Did Aunt Bessemary really watch over me? I like to imagine that she did. You decide. Perhaps someday in a more perfect world or place I can thank her.

- JIM CAMPBELL

EPILOGUE

I've saved the worst for the last so the following few pages are not required reading. Just a lot the reminiscing from one who has had the good fortune to lead a pretty darned good life. Perhaps however, some of you old guys (and I believe I am included in that category) might read a passage and say, "Yea, I remember that!" As for you of the younger generation, don't bother - you'll probably be bored to death. The world today is so far from my world as a kid growing up in the forties as to be unimaginable to the current crop of youngsters.

In those days, we came home from school to a waiting and loving mother. We played outdoors in the fresh air inventing games and ways to amuse ourselves. Bag swings (one of my buddies broke a leg jumping for one), bike races, tag football, marbles, Boy Scouts and Sea Scouts, sailing, swimming, working, camping, etc. The local college had a dock on the lake with a 60-foot diving tower. During WWII, Navy recruits were brought over from a nearby naval station and were required to jump from that platform so that they would have no fear of heights should they have to abandon a sinking ship. We DOVE from it. Now THAT was entertainment.

There were radio programs that were entertaining and scary like "Lights Out." We would huddle around so as not to miss a word. Or great music like the Saturday night program, "The Hit Parade." What music! To our young ears it was wonderful. That was the era of the Big Bands like Tommy and Jimmy Dorsey, Glen Miller, Ray Anthony, Nelson Riddle, Les Brown, Paul Weston, Artie Shaw and on and on. And of course, there was Jitterbugging. Music of those days (for the most part) had melodies and words that made sense. Not now. WWII produced some of the most beautiful and romantic love songs ever written.

As for work, most of us had part-time jobs. An allowance for a kid was pretty much unknown. My buddy, Johnny, was an usher in the only theater in town. I was a soda jerk in the drug store across the street. In those days, a drug store was also the forerunner of what we now call a fast food place. We served sandwiches (no hamburgers - I don't believe they had been invented at that time!), ice cream, sundaes, sodas, etc. A chocolate soda would consist of a couple of scoops of ice cream, two or three shots of chocolate syrup in a tall glass, which was then filled with soda (carbonated) water. The soda water was dispensed from a sealed container under the counter by jerking the handle - thus the name, soda jerk. Bottled drinks like Coca-Cola were of course plentiful. But nothing surpassed the taste of a "Fountain Coke" - a glass full of ice with a couple of squirts (from the fountain) of Coca-Cola syrup and then filled with carbonated water. Unbelievable.

We did other jobs as well. An unforgettable one consisted of spending most of a summer cleaning equipment in the local orange packinghouses. In those days, oranges were run through a huge overhead metal vat and sprayed with wax and an orange colorant. Our job (about six of us kids) was to get inside the vat and scrape all the orange wax off of the four walls, ceiling, and floor. It was a nasty job and we would return home in the evening looking like imitation Indians. And worse, the dye was almost impossible to wash off even with constant scrubbing. And what pretty girl would have a date with a guy looking like a Caucasian Comanche (if there were such)?

So you young folks are excused. Go back to your computers, your cell phones, IPod, IPhones, IPads, Twitter, Texting, and YouTube. Blackberry, TV, computers, computer games, etc., etc. But when you see someone in the uniform of our armed forces, shake his or her hand and thank that person for literally putting their lives on the line to give freedom to those in this world who don't have it - and for protecting ours. Should you have the good fortune to see a WWII veteran, give that person a special hug. Had it not been for their sacrifices, you might never have been born.

World War II ended in the summer of 1945. I was sixteen years of age and like most kids of that era, was disappointed that I had not had an opportunity to serve our country. The summer before I had thought of signing on with the Merchant Marine as I figured they had

Epilogue

no age requirements. One of my high school buddies had joined them in his junior year of high school. He was probably the dumbest kid in our class; I ran a close second. Anyway, Charlie came home on leave and I asked him what was his job on board a ship. Turns out he was an oiler which he described as standing in the engine room and oiling (with a big can and spout) the pistons and other moving parts of the equipment for about ten hours at a stretch. That didn't sound too exciting so I gave up on that plan. The idea of being sunk by a German U-Boat in the middle of the cold North Atlantic wasn't very appealing either.

Instead I, along with my good friend Johnny Girardeau, decided to join the Army. I had to wait to turn 17 and also had to have the approval of my parents. My mother was not at all happy. She hated to think of her little boy going off to some faraway land. We were not wealthy, not poor, but my mother knew the value of a dollar. She had to be frugal as we lived on my father's retirement pay, which wasn't much. Also this was a time of rationing - sugar, meat, cigarettes, gas, heating oil and on and on. A family had to be thrifty with the ration stamps as well. When I reminded her that I would be eligible for the GI Bill and a college education after my tour of duty, she promptly approved. I did have enough common sense to know that a college degree was something of value and that it would be worth the effort to get one.

Our parents saw us off on a Greyhound bus heading for Boca Raton, Florida, where we were to be inducted. I remember that the Army had taken over an old and large hotel for their purposes. There wasn't much else around the area. Our first experience was the physical exam including every shot known to mankind. It seems that the biggest, toughest looking recruits were the ones that passed out when they approached the needle. One of the medics pretended he had palsy with his hands shaking fiercely as he got ready to jab the victims arm. That really looked ominous and scared the Hell out of a few more recruits.

We then stripped with just a towel around our waists and were told to walk toward a couple of doctors seated at desks across what must have been at one time the ballroom. There the doctors dispatched the recruits to one of two lines – one left and one to the right. I noticed that the left lane seemed to be made up of rather poor specimens and figured they were going to be assigned to non-combat units. I wanted to be an Infantryman but knew my flat feet would be a problem. So I kind of duck walked by trying to pull up my flat arches while walking toward the doctor.

As I approached he said, "Son, what is the MATTER with your feet?" I readily replied that my feet were fine and had never given me a problem. I could see that he was having difficulty containing a smile and I suppose he knew what I was about. He promptly directed me to the line of future combat soldiers for which I was most pleased. After all the medical stuff, we were sworn in and became soldiers in the United States Army. It was a proud moment.

Then we were loaded on a bus to Fort McClellan, Alabama, where we would take Basic Infantry Training. I was delighted though it was June and hotter than Hades when we arrived at our destination. We were issued uniforms, bedding, rifles, etc. and assigned to a training company. As I recall, the living quarters were fairly small with a mattress, cot, footlocker, etc., for each of us. When making up the cot in the morning, the blankets had to be tight to the point that when the inspecting sergeant dropped a quarter in the middle of the cot, the quarter had better bounce. Otherwise, the miscreant would find himself doing laps around the area.

The chow hall was close by and if we weren't in the field, took all of our meals there. We quickly learned to keep a 25-cent pocket novel with us at all times as we stood in interminable lines for one thing or another - including food. I don't remember much about the chow - it must have been edible as none of us starved. However, if you were unlucky enough to be toward the end of the line you'd have scant minutes to eat before having to head back to training.

Epilogue

Basic lasted eight weeks but those were two of the hottest months in Alabama - June and July. Looking back, I sometimes wonder how we endured the heat. Most of our training was outdoors with very little classroom work. We were required to take salt tablets every morning and I suppose that was part of our salvation. Also, the cadre was very careful to give us a fifteen-minute break every hour. If we were doing bayonet drill or something strenuous of that sort, those breaks were lifesavers. We'd flop down on the ground, helmet for a pillow, and be asleep in a matter of seconds. And that 15-minute break seemed Heaven sent.

As for bayonet training it was pretty tough. The instructor was on a large raised platform with all of us neophytes surrounding him. The M-1 rifle (which weighed nine pounds plus) had a hinged metal butt plate. The wooden stock was drilled out to hold a metal cleaning tool, which weighed several ounces. The hinge was very stiff and required a lot of broken thumbnails to open and remove said cleaning tool.

The instructor would give a command such as, "Long thrust, vertical butt stroke, slash, withdraw, and recover!" On the withdrawal command, the recruit was supposed to snap the rifle backward so sharply that the cleaning tool would fly out and hit the ground. That was almost impossible particularly since none of us had the good sense to lubricate the hinge and make it easier. At any rate, one hot afternoon I succeeded in popping the hinge open and out flew the cleaning tool! The instructor stopped, looked down, and announced to all 200 of us: "What's the matter with you guys? This little 110 pound 15 year-old kid here snapped his out with no problem. Get with it!" I didn't know whether to be embarrassed or proud - but I felt pretty good about myself. No one else did it at any of the following sessions, including me.

My favorite part of our training was learning to use the various Infantry weapons: the M-1 rifle, the M-2 carbine, the BAR, 60mm mortars, .30 caliber light machine gun, grenades, .45 caliber pistol, etc. We spent hours on the rifle range and I loved it. I was probably the only recruit in the Army that even enjoyed pulling targets in the pits. I fired expert with the M-1 rifle and was very proud of that achievement, as it was difficult to attain that level of marksmanship. I also received the Expert Grenade Badge. I always laughed about that. The recruit would get into a large deep hole with the instructor. He would hand a grenade to the recruit who would then pull the pin and throw the grenade as far as possible. If the young trainee didn't panic and drop the grenade in the pit with the instructor and himself thus killing both, he was awarded the Expert Badge!

Occasionally in the evening at the end of a hard day in the field, our platoon sergeant would break out the boxing gloves and ask if anyone wanted to go a few rounds. I was probably the smallest kid around but figured I was tough as anyone. So one evening, I said, "Give me the gloves, Sarge - I'll take on anyone here!" A tall, gangly, fellow recruit stepped forward, put on the gloves, and proceeded to beat the crap out of me. The sergeant wisely stepped in before I got killed and a few minutes later, we all returned to our barracks. I discovered later that my young opponent had been a Junior Golden Gloves champ from New Mexico! That made me feel a little better about my poor performance.

Our eight weeks of training soon ended and after a short leave (of which I remember very little) we were on our way by troop train to San Francisco, California! I believe it took five days to reach our destination and that trip was so horrible I remember little of it. We were packed into day coaches that were probably meant to seat 80 adults. There must have been 200 of us in each car. We sat on our duffel bags in the aisle and I don't know how we slept. Those who were lucky enough to get seats had a little comfort but very little. As for using the bathrooms (two per coach), I don't even remember how that went. Nor do I remember what or where we ate - there was certainly no dining car with white tablecloths. Whoever was responsible for that disaster should have been court-martialed.

We finally arrived in Frisco exhausted and in ill humor. Then after getting off the train, we had to walk carrying our equipment

Epilogue

about a mile in steaming heat. My duffel bag probably weighed as much as my small body. In fact, some of my buddies offered to help but I was too proud for that and struggled along with the rest of our group. I would have eaten dirt before accepting any assistance. I don't remember what happened after that but we obviously reported to some higher authority and there we were given three-day passes! Johnny was still with me so the two of us immediately took off for Los Angeles to see Hollywood.

We had very little money so we must have slept in the cheapest hotel in town. We walked around taking in the sights and gawking like any tourist. One night, we went to a radio show (which was free). In those days, radio programs were broadcast live and generally in front of an audience. I believe one of the most popular was the Saturday Night Hit Parade sponsored by Lucky Strike cigarettes. Their slogan during the war years was "Lucky Strike Green Has Gone to War." Their cigarette packages prior to the war were predominately a dark green. It seems that the chemical needed for that color was also needed for the war effort in some form. So Lucky Strike packages dropped the dark green and were predominately white during those four years.

The show we happened upon was "The Studebaker Hour," which consisted of a lot of big band music provided by a great orchestra and a beautiful young blonde vocalist. She was drop-dead gorgeous. I suppose, as we were in uniform, we were given seats dead center, and about three rows back from the stage.

I was enchanted with the young singer and could not take my eyes off of her. At the conclusion of the show, the curtain was drawn and we stood up to leave. As I got to my feet, the lovely young vocalist parted the curtain, looked at me, and said, "Come back stage!" I grabbed hold of Johnny and told him; he promptly said I was bonkers and proceeded to walk down the aisle toward the exit. Johnny was an experienced ladies' man - I was a klutz. Without his support I was way too shy, bashful, and dumb to go alone. Reluctantly, I followed him out the door. Man, was I ever disappointed. I've always wondered what would have happened that night had we accepted her invitation. I'm sure she felt sorry for us, as we obviously were a couple of very raw recruits – shaved heads, ill-fitting new uniforms, awkward and heading for parts unknown. But she sure made me happy for an hour or so.

We reported back to our unit and soon found ourselves at Camp Stoneman, California, where we shipped out for our next destination. Johnny was to leave at a later date so I doubted we'd ever see each other again. Our ship was bound for the Philippines, which sounded pretty good to me. I remember passing under the Golden Gate Bridge and standing at the fantail of the ship until the bridge was no longer visible. A somewhat sad moment as that would be my last sight of the good old United States for quite a while.

The voyage was actually pleasant. The weather was warm and sunny and the food pretty decent. We had nothing in particular to do so we sat around on deck playing cards or shooting craps. Since none of us had much money, gambling losses were pretty minimal. Most of us slept on deck at night as the troop compartments down below were stuffy and dismal, not to mention the fact that some of the guys were seasick and throwing up all over the place. Not a nice odor plus it made for a very slick and dangerous flooring.

One of the amazing things about the voyage was the fact that when we crossed the 180th Meridian, a ceremony was held topside and every GI on that ship received a colorful 8x10 certificate entitled, " Domain of the Golden Dragon" with a lot of pre-printed humorous verbiage. More amazing was that every certificate had information TYPED on it giving the name of the recipient. the day, month and year of the crossing, the latitude and longitude, the name of the ship (USAT J.H. McRae), and the signature of the issuing officer (The Golden Dragon), Darwin L. Coleman. I think Captain Coleman cheated and used a rubber stamp. Some poor bunch of Army guys were drafted to do all that typing. They must have been at the job for days considering that there were probably three or four thousand men aboard the ship. I was thankful I didn't get that duty! Playing poker topside was a lot more entertaining. Oddly enough, I still have that certificate, framed and hanging in my den.

The voyage was probably two weeks in duration. We finally reached Manila where we debarked and headed for the Replacement Depot to receive our orders. It didn't take long for the rumors to start - we were going to be assigned to the 86th Infantry Division, the Black Hawks. Our mission was (supposedly) to seek out and destroy the Hukbalahaps. The Huks were a communist group formed in 1942 shortly after the beginning of WWII to fight the Japanese who had invaded their islands. After the defeat of the Japanese, the Huks goal was to overthrow the pro-western leaders of their newly independent country. In a conversation with a lady who lived in the Philippines during that era, she claimed that the Huks were simply an extreme nationalist movement. Darned extreme I would say as we heard rifle fire almost every night. They didn't like Americans.

We slept in open sided 12-man squad tents. Our canvas cots had mosquito nets suspended from T-bars at each end with the nets draping to the wooden floor. One night after about four hours of sleep, I became aware of a presence standing at the head of my bunk. I opened my eyes just enough to make out the form of a man inches from my head. Not good. My rifle was under my cot out of reach. I pondered a few more seconds but knew that I was not going to lie there and get my throat cut. I came leaping out of the bed enshrouded in my netting and screaming like an Apache. The bad guy took off and all my sleeping buddies hit the floor. I told them what happened, things calmed down, and we went back to our bunks. Apparently, our perimeter security was not very good!

However, the rumor that we would be fighting the Huks was, as usual, not true. Most of us were truly disappointed that we were not going to become real combat soldiers and fight somebody! Pretty crazy. Instead, our group was assigned to sort mail in the Army Post Office for the next couple of weeks! What a letdown. A few days later I was standing in the chow line when someone tapped me on the shoulder. I turned and there was my buddy, Johnny. His ship pulled out a day or so after ours, broke down a few hundred miles out and was towed to Honolulu. All the troops were given shore leave and had a great week of enjoying the beaches, the beautiful women, good food, etc.; I was envious needless to say.

Our third week in Manila brought new orders. We were going to Korea. Where in the Hell was that? World maps came out and we found it - not far from Japan so it couldn't be too bad. Little did we know. We loaded aboard ship and a few days later landed at Inchon on the west coast of Korea. At the Replacement Depot I was assigned to the 7th Infantry Division, 32nd Infantry Regiment. Johnny was assigned to a Military Police Company so we split up once again.

I reported to Regimental Headquarters. The Regimental Sergeant Major's name was also Campbell. He had looked at my records and saw that I (in addition to high school) had also attended a business school. So I got stuck in the Regimental S-1 office (Adjutants Office) as a clerk-typist. I was not too pleased with the assignment, as I wanted to be a rifleman - even though there was no war on going. Of course, I wasn't given a choice - the Army is peculiar that way.

We were billeted in old Japanese Army two-story brick barracks. They were well built but had a few flaws - no heat, no plumbing, no running water, no electricity, no toilets. Nothing. Each building did have its own mess hall and kitchen. The food was fairly awful - powdered eggs, instant coffee, dehydrated mashed potatoes, etc.; the powdered eggs always had somewhat of a green tint about them. I learned to drink 180° coffee from a metal canteen cup at breakfast - for warmth. Huddled over the cup, it was a great hand warmer as well. Like the rest of the building the mess hall had no heat and at six AM on a winter morn, the temperature inside was the same as outside - 20°, more or less.

Our sleeping quarters consisted of squad size rooms with bunks, footlockers, wall cabinet, and a warm sleeping bag. Heat consisted of a pot-bellied stove and firewood. Bathing was done from heating water in our helmets on the stove. There was always a water trailer parked in front of the barracks from which we would draw water for bathing, brushing our teeth, etc., but there was a small problem; the faucets of the trailer would generally freeze and often, the water in the trailer would do the same. The few months that I was in that assignment I never remember having a real bath or a shower. We must have used a lot of after-shave lotion.

One of the guys had a battery-operated radio and every morning at 0600 (6:00 AM) we were awakened to Stan Kenton's Big Band playing his famous rendition of "Intermission Riff" - and the announcer saying, "This broadcast is coming to you courtesy of your Armed Forces Radio Network, from Seoul, Korea." A touch of home and when I hear that song even now, I can't help but think of those long ago lonely days.

Somehow, Johnny and I got in touch with one another and I visited him at his MP Company, a few miles from our headquarters. His assignment was pretty neat - he was being taught to train dogs for various duties such as scout dogs, attack dogs, sentry dogs, etc. Most of the dogs were German Shepherds. Johnny brought out two beautiful animals and he told me that those two dogs had once belonged to Adolph Hitler. I read that Hitler kept quite a number of shepherds on hand. If he was a true animal lover, that would have been the only decent thing about the man. I returned to my unit and the next time I saw Johnny was some fifty years later. We had finally reconnected in civilian life but sadly he died a year after our reunion. We had looked forward to continuing our almost life-long friendship.

Being stationed at Regimental Headquarters did have one advantage. The Army had taken over a fairly decent building not far from our area and set up a pretty good library. Since there was no other form of entertainment, I made frequent trips there and kept a stock of reading material on hand. I found out that being somewhat educated had its advantages. One afternoon while I was browsing the aisles, lo and behold, there in front of me was a beautiful young blonde American girl of about sixteen. I was awestruck. Somehow, I mustered the nerve to speak and we struck up a conversation. Turns out her father was a Lt. Colonel in our division and mother and daughter were there with him living in dependent housing quarters not far from our barracks. I guess we met a couple of times at the library and then one afternoon, she asked me over to have dinner with her and her parents. I was bashful and inept with the opposite sex but I readily accepted her invitation. Her parents were very nice and I enjoyed the visits. However, they shortly came to an end as I had asked my CO to transfer me to a line company.

I was bored to death with my job as a clerk even though I had by that time earned three stripes. He approved my request and I was on my way to Fox Company, 2nd Battalion, 32nd Infantry Regiment. I said goodbye to Joan, promised to write, and was on my way. I never wrote her and always felt guilty about not corresponding. So Joan McLendon, where ever you are, please accept my long delayed apologies.

Fox Company was situated practically on the 38th Parallel, the demarcation line between North and South Korea near Kaesong. My assignment was squad leader in a rifle platoon of the company. Living conditions weren't great but compared to what I had been used to, not bad. Our quarters were Quonset huts, we had a mess hall and kitchen, and the weather had warmed up so being cold was no longer a problem. But we still had no running water, no showers, and no bathing facilities. I don't remember anything about the food, but since someone was always on guard duty, the mess hall always had something ready for the changing shifts.

Our company was at the base of a small hill and the 38th parallel ran right across the top of it. We would often go up there and look at our future adversaries a couple of hundred yards or so on the other side of the hill. The Russian advisors could be clearly seen in training sessions with their North Korean protégés. This was early 1947 and we were certainly not geared up for a fight, which came only three years later.

Epilogue

We had no defensive positions in place, no artillery support, no patrol activity, no minefields, no barbwire, no trenches, no nothing. Occasionally, out of boredom I'd grab a couple of guys and take off in a jeep driving for miles alongside the parallel and never see another American unit. We were more like a stateside garrison outfit. We didn't even train. Even odder, our ammo was locked up in a storage room due to the fact that one of the men went berserk a couple of months before I arrived and murdered his platoon sergeant. Had the North Koreans attacked along the parallel in those days, I don't think we could have stopped them until they got to Seattle. I know our unit would have been annihilated in a matter of minutes. Bad situation.

My tour of duty in Korea ended and I was soon back in Inchon boarding a troop ship for home. I don't recall much about the voyage other than we hit a sizeable storm. I was in the chow line at the time. The mess hall floor was slick with spilled liquids of all sorts (including men vomiting) as the ship rolled from side to side. My feet went out from under me and I shot across that mess hall on my butt and slammed into the bulkhead. My right foot took the brunt of the impact and crumpled under me with much pain. It felt as though something might be broken but I was afraid to report it to the medics for fear my discharge might be delayed. So I limped off the ship, went through all the paper work and once again found myself a civilian.

Four of us hopped a Greyhound Bus and headed for the East Coast. Our first stop was Denver, Colorado, where we stayed in The Brown Palace Hotel. We were too tired to enjoy the town but I do remember luxuriating in a hot bath and a good meal. We rented a car, drove it to Atlanta and there took a commercial flight home. My short tour in the United States Army had, to say the least, been interesting. Our government kept its promise and I began college on the GI Bill shortly after my arrival back in civilization.

In the summer of 1950, I was at Laval University in Canada, trying to master the French language (I never did). The Korean War broke out in June of that year, and a couple of months later I was called back to active duty. I had completed my sophomore year at the School of Foreign Service, Georgetown University, in Washington, D.C. I was to enter advanced ROTC (Infantry) the coming fall semester and would receive my commission as a 2nd Lt. upon graduation.

I was torn between going back on active duty as called or continuing my education and getting my commission. Fortunately, I had time to go back to Georgetown and told our PMS&T (Professor of Military Science and Tactics) a Major in the Army, of my dilemma. I felt duty bound to go but I wanted that commission. The Major said to me, "Jim, finish your education and get your commission. The war will still be ongoing when you graduate and you will probably be needed more then, than now." His meaning was pretty clear - 2nd Lieutenants are very expendable so there will always be a demand!

I took his advice with some sense of guilt, finished my college education, received my commission as a young 2nd Lt. of Infantry (to use an old term), Regular Army, which is what I wanted, and rejoined the military in June of 1952. And true to the Major's words I soon found myself back in Korea as a young combat platoon leader. Fortunately, his inference concerning the premature deaths of many young lieutenants did not come true in my case. For that I was grateful but I often think of those many brave members of our military who were wounded or gave their lives in Korea, "to defend a country they never knew and a people they never met."

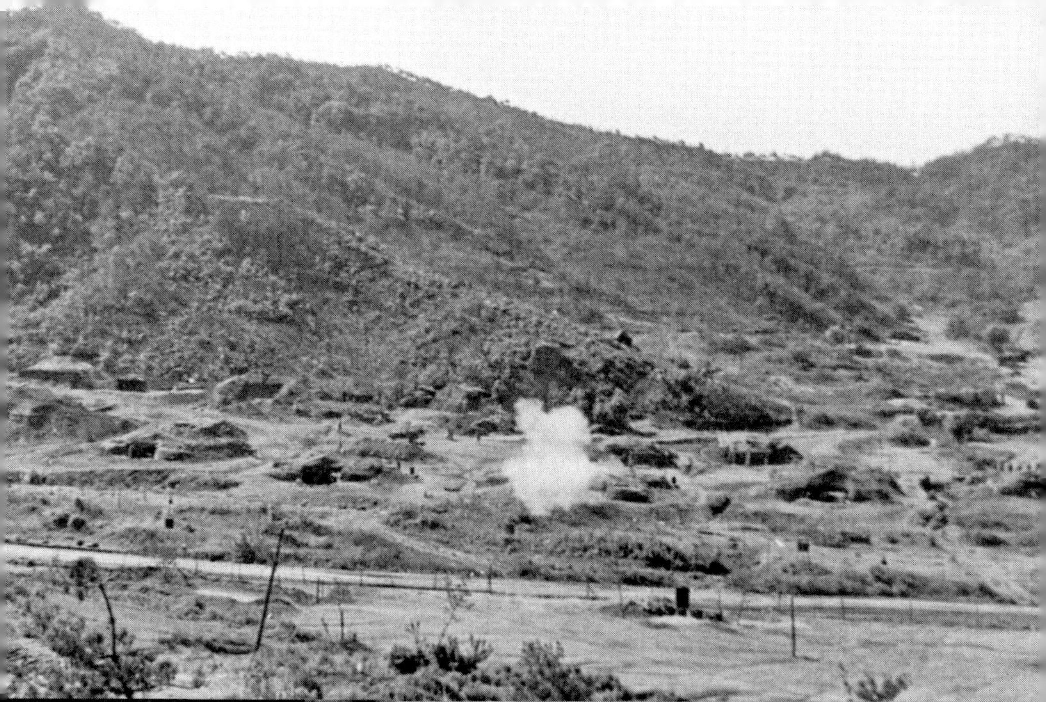

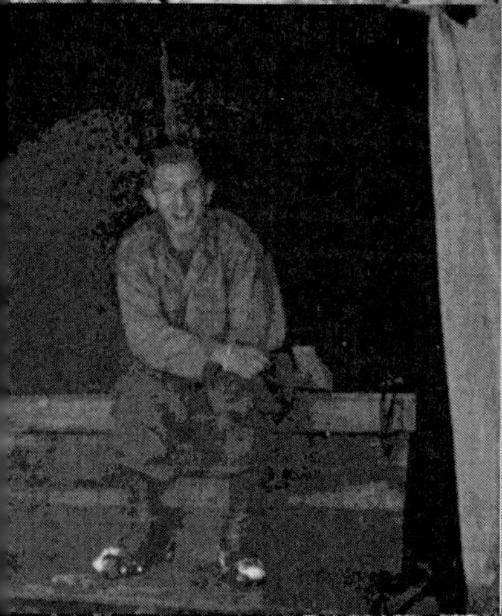

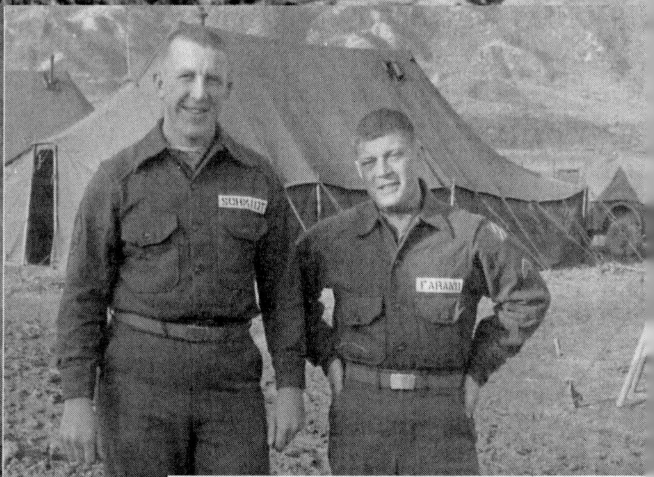
SCHMIDT

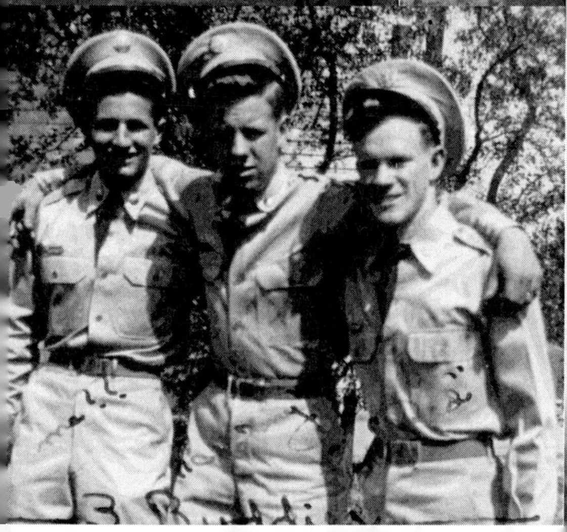

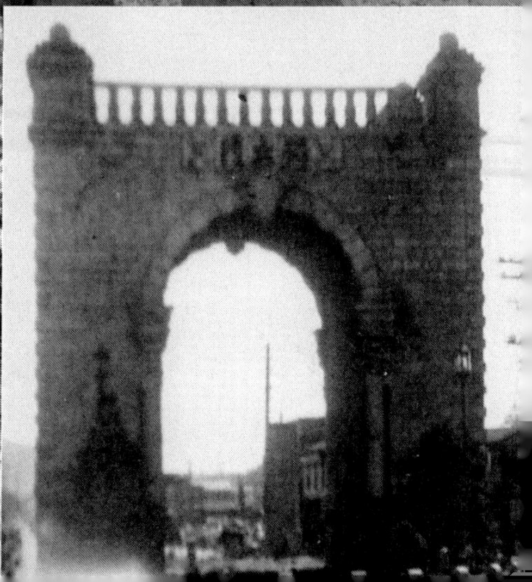

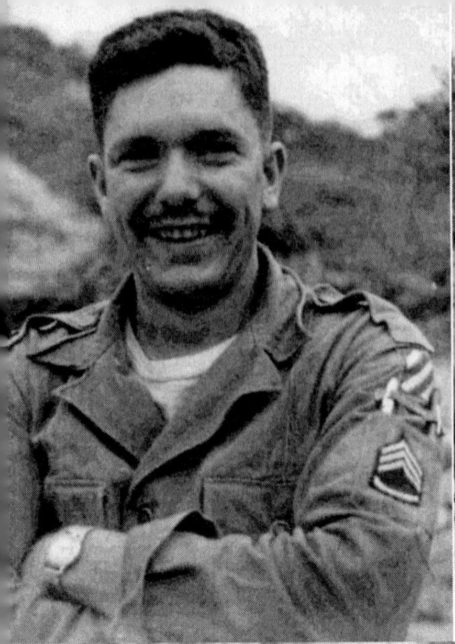

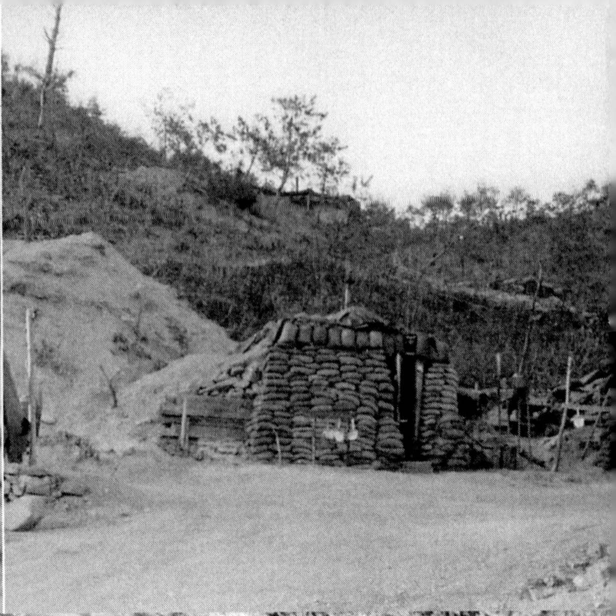

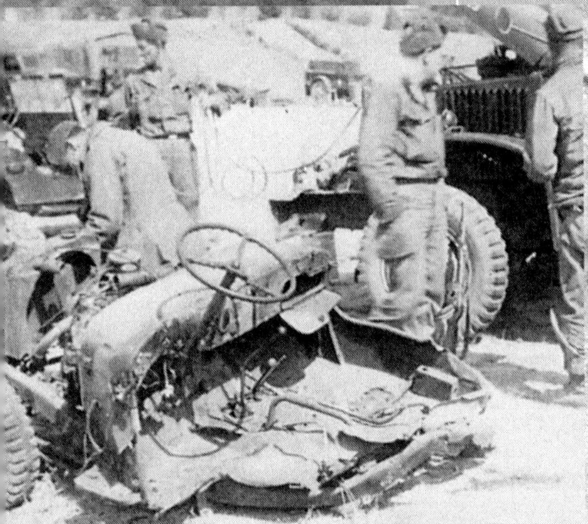

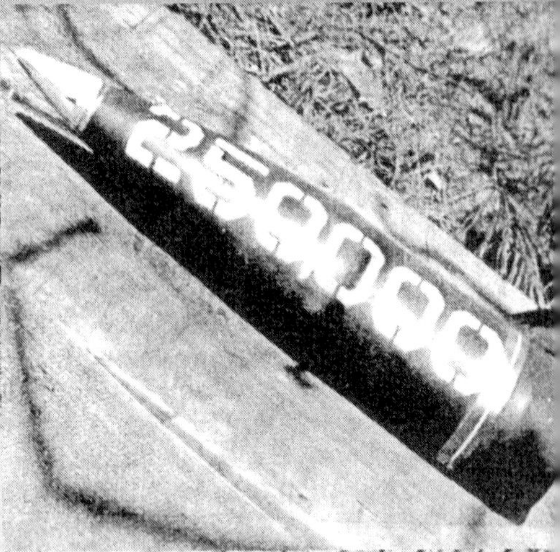

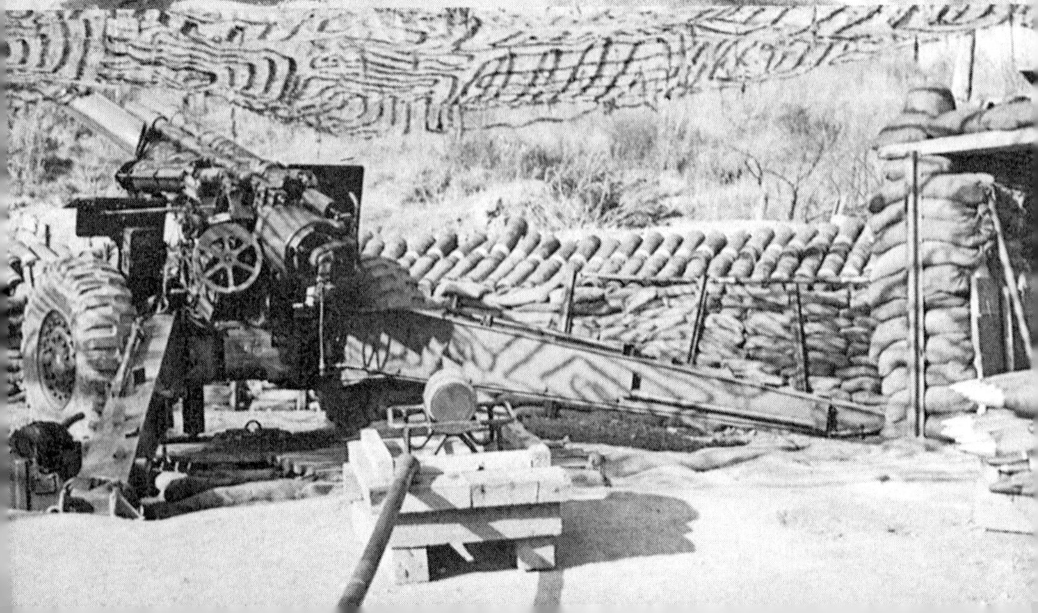

ORDERING INFORMATION

You may order additional copies of *'War in the Land of the Morning Calm'* for $19.95 plus $3.25 shipping, simply by copying this page, and mailing your cashiers' check, money order, or personal check.

NAME

_____

SHIPPING ADDRESS

_____

_____

PHONE & E-MAIL (OPTIONAL FOR SHIPMENT TRACKING AND VERIFICATION)

_____

		$19.95
# of books	x	
SUB-TOTAL		
Shipping	+	$3.25
TOTAL ORDER		

MAIL YOUR ORDER TO:
JAMES CAMPBELL
1126 SOMERTON PLACE
CUMMING, GA 30040
CAMPBELL_JAMES@BELLSOUTH.NET

U.S.N.T.
GENERAL JOHN POPE

USA
8157283 S